THE CREWE MURDERS

KIRSTY JOHNSTON & JAMES HOLLINGS

THE CREWE MURDERS

INSIDE NEW ZEALAND'S MOST INFAMOUS COLD CASE

It is impossible to satisfy the nobles
honourably, without doing violence
to the interests of others; but this
can be done as far as the people are
concerned. The people are more honest
in their intentions than the nobles are
because the latter want to oppress the
people, whereas [the people] want only
not to be oppressed.

— Niccolò Machiavelli, *The Prince*

CONTENTS

Introduction	9
1. TE AWA, TE WHENUA	15
2. RETURN TO PUKEKAWA	41
3. A TERRIBLE BLOODY MESS	54
4. THE INVESTIGATION	63
5. THE ARREST	93
6. THE FIRST TRIAL	112
7. THE BACKLASH	134
8. THE SECOND TRIAL	144
9. THE GATHERING STORM	167
10. THE PARDON	183
11. THE ROYAL COMMISSION OF INQUIRY	199
12. INTEREST REKINDLED	211
13. SHORTFALLS	229
14. BULLETS, WIRE, AXLE	247
15. A DISTRICT DIVIDED	274
16. THE COURT OF LAST RESORT	286
Notes	297
Bibliography	308
Acknowledgements	310
About the authors	312
Index	313

INTRODUCTION

For all the infamy surrounding their murders on a cold winter's night in a country farmhouse 50 years ago, only a handful of photos of Jeannette and Harvey Crewe remain. In these black-and-white images we see Jeannette as a teenager, smiling, in a fancy dress and white gloves at her debutante ball; the couple on their wedding day, cheeks flushed and eyes bright; their daughter Rochelle as a toddler in overalls, her chubby hand to her mouth. And Harvey holding Rochelle, who is wearing a smock and squinting at the light.

The Crewes have now been dead longer than they were alive. They were almost certainly shot on 17 June 1970, after dinner, Harvey in his armchair by the fire while Jeannette knitted on the couch. Harvey was 28 and Jeannette was 30. An orphaned Rochelle was found five days afterwards, crying in her cot, alone. Her parents' bodies were pulled from the Waikato River months later.

Initially, the public was fascinated by the young farming couple from Pukekawa and their tragic story: Who were they, and who despised them enough to want them to die? But by the end of that year, after police had arrested local farmer Arthur Thomas for their murders, the Crewes' lives became a backdrop for a bigger drama, a fight for justice for a man many argued was wrongfully imprisoned. When that was finally won, a new battle began, this time to establish who was truly responsible. It has so far proved a futile venture.

In the myriad court cases, newspaper articles, books and the royal commission of inquiry in 1980, Jeannette and Harvey Crewe were often reduced to caricatures of themselves, speculative outlines no longer based on fact. She was a rich snob, grown slovenly since marriage. He was ambitious and angry; he married her for her money. The killer, rumour ran, was her curmudgeonly old father, who didn't want to give up his farm. Later, the accused, Arthur Thomas, faced the same reductive fate: he was a local simpleton who had never given up his childhood crush, Jeannette, who he killed out of jealousy. His wife was the 'brains of the operation'; she covered up for him.

It was a seductive story with a compelling cast of characters. But look closer at the photo of Harvey Crewe holding his daughter opposite. The pair share the same dark hair, swept sideways. It's a warm day, they are outside in the sun. As he lifts her up, Harvey is laughing, his eyes wrinkling at the corners. Rochelle extends her little arm towards the camera, reaching for something just out of sight.

That photo was, in some ways, the catalyst for this book. James came across the image in 2018 while researching an obituary for the journalist Pat Booth. Booth had argued that the Crewe murders were actually a murder–suicide. He believed Harvey had hit his wife, prompting her to shoot and kill him, and then, stricken with grief, kill herself. James, who has two daughters, looked at that photo, saw a loving father, and wondered how that photo fitted that scenario. He began to read more carefully about the investigations into the murders, and then contacted Kirsty to see if she wanted to jointly investigate the case.

An examination of the early police files found it wasn't only journalists who had sought to characterise the Crewes and the other suspects and witnesses as best fitted their stories. Although some of the detectives were thorough and open-minded, many were quick to make sweeping judgements based on questionable assumptions about the couple whose killer they were seeking to find.

The officer in charge of the case, Detective Inspector Bruce Hutton, fell prey to tunnel vision, which tainted the trajectory of the investigation from the very start. When his theory refused to stack up, he was found to have almost certainly used fake evidence to frame Arthur Thomas, causing the most famous miscarriage of justice case in New Zealand history.

When we first began to consider the case, we planned to write an article on just one aspect: the axle found with Harvey Crewe's body in the Waikato River in 1970. No one needed another retelling of a cold case, we thought, particularly not one that had already had its bones picked over so many times. But gradually, as we read more and more,

Harvey Crewe and his daughter Rochelle on their farm in Pukekawa. This photograph was probably taken in the summer of 1969/70, six months before Harvey and Jeannette Crewe were killed.

Many ordinary New Zealanders were disturbed by the conviction of Arthur Allan Thomas, and signed petitions asking for a retrial.

we realised this was much more than just another cold case — much more, even, than just another account of police mistakes.

This story had layers, its roots deep in the subsoil of New Zealand society, in the latent class divisions of farm and city, of sheep farmer versus dairy farmer, landowner and leaseholder. More, the reverberations caused by growing public concern over what many saw as a police lynching ran up through the trunk of New Zealand, through the solid middle wood of urban people to the top branches — the police bosses, the judiciary, the mandarins of the civil service, and finally to the prime minister. Everyone had an opinion; everyone, including the prime minister, had to take a side.

Thus we had the first, and still only ever, free pardon granted to a living prisoner in New Zealand history. That some police made mistakes and tried to cover them up is well known, but, we wondered, what other mistakes were made? Why did politicians eventually step in and effectively overrule the courts and free Arthur Thomas? That story has never been told until now.

And why Thomas? What was it about this case that caused over 2000 people to pack the Auckland Town Hall in 1973 in support of him? There have been plenty of apparent miscarriage of justice cases — what was it about this one?

A s we delved, we saw there was a historical context that has not been explored fully: two high-profile murder cases nearby, just a few years before; cases with many similarities. What role did they play? And the land itself, we realised, has many stories that influenced this one. Pukekawa, as the stage, is where some of the country's most dramatic events have played out.

We also realised, remarkably for a story which has generated so much attention, that there was still no comprehensive account of the Crewe story — and in particular, not one that sought to examine the political aspects, its impact on New Zealand society and its constitution.

The police corruption exposed in the Crewe case is often referred to as the country's 'loss of innocence', prompting protest, as former Prime Minister David Lange once said, 'not from urban agitators, not people who demonstrate, not people worried about apartheid or

Vietnam but by people who had shares in dairy companies'.[1]

Before Thomas was pardoned, the books published about the case tended to campaign for his freedom. Arguably, without the works of Terry Bell, David Yallop and Pat Booth, Arthur Thomas would still be sitting in a jail cell. Their investigations were vital, but not neutral. Equally, most of the books written after the pardon carried their own theories about the killer. While we are indebted to all of their work, and in particular to the work of former journalist Chris Birt, whose skills using the Official Information Act brought to light many of the documents we relied on from the police file, those books were written with a specific suspect in mind. The evidence was marshalled in a certain direction, which by definition means that some facts were left behind. In contrast, from the outset, we resolved to write a history, not a whodunnit.

We also wanted to consider the unanswered questions that lingered, of which there are many. At the end of the 2014 police review is a list of 80 issues police were unable to resolve when they reinvestigated the case file at the behest of Rochelle Crewe. We had additional questions, some arising from that same review report. We sought to answer some of them, re-examining old evidence in light of what we have found.

In Pukekawa, many of the key witnesses are now dead, and those still alive are often elderly or sick. That only gave us further impetus to gather what they might have to say before it was too late. Some people did not want to talk. Rochelle Crewe, for example, has never given a full interview to anyone, preferring that her identity remains secret. Others asked us to let sleeping dogs lie, saying the case was firmly in the past. But some people decided they had faith in our project and agreed to be interviewed. They told us of lingering bitterness between families, and towards some witnesses, and a sense of hostility and heaviness surrounding the case that has yet to fade. Some told us things they hadn't said in public before.

And of course, there is the final question, the one everyone has sought to answer: Who killed the Crewes? There is still no definitive answer to that question, but we hope at least to have brought more light to bear on who *didn't* kill them, and thus who might have.

CHAPTER ONE
TE AWA, TE WHENUA

I t all starts with the river, te awa. The Waikato. The country's biggest, longest and — for much of our history — most contested. It begins at Taupō, heads north for almost 400 kilometres, as if determined to cut a path to Auckland. About 70 kilometres before it would have reached the Waitematā harbour, it meets the rising ground of the Bombay Hills, which mark the line between Waikato and Auckland. Thwarted, it takes a sharp left and heads straight for the Tasman Sea, just 20 kilometres away.

At this bend in the river, the banks are low, the river wide and slow. Just to the west there is a hill from whose top you have a good view. If you look south, on the river's right-hand side there is a distinctive dome-shaped mound, rising from the surrounding farmland. This is Pukekawa, which gives the district its name. It is an attractive landscape: the lazy swing of the river, the rich green rolling hills. In 2012 the composer Sarah Ballard, who grew up here, wrote a symphony, *Bitter Hill* (Pukekawa is sometimes translated as 'the hill of bitter memories'), about what she called its primal beauty.[1]

It is at this bend in the river and the land to the west and south of it — known as the left bank — that this story takes place. It is land with, by New Zealand standards, a very storied and bloody history. The worst battles of the colonial wars took place here, the first beginning on 17 July 1863 at Koheroa. So did the biggest land confiscations, as the Crown sought to crush the Kīngitanga or King Movement. Here, also, in the next century, there were three sets of murders, two of them double murders. Each became notorious, each more infamous than the ones before; the third, the subject of this book, became the most controversial, most written-about, murder case that this country has ever seen.

Until the arrival of Europeans in the early nineteenth century, these rich lands, noted for their fertile red soil, were occupied by Māori. The predominant iwi or tribal group was Ngā Iwi o Tainui. It was productive country, the river a source of fish, the land excellent for growing crops such as kūmara. In the 1840s, a few Europeans settled in the area, buying land and establishing farms. They lived peacefully alongside Māori, often becoming fluent in te reo. One of the first was Charles Marshall, who in 1839 purchased the Paraparaumu Block at Pukekawa for £75 from Totaha and Kauahi.[2] Wesleyan missionaries arrived soon after, and found that Māori had 'great desire to learn [to read and write] and the facility with which some advanced was astonishing'.[3]

Māori welcomed the new settlers: their number was manageable and they brought trade, knowledge, skills, and generally enhanced the mana of the iwi. Māori were quick learners, and began to grow and export crops, particularly wheat, to Auckland and beyond. European visitors to the Tainui lands at this time were astonished to find flour mills and hundreds or thousands of acres of crops. One flour mill was at Tūākau, while the Raglan and Waikato Native Company was trading goods such as timber, wheat, pork and flax.[4]

The area's produce was sent downriver by waka to Auckland. Waikato was the breadbasket of the rapidly growing city; in 1854, it was estimated that £16,000 worth of produce was sent to Auckland.[5] In this era Europeans had Auckland; Māori had the Waikato and beyond. Although nominally under the rule of the Crown, the colony's governor, Thomas Gore Browne, left Māori alone to govern their land and both sides benefitted from a mutually profitable arrangement.

It could have carried on like this for decades, the Waikato becoming a self-governing, economically autonomous province under the overall rule of the Crown. Indeed, there was provision for just such an arrangement in the New Zealand Constitution Act, passed by the British Parliament in 1852. Section 71 of that Act allowed the government to declare native districts where it 'would be advisable to maintain the customs and laws of the natives until the whole Colony had become more or less incorporated with the European inhabitants'.[6]

That version of history was not to come to pass. What happened next was described by historian Vincent O'Malley in his 2016 book *The Great War for New Zealand*. Although the Act envisaged that Māori could vote and be represented in the General Assembly (an earlier form of a parliament with an appointed legislative council and a House of Representatives), in practice few met the property qualification. Māori were suspicious of the Assembly and worried that the rapidly increasing number of settlers (exceeding 28,000 by 1852) were after their land, a view shared privately by the governor.

Browne, although sympathetic to Māori, was under pressure from the settlers to open up more land, but Māori were increasingly resistant to selling. So alarmed were they by their exclusion from the new settler Parliament, the increasing demands for land, and the increasingly hostile and aggressive attitude of many Europeans, that many decided to resist. And thus the Kīngitanga, or King Movement, was born.[7]

At a series of large hui in the 1850s, where many of the leading tribes met, they decided to elect a king to represent them and ideally negotiate directly with the Queen, or her representative, the governor. Not all Māori supported the movement, but by the late 1850s and early 1860s, a significant proportion of those in the central and lower North Island did. Under their king, Pōtatau, and his successor, Tāwhiao, they declared an aukati, a line that marked the boundary between European- and Māori-controlled land. It ran along the Mangatāwhiri River, north of Tūākau, near where the Waikato River turned to the sea. Europeans could trade across this line, with Māori permission, but if anyone bore arms across it, it would be considered an act of war.

For Browne, this was a direct challenge to the Crown's authority. He demanded the submission of the Kīngitanga to the Crown and compensation for losses suffered in the recent Taranaki war.[8] This was unacceptable to Māori, not unreasonably, given they had effectively been excluded from the legislature. Browne began preparing to invade the Waikato as early as 1861, but he did not get to see his plans realised; he had lost the confidence of the settlers and his colonial masters in England and was replaced in 1861 by George Grey. The new governor came with a big reputation, having subdued the Xhosa people during his tenure as governor of the Cape Colony in South Africa. Publicly he talked peace with Māori, but privately he wanted to crush the Waikato movement once and for all.[9] Negotiations failed, and the most bloody fighting in New Zealand history began. Tūākau and the river to the south was ground zero.

When British troops, under General Cameron, crossed the Mangatāwhiri on 12 July 1863, the heights around Tūākau were his first target; an ideal place for a redoubt that could control the river and secure it as a thoroughfare for British ships and troops. The Māori inhabitants of the kāinga at Tūākau were told to surrender or be considered rebels and leave. What happened next was witnessed by Charles Marshall: '[Resident magistrate] Mr [James] Armitage was sent to Tuakau to demand their arms, but they refused to give them to him as they were their own private property. He then told them to leave Tuakau, their home, which at that time they also declined to do as being their own property.'[10]

The next day, 300 soldiers of the 65th Regiment began building the Alexandra Redoubt on the hills overlooking the settlement. All the Māori in the settlement evacuated when they saw the troops advancing. 'They came across the Waikato to me,' said Charles Marshall, 'and they had no alternative but to join the rebels. They were passing the Koheroa in canoes at the time of the fighting and were fired on by the soldiers, fortunately without anyone being hurt.'[11]

The Kīngitanga built formidable defences at Meremere, 6 kilometres to the south, and at Rangiriri, about 10 kilometres south of that. Imperial troops based at Tūākau brought gunboats up the river and laid siege. The Kīngitanga was pushed back, making a final stand at Ōrākau, 60 kilometres south. Along the way, British troops burned and pillaged undefended villages, including hundreds of acres of orchards and gardens, in a notorious incident at Rangiaowhia. Women and children caught up in the fighting were bayoneted or shot by British troops at Ōrākau. Vincent O'Malley estimates that around 400 Māori died in the fighting in the Waikato: about 4 per cent of the population, a figure he points out eclipses the 1.7 per cent of the population killed in the First World War, robbing, as all wars do, hapū and the iwi itself of current and future leaders.[12]

Having been pushed out by the fighting, on their return Māori found that their land and belongings had been pilfered or destroyed by settlers. Over 1.2 million acres in the Waikato region alone were confiscated by the government as punishment for the rebellion and given to European settlers, particularly soldiers.[13] Around Pukekawa, a large block of 34,330 acres, known as the Onewhero Block, was taken on 16 May 1865. It is a vast piece of land, stretching west from the river to the sea; rich, highly fertile volcanic loam. For Europeans, the land now opening up for settlement was alluring.

As the district government surveyor, A. K. Churton, noted that year, when measuring it up: 'I would particularly direct attention to the fine district lying around Pukekawa, and extending from Kohekohe, past Kohanga, to the Waikato Heads. Pukekawa is an old point of eruption, and around it there is an extent of about 5000 acres of first-rate volcanic land. The whole district is interspersed with forest, and lying as it does between the Port of Waikato Heads and the termination of the Great South Road, it is of easy access. I would strongly recommend an effort be made to extend settlement in this direction; no very great outlay would be necessary in roadmaking, as the district extends along the river, and with but short branch roads, water communication from its most fertile portions to the Waikato Heads would be available.'[14]

Settlers were already lining up to fill the 'empty' lands. That year, Joseph Newman, the Provincial Council[15] member responsible for settling the rising tide of immigrants flooding into the Waikato, many of whom had themselves been cleared from the highlands of Scotland or Ireland, had a shipful ready to land at the settlement of Camerontown, near Tūākau. But the government, perhaps nervous about a Māori backlash so soon after the end of the fighting, refused to let them south of the river onto the Onewhero Block, and Newman resigned in protest.[16]

Nonetheless, the Onewhero Block was eventually carved up and parcelled out, mostly in 300- to 400-acre lots. A government map of the district shows it diced into 'blocks' marked in neat Roman numerals from I to XVII, with the blocks then subdivided into farm-sized pieces, each marked with a lot number and acreage.[17]

According to local history, 'friendly Maoris' were granted land within the Onewhero Block, with lots 29 and 31–48 set aside. Charles Marshall's Māori wife Tiramate was given 1409 acres, for example. Nearby, in Ōpuatia (next to the Onewhero Block), Waata Kukutai and others were said to have been given 45,500 acres. But most of the land went to Pākehā settlers.[18]

On the government map, in block XVI, to the south of Pukekawa and just to the right of a now thin squiggle that marks Highway 22, there is one piece of land named section 7, of 364 acres. Unlike all the other sections in this block, it has the letters 'E.R.', for educational reserve, written across it. It was set aside in 1899 as an endowment to fund primary education, the land to be leased and the funds to be used to support a local school.[19] The reserve is on the crest of the ridge that overlooks the Waikato River. There is a gully, thickly forested, running down the middle, almost west to east. It is an attractive site for a farm, with views out across the river to the east and north to the distinctive mound of Pukekawa Hill.

This piece of land was to become the site of the Crewe murders.

For the Kīngitanga, the loss of land after the war was devastating. As O'Malley writes, efforts to regain the land dominated Māori relations with the Crown for the next 120 years. Tāwhiao, the second Māori King, moved to Pukekawa in 1888 with his followers and established three settlements, about 2 kilometres apart, with around 80 whare and many acres cultivated in gardens. His own settlements were on the river side of the road, at Kohekohe, opposite Meremere, and at Te Karaka, at the end of what is now Mercer Ferry Road. They worked a thriving industry cutting flax. Tāwhiao's followers were often

A section of the map of county boundaries produced for the 1927 Royal Commission on Confiscated Lands and Other Native Grievances, which met at Ngāruawāhia. What would become the Crewe farm is located near the middle, marked '7 E.R.' ('educational reserve'). A small triangular section just above is marked 'Cem Reserve' — it appears a cemetery was planned for this section, but it never eventuated. The full map is available at Archives New Zealand (item code R23895950).

known to cut 50 tons a day, at 12 shillings a ton, a profitable trade for local storekeepers.

In the *Pukekawa Profile*, a history of the district published in 1970, a settler described how Tāwhiao did business at the local store, M&S Hunter, at Mercer: 'Tawhiao and his followers would arrive early in the day and in the afternoon the store would be closed to everyone else. Then the King's party, several at a time, would pass through the store selecting their items . . . each was entered in a book by the storekeepers. This procedure went on until the last customer had been served. Then the King would rise from his seat near the door and ask what was to be paid. On being told the amount his own treasurer would come forward with his gladstone bag crammed full of money and the account would be settled. There was no arguing or queries; each party trusted the other implicitly.'[20]

From his Pukekawa base, Tāwhiao continued his attempts to gain British government recognition of the Kīngitanga. In 1884, he led a delegation to England, hoping to meet with Queen Victoria, but intense lobbying from the New Zealand government blocked that meeting. Back in New Zealand, the government tried to woo him, a series of ministers making their way north with various offers of an annual pension and titles and small parcels of land in return for abandoning the Kīngitanga. All were refused unless the central issue of the return of the confiscated lands was settled.

Just how steadfast Tāwhiao and his supporters were in their determination to regain their lands was demonstrated in a volatile incident in 1890. That year, Tāwhiao's secretary, Henare Kaihau, pulled up a government survey trig on Māori land. The government sent in 41 of the Permanent Force to arrest him in what the Christchurch *Star* decried as a 'ridiculous parade of force' executed mainly for electioneering purposes.[21] Kaihau gave himself up peacefully.

Tāwhiao moved to Parawera, south-east of Te Awamutu, in 1893. However, it was to be over a century before the government finally made a settlement with Waikato Māori. In May 1995, Queen Elizabeth II signed the Waikato–Tainui Raupatu Claims Settlement, valued at $170 million, returning land and cash payments to Tainui. This was the first historical settlement under the Treaty.

As the twentieth century dawned, Pākehā residents of Pukekawa could reasonably have expected that the years of bloodshed were behind them and prosperity lay ahead, the next few decades a time of peaceful development. But, for Māori, the lands around Pukekawa were still contested. Just as A. K. Churton had foretold when looking through the lens of his theodolite in 1865, the land quickly proved its worth once transport links were built.

The railway reached Tūākau in 1875, and the first bridge across the river was built in 1904. The main road, which was to become Highway 22, snaked south through Pukekawa towards Glen Murray, 38 kilometres away, along the left, or western, bank of the river. Off this access roads were built, often taking the names of the first Europeans to settle farms on them: Brewster, Churchill, Sharpe, Logan, Clark and Denize, Hunt, Fleming, Thompson and Tonga. Many of those families are still in the area today.

For those early settlers, life was isolated. In 1970, Mrs Mullins, a daughter of Richard Underwood, one of the first to settle at Pukekawa in 1859, gave this account of life before the Pukekawa School was opened: 'Until then we children had to cross the river every day and then walk three and a half miles to Whangarata School and back. We had a very good home at the back of Smeed's Quarry . . . on top of our big rock that was destroyed when blasted for the quarry was a real redoubt, and we used to run there as children and see the big Maori war canoes going down the river, canoes fifty feet long, like we could only see in the museum today.'[22]

As the land was cleared and farms brought into production, the population grew. A school was established at Pukekawa in 1894. And, in 1920, the Onewhero Rugby Club. Like many country districts around New Zealand, social life revolved around the school, the golf club and the rugby club. Children attended the local school until they were about 12, then went to either the local college in Pukekohe or, if their parents had money, a private boarding school in Auckland such as St Cuthbert's (for girls) or St Kentigern (for boys). In the days before television, radio and the internet, an elaborate staircase of social rituals escorted young men and women from the casual friendships of school into courtship and then marriage — there were coming-out parties, twenty-first birthday celebrations and engagements, as well as a series of annual dances and events at which young men and women could mingle and match.

All were rigorously photographed and published in local magazines such as the *Franklin Times* alongside advertisements for tractors and fibre cement. In 1921, the front page of the *Times* included an advertisement for a 'new lightweight car', the Nash 6, 'featuring astonishing qualities in a new style of springing'.[23] Clubs such as tennis and table tennis sprang up; for the older citizens, social contact came through the tapestry of civic business required to keep the district running, such as stock sales in Tūākau or nearby Pukekohe and regular ratepayers' association meetings. For young men, socialising occurred at the rugby club or pub, where talk about cars, and doing up old jalopies and driving them on under-policed country roads, was as popular in Pukekawa as anywhere in New Zealand.

At about this time, four families moved into the district whose destinies were to become entangled: the Thomases, the Eyres, the Chennellses and the Demlers. The Eyres were there first, Sydney Eyre buying his farm in the early 1900s, beside what is now Highway 22, a couple of kilometres south of Pukekawa. The Chennellses came next, around 1922, leasing a farm very close to the Eyre farm.

In 1926, Edward Thomas, a former miner, moved his young family of six boys and five girls onto 160 hectares of leased farmland at Ōpuatia, a few kilometres south of the Chennellses' farm. The oldest son, Allan, went to Pukekawa School and played rugby for Onewhero. Seven years later, in 1931, William Demler bought the property next to the Thomas farm, and Lenard, his 22-year-old son, arrived the following year.[24]

All four families were now in place, but just before they arrived, an event occured that shattered the 50-year peace the district had enjoyed since the end of the land wars.

When Syd Eyre arrived in the district in search of a farm, much of the land south of Pukekawa was still in heavy bush, including big rimu with trunks up to 1.8 metres wide. As local historians described it: 'South of Pukekawa School Site, apart from the track marking the present Main Road, which was to replace the Mission Track, only survey lines had been cut . . . when [local bushman]

Tom Murray took Syd Eyre to inspect the land which Syd ultimately purchased, both became lost and benighted in the heavy bush. They circled round the western slopes of Pukekawa Hill and finally came to open land on Mr Din Hunt's the next day.'[25]

By 1920, Eyre had carved out a working farm, and he and his wife Millicent were parents to three boys: Philip, born in 1904, John, born in 1908, and Annesley, known as Joff, born two years later. On the night of 25 August, Syd Eyre went to sleep as usual in his single bed by the window, while Millicent slept in hers on the other side of the room. At about 9 p.m., Millicent was woken by a shot. She called Syd, but getting no reply, lit a candle and went to his bedside to find that the top of his head had been blown off.

The Eyres' older sons, Philip and John, ran to a neighbouring farmhouse to phone the police. They got through to the Pukekohe station, which then alerted Auckland. At 2 a.m., in what is believed to be the first use of a police car to attend a crime scene in New Zealand, Detective Sergeant James Cummings drove south to Pukekawa. Tūākau's constable, Bruce Thompson, and the Pukekohe officer, John Cowan, were already at the Eyre farm and had had the presence of mind to secure the crime scene. Crucially, they put covers over a distinctive set of horse hoofprints found near the house, to protect them from imminent rain.[26]

Cummings soon established that while Eyre had been on war service, Millicent had become close to Eyre's former farm manager, Samuel Thorn. Eyre had dismissed Thorn when he returned from the war and Thorn had taken a labourer's job on a nearby farm.

What ensued has gone down as a landmark in detective procedure. Police followed the hoofprints 29 kilometres to the farm of James Granville, where Thorn worked. The horseshoe print was found to match one of Granville's horses, Mickey. Meanwhile an unusual shotgun cartridge known as 'Peter's number 7' had been found at the scene. All of the 176 local homes were searched and the only people found to be in possession of such a cartridge were the Eyres' son Philip, and Thorn. Tests revealed Philip's cartridge had a different wadding; Thorn's was a match. Thorn's gun had recently been fired, Philip's had not. Thirteen hundred horses in the district were examined but only Mickey's shoes matched the hoofprints found at the scene. Thorn was charged with murder and taken to Mount Eden Prison in Auckland to await trial.[27]

Despite the apparently overwhelming weight of forensic evidence against him, Thorn's trial did not go smoothly. The prosecution, which described the case as a 'strong circumstantial one', said that Thorn murdered Syd Eyre in revenge for his dismissal, and because he was in love with Millicent. She gave evidence that he had often told her he loved her, and had asked her to live with him. She explained that the relationship had continued after Eyre's return from the war and that she could not prevent him because he would have told her husband and 'have her name dragged in the gutter and get divorced'. Although she had liked Thorn at first, when she tried to break off the relationship he had threatened her and struck her.[28]

A series of experts contended that Eyre must have been shot by a left-hander as the shooter held on to the windowsill with his right arm (Thorn was left-handed), and that cartridges found at the scene matched his gun. Philip Eyre testified that Thorn had gone into his mother's room 'frequently' and had said he would kill Syd Eyre. John Eyre said he had also seen Thorn kissing his mother. The pathologist considered it impossible that the shot was fired from inside the room (although no explanation was given), and a witness claimed he had overheard Thorn tell someone at the pub that, 'If they get me, I'll drag some other . . . into it.'[29]

But Thorn's lawyer ridiculed and undermined this evidence, noting that another set of hoofprints had not been followed, and that Mickey's prints had only been tracked for four of the 30 kilometres to Thorn's cottage. No footprints had been found outside the window under which Syd Eyre had been sleeping. Furthermore, no one had seen Thorn during the 60-kilometre round trip he was alleged to have made on the night of the murder. Cartridge wads had been found at the Eyre house, as well as at Thorn's. If Philip Eyre had a gun that also fired them, could it not have been him, or Millicent herself, from inside the house?

Thorn's counsel argued that if it was a left-handed shooter, Eyre would have been shot through the right eye, not the left. Millicent Eyre admitted she had told her sons not to mention her familiarity with Thorn 'because they might be the means of having an innocent man hanged'. Furthermore, Thorn's employer, and Mickey's owner, James

Granville, gave evidence that Thorn did not ride Mickey, preferring another horse, Dick.[30]

After five hours' deliberation, the jury couldn't agree and the Crown applied for a new trial.[31] That second trial took place two weeks later. This time the Crown made no mistake. Although the defence tried to cast doubt on the ballistics evidence, particularly the claim that the shotgun shell used was rare, the jury seemed to have little doubt. At one point jury members chorused 'Hear hear' when a Crown ballistics witness gave evidence.[32] Even so, the jury took four hours to reach a verdict, returning at 8.30 p.m. Thorn took it calmly. He did not respond when the death sentence was pronounced.[33] Barely a week later, James Granville killed himself with his own shotgun.[34]

On the morning of his execution at Mount Eden Prison, 20 December 1920, it was reported that Samuel Thorn woke at 6 a.m. and breakfasted. He asked to see a clergyman before he walked to the scaffold 'without a tremor'. His final moments were described by a reporter: 'Thorn mounted the steps firmly, and when asked by the sheriff if he had anything to say, replied, "Yes I want to thank the gaol officials, especially the three warders who attended on me, for their kindness. But it is unjust — very unjust — of the police the way they have treated me. I am not guilty. I do not know who did it. I am prepared to meet my God; I have made my peace with Him."'[35]

The public did not know it, but only a last-minute scramble by officials had enabled the execution to take place; just days before, the usual executioner had resigned. A stand-in was procured, but he had no experience in the role. When this man presented himself for training the day before the execution, the reality of what he was about to do caused him to have a panic attack. Desperate officials managed to persuade one of the inmates, a convicted burglar, to pull the lever in return for a one-way ticket out of the country.[36]

Detective Sergeant James Cummings' work on the case was commended by the judge, Mr Justice Chapman, and within two years he was promoted to chief detective. He was to become legendary as the 'Sherlock Holmes of New Zealand and the country's most successful detective', eventually becoming commissioner of police in 1944.[37]

For the residents of Pukekawa and beyond, the murder was a dark spot on an otherwise prospering district. It was not to be the last.

On 20 July 1934, just after 7.30 a.m., a man was led out of his cell at Mount Eden Prison. He was slim, with thinning, neatly cut hair. He wore white prison trousers, a blue shirt and a grey jacket. He smoked a cigarette as he walked the short distance to a solitary confinement cell. Nearby was the makeshift wooden platform on which stood the gallows. The prisoner's name was William Alfred Bayly. He was 28 years old, a farmer from the remote rural area of Ruawaro, about 20 kilometres south of Pukekawa. Bayly was a husband, and a father of two small boys. He had been convicted of the murder of Samuel and Christobel Lakey six months previously.

The Lakeys lived on a 100-acre dairy farm next to William Bayly. On 16 October 1933, a Monday, another neighbour, John Slater, noticed the Lakeys' cows hadn't been milked and went to investigate. When he couldn't find the Lakeys, the police were called. By late morning, a search of the property uncovered Christobel Lakey's body face down in a duck pond near the farmhouse, covered in sacks. She was in her milking clothes. There was a small mark on her chin, and blood coming from her nose. There was no sign of her husband.

Inside the house, a cooked meal was on the stove, untouched. Three plates were in the rack above the stove, suggesting the Lakeys were expecting a visitor to dinner. Enquiries with neighbours revealed the Lakeys had last been seen going to their cowshed at about 4.30 p.m. the previous evening. A neighbour saw someone turning out their cows about 6.30 p.m. The dairy separator had been cleaned.

At first, police thought Christobel Lakey had had a seizure and fallen into the pond and drowned and that her husband had simply disappeared in distress. However, no one could explain why he would have covered her body with sacks. Also, he had evidently changed from his farm clothes into a good suit, and his prized shotgun was missing. The cream cans had been put at the gate for collection, but not in their usual position and not covered with sacks, as was Lakey's habit.

Then, on 18 October, a close examination of the property revealed bloodstains on a wheeled frame near the boundary with the Lakeys' neighbour William Bayly. Police extended their search to Bayly's farm, where they found a drum containing charred bones. By now, police suspected a double murder and the surrounding farmland was combed in the hopes of finding Samuel Lakey's body. Over 50 police camped on the farm and dozens of locals joined, probing swamps and caves in the difficult hill country. Nearby Lake Whangapē, particularly its south-western shores, was searched in the hope that the prevailing wind might have blown his body across the lake.[38]

William Bayly remained the chief suspect. Seven weeks later, police arrested him in Auckland, to where he had fled after leaving a suicide note. His trial, which began in Auckland on 21 May 1934, was, in every sense, a national spectacle. While the country was in the grip of the Depression, the court case set all the worst kind of records — for length, ghoulishness and, to the modern eye, a bizarre concatenation of pseudo-science that helped send Bayly to his death. Large crowds gathered outside the courthouse each day and hundreds of people pushed and shoved to gain entrance to the courtroom.

The Crown case also set a new standard in attention to forensic detail. It contended that Bayly had knocked Christobel down, and then asphyxiated her in the duck pond. He then shot Samuel Lakey with a .22 rifle and burned his body in a steel drum on his farm. The Crown called 68 witnesses, several of them forensic experts, and presented more than 200 exhibits. Many were from the drum allegedly used to burn Lakey's body, from which a government analyst identified human fat, the charred remains of a watch, parts of a shoe and even a rosewood pipe. Experts testified as to the way in which tin snips had cut the drum, and what could be ascertained from various fat deposits and shards of bone found in it; one 'expert' even produced a spirit lamp in court and conducted experiments to test the effect of fire on bone. Glass jars containing exhibits were lined up on a table between the jury and the accused.

A Constable Elms gave evidence that he had found a .22 shell in the Lakeys' garden, and one Gregory Kelly, an Auckland sports goods dealer, examined Bayly's rifle, a Winchester model 1902, and cleaned it of mud and rust. He testified that he had been shown a .22 cartridge shell with ICI on the base by one of the detectives, and that after firing other similar cartridges from the rifle he was confident that the cartridge had been shot from that rifle.[39]

A dairy factory manager told the court that the Lakeys' cows' cream was underweight the day after the murders, and that this was because the cows must have been 'uncomfortable'. A friend of the Lakeys said he had heard Bayly threaten to fight Lakey after his bull had been found on the Lakeys' farm.

Such a mountain of evidence completely swamped the defence, which called no witnesses of its own. The trial lasted 29 days, a record for the time, and depositions alone amounted to 483 pages, totalling 200,000 words.[40]

On the last day, after five weeks of hearings, public interest was undimmed. People had begun queuing outside the court at 6 a.m., several with thermoses of tea and coffee. The jury took barely 90 minutes to make its mind up. According to reports, the court was silent as Bayly was found guilty, and the sentence of death by hanging was delivered. His father, Frank, and his wife, Phyllis, were with him, as they had been throughout the trial. Bayly said nothing as the sentence was issued, although he did look back once as he was led away.[41]

His lawyer decided there were no grounds for an appeal, but a plea for a new trial was entered in early July. Phyllis Bayly said her son had been with her all that evening; there had been no fire in the oil drum as the prosecution had alleged; that in fact half the drum was being used to grow vegetables.[42] The plea was denied. A couple of weeks later, Bayly's farm and that of the Lakeys were sold to two brothers, one a former policeman, for £1700 each.[43]

O n 20 July 1934, the day of Bayly's hanging, a crowd of about 60 people had gathered outside the prison. Police and warders patrolled the walls. It is not surprising there were precautions. Despite the times, capital punishment was by no means universally popular in New Zealand and public unease about the safety of convictions (whether a person is actually guilty or not) was never far from the surface. Just 20 years earlier, the execution of a Māori teenager, Tahi Kaka, for a murder many thought was manslaughter in self-defence, had aroused widespread disquiet. The working-class *Truth* newspaper had even uncovered the identity of the hangman, a bricklayer who had taken on the job for the extra cash. He lost his job after *Truth* revealed his moonlight occupation.[44]

Bayly's fate had been in doubt until hours before, when a last-minute plea for a stay of execution had been put before the government by his chief counsel, Mr E. Northcroft. Bayly was still protesting his innocence, his wife had remained loyal and his fate obviously made some officials uneasy. There had been numerous meetings between Cabinet ministers and the commissioner of police and the comptroller of prisons. Evidence had been presented after the trial that someone had told police before the murders that they had intended to scatter bones. This could not be verified, Prime Minister George Forbes told waiting journalists at Parliament.

At 10.30 p.m., the commissioner of police and the comptroller of prisons went to consult the governor-general at Government House in Wellington. They returned at midnight and there was another conference with the Executive Council, consisting of George Forbes and three Cabinet ministers. By one in the morning they emerged; they would not interfere with the sentence. Bayly's fate was sealed.[45]

According to the *New Zealand Herald*, Bayly had spent most of the night before his hanging playing draughts with his warder.[46] He had gone to bed at 2.30 a.m. and was woken at seven. He was given a basin in which to wash and a breakfast of poached eggs on toast and a cup of tea. He rolled a cigarette and was offered a 'stimulant', which he took. Then he was taken from his cell to the solitary confinement cell to prepare for his hanging. The newspaper went on to say that Bayly was calm as he walked to his death. He was accompanied by a minister, Reverend G. E. Moreton. 'Just before he was executed Bayly raised his arm,' the *Waikato Times* reported that evening. 'Led by Mr Moreton . . . Bayly . . . was followed to the gallows by three warders. [Moreton] recited as he walked the opening sentences of the burial service, and then Psalm 130. "O Israel, Trust in the Lord, for with the Lord there is mercy and with him is plenteous redemption." Placing his hand on Bayly's head as he stood on the gallows, Mr Moreton gave him the blessing.'

The sheriff, C. J. Hewlett, asked him if he wished to say anything. '"Yes," said Bayly. "I would like to say that I am entirely innocent. The circumstantial evidence may appear to be entirely against me, but there no tittle of truth in the circumstantial evidence which has been produced against me. If I had received the treatment outside which I have received in this place I would never be here to-day. Everybody has done all they could for me, and I do not think anybody who has helped me here could have done more."

'After a pause, he said: "I don't think I can say any more, but I do repeat that I am innocent. A fair and dispassionate statement of the evidence is as much against my accusers as it is against me."'[47] Bayly shook hands with two warders and thanked the prison chaplain. Less than a minute later, the wooden trapdoor on which he stood fell away.

A macabre postscript was to come. Henry Ernest Johnson, who ran a waxworks show at the Waikato Winter Show in Hamilton, created a waxwork effigy of Bayly, which he hoped would be a hit with the public. The proprietors of the Winter Show closed the display down on the grounds of indecency and that it might offend patrons. Johnson sued for damages of £90, saying he had taken only £27 without the effigy. A magistrate awarded him £50 with costs.[48]

The Lakey investigation is still lauded as a landmark in the development of forensic investigation, yet much of what passed for evidence would not stand up in court today: there was, for example, no DNA evidence nor analysis of blood groups. The supposedly telling bloodstains found near Bayly's boundary could well have been animal blood. The supposedly human remains found in the drum on Bayly's property could have been animal bones, and the remains of clothing were not positively identified. Even the most damning evidence, the cartridge case, was of dubious reliability given the state of ballistic forensics at the time.

Once labelled criminal, the reputation of suspects and accused becomes fair game. William Bayly was no exception. Despite the relatively restrained newspaper coverage at the time, subsequent writing has not held back from repeating gossip about his 'evil character'. In 2015, 82 years after Samuel Lakey's death, police agreed to release what they believed to be Lakey's remains, which had been held as an exhibit in the police museum, for burial alongside his wife in the Huntly cemetery. A newspaper article about the burial quoted a local woman who said her mother told her he was a 'scary and arrogant man ... always riding his horses around the area'.[49] New Zealand's online encyclopedia, *Te Ara*, repeated unsubstantiated accusations that in 1928, Bayly had been a suspect in the death of his niece.[50]

The Lakey murders and the subsequent trial were widely known throughout Pukekawa, and had been well covered in local newspapers. Among those who would have followed them were the three farming families, the Chennellses, Demlers and Thomases.

Newman Chennells had emigrated from England around 1910 with his wife, Nellie, and first child, May, also known as Maisie. They arrived in Auckland, where Newman Chennells set up as a land agent. Their second child, Howard, was born in 1911. By 1920, Chennells had accumulated enough capital to lease a farm at Pukekawa. Howard was enrolled at Pukekawa School in 1922.

There are glimpses of the family's progress in the next few years from various newspaper reports: regular school prizes for May; cricket and athletics success for Howard, who was sent to board at King's College in Auckland; successes at golf for Newman. He was clearly popular in the district, elected chairman of the Ōpuatia School Committee in 1928 and appointed a Justice of the Peace in 1930. The Chennellses were keen supporters of the new tennis club and Newman and May represented Ōpuatia against Glen Murray in 1932.

In 1931, William Demler moved into the Pukekawa district. His son, Lenard, arrived soon after and they set to work to break in their farm, a few miles up the road from the Eyre farm. Their neighbours were the Thomas family. Demler was a hard worker, even by the standards of the day. As Chris Birt wrote in his 2001 book about the murders, 'The work pace set by the Demlers was known throughout the district. The older Demler would walk through the bush for two hours and be ready to start work in the middle of nowhere at dawn. He'd slash and burn all day and would get home well after dark. It was a seven-day work week.'[51]

By the late 1930s, many in the district must have felt things were finally starting to turn a corner. After the hard years of the Depression, farm prices were rising. The economy improved, more people came to work on local dairy and sheep farms and in the expanding town of Tūākau, and the local population grew; the district by then had its own hall, which was the centre of many social events, as was the new Ōpuatia Hall, just a few miles south.

In 1934, Edward Thomas's eldest son, Allan, left home and moved to his own leasehold dairy farm, 16 kilometres down the road, close to

Mercer. A year later he married Ivy Wilkins, who came from Pātetonga on the Hauraki Plains. One of the guests at the wedding was their neighbour, Len Demler, who was courting May Chennells at the time. Len's nickname was 'Merry' because he had a habit of laughing, no matter what happened to him.[52] The couple shared a love of tennis; as early as 1931 they were playing together on the Ōpuatia team. Both were sporty; Len had been a keen hockey player and in later life was a noted bowler. Perhaps Allan Thomas's wedding spurred Demler into action; the next year, 1935, he and May were engaged and they married a year after that.

On 17 October 1936, the *Auckland Star*'s women's pages reported that May entered the Pukekohe Anglican church on her father Newman Chennells' arm, 'a charming picture in her beautiful gown of ivory lace cut on classical lines, with a long graceful train, in which were appliqued godets of georgette. Her long tulle veil was caught to the head with a halo of orange blossoms ... [the bridesmaids] were dressed alike in picture frocks of water lily green and lavender, slim fitting to the knees, from where they flared to the hemline, with large taffeta flowers toning in deeper shades towards the centre. Halos of velvet flowers were worn on the hair ...'[53]

In 1937, the young couple moved onto their own farm, a 465-acre-block next door to May's parents' 340-acre property. Their other neighbour was Herman Sharpe. Len and May were a social couple, active in local sports and events such as the annual ball of the Maramarua Hunt Club, the *New Zealand Herald* recording the ball in 1937 as 'a success in every way'.[54]

Newman Chennells died in 1938, and the lease on his farm went to his two children; Howard took over the running of it.

During the Second World War, a Home Guard unit was formed in Pukekawa and a local farmer donated some land to be used for a rifle range. Many men in the district served overseas in the armed forces, Len Demler and Howard Chennells among them. They both survived the war, and on their return settled back into the familiar rhythms of rural life: stock sales, shearing, lambing, local dances, rugby and regular trips to Tūākau for shopping and a night out. The Demlers were contributing to the country's baby boom, with their first daughter, Jeannette Lenore Demler, born on 6 February 1940, and their second,

Heather, on 20 January 1942. Jeannette started at Pukekawa School in 1945, aged five. Heather followed two years later.[55]

By 1950, wool prices in New Zealand were booming, the population was increasing, and the golden years of the 1950s and 1960s lay ahead.

Early in the afternoon of 20 May 1950, Howard Chennells was out working on a steep slope in the gully just behind his house. He had recently bought a new Ferguson tractor, which the salesperson had assured him could go anywhere. A local boy, Eric Rumble, was cycling up Highway 22 to see his elderly neighbour, Herman Sharpe. When he arrived at Sharpe's house, he could see him working by his woolshed and walked across the paddock towards him. As he did so, he noticed Chennells driving his tractor up a gully. It went out of sight behind some trees and then Rumble heard someone calling for help from the gully.[56]

Sharpe and Rumble arrived to find the tractor upside down, with Howard Chennells pinned beneath it. Using a fence stay, Sharpe was able to lever the weight of the tractor off Chennells, and he and the boy managed to pull him out. Neighbours came to help carry him to his house, then an ambulance took him to Middlemore Hospital 54 kilometres away in Auckland. Chennells had a broken hip and severe lacerations. His condition deteriorated, and he died the next morning. He was only 39.

At the coronial inquest, the Tūākau constable, Thomas Magon, reported: 'At the place where the accident occurred, the hill was very steep, and I would say a grade of about one in two and was very rough. It could be seen where the tractor had come down the hill, prior to the accident, as there were marks made by the back wheels, which had apparently both been locked, and they ploughed their way down the hill. I would consider it impossible for a wheel tractor to climb up the hill, which the deceased was attempting to do, in safety.'

Len Demler was called to identify his brother-in-law's body. He told the coroner that Howard had been in good health and was a very experienced tractor driver.[57]

Howard's death must have come as a terrible blow to Len and May and their daughters, now eight and ten years old. Howard, who had never married, was kin and neighbour, a hard-working and successful farmer, and an excellent cricketer. And, as it turned out, a concerned and caring uncle: when his will was read they discovered that he had left the farm, valued at around £16,000, to his two nieces, Jeannette and Heather.

The executors of his will, local Tūākau solicitor Colin Sturrock and Howard's neighbour, Alfred Hodgson, made a significant decision. Because the farm was not owned by the Chennells estate but rather leased from the Crown, Sturrock and Hodgson sought — and were granted — permission to buy the land, all 361 acres of it, from the Crown for £3090.[58] A year later, the title was transferred to Len Demler as the trustee of the estate.

The two Demler girls had become owners of a substantial block of land for what was clearly a bargain-basement price; Demler's own 420-acre farm was worth £18,900 just five years later. At £45 an acre, that would make the Chennells farm worth £16,245 — more than five times what the government was paid for it. It was undoubtedly a providential windfall. The land would now be worth $7.18 million, based on the average price of Waikato farmland in 2021.[59]

Demler also took the opportunity to expand his own farm: he sought and was given approval by the trustees to carve 27 acres off the girls' farm and add it to his own land. Solicitor Colin Sturrock told the Land Valuation Court, which approved the sale, that this was bare land cut off by a gully and suited only for farming as part of Demler's adjoining farm. He paid £1050 for it.[60] The trustees of Jeannette and Heather's inheritance had done exceptionally well for them: they had bought them a substantial farm for one-fifth of its probable value, from the government, and then flipped 27 acres for about five times what they paid for it, within two years.

I f any of the descendants of the original Māori owners of block XVI section 7, which had been confiscated from them in 1865, were aware of the sale — let alone if they had known what was to happen another 40 years on — they might have had reason to object. For Ngā Iwi o Tainui, as part of the Waikato–Tainui Raupatu settlement for redress of the land confiscations, any land in private ownership could not be subject to claim, and that included most of the Onewhero Block confiscated in 1865. Had the Chennells farm been retained by the Crown in 1952 and not sold, it could well have been returned to Tainui in the 1990s, or at least be subject to claim.

It is not known why that land had been kept in Crown ownership. It could have been randomly chosen out of all the Onewhero land as one piece, as an endowment to provide income for the Auckland Education Board. Such endowments were customary at the time. But why *that* specific piece of land? Given the historical significance of the land to Tainui, and the fact that Tāwhiao had spent some time close by at Meremere in the 1890s, could it be that he had somehow been promised this piece of land would not be sold? It was common for surveyors to talk to local Māori — it is possible there had been communication about this land being put aside.

And if so, why? The land may have been wāhi tapu, sacred; perhaps because it held an urupā, a burial site. There is known to be an urupā less than a kilometre south of the land, along Highway 22.[61] We made some efforts to speak to mana whenua about this, but were unsuccessful. It may be that this knowledge of the whenua is also tapu, and not to be shared in this place or at this time.

What *is* known is that while Pākehā families around the district were enjoying the fruits of a steadily improving economy and social structure, many Māori were not. As late as the 1960s, Pukekohe, a few miles from Tūākau, was viciously racist; so racist that its apartheid-like treatment of 'natives' would not have been out of place in South Africa. Barbers refused to cut Māori hair, cinemas were segregated, businesses would not let them use toilets. (The local Indian farmworkers were also treated badly.) The local school had separate bathrooms for Māori; those entering white bathrooms were strapped.

Historian Dr Robert Bartholomew detailed how bad it was in 2020: 'While other students could swim in the baths Monday through Thursday, Māori were only allowed in on Fridays — just before the dirty water was drained . . . between 1952 and 1964, Pukekohe housed the only segregated Māori school in the history of the country. Worst of all, 237 Māori infants and children died from preventable conditions linked to the atrocious housing — 73 per cent of all deaths during this period . . . For over 40 years, a group of poor, nomadic Māori farm workers were forced to live in filthy, disgraceful conditions in run-down shacks and manure sheds near the fields where they toiled, picking vegetables on the outskirts of Pukekohe. They were confined to an area known as the Reservation, strategically separated from European houses where no one would lend them money or allow them to rent.'[62]

Despite the pain of Howard Chennells' death, the remainder of the 1950s were presumably happy years for the Demler family. Len and May's farm was doing well, their lambs fetching good prices at the local Pukekohe and Tūākau stock sales. Len Demler represented Tūākau at the national bowls competition in 1957; the district at that time boasting the national bowls champion, J. Pirret.

Both girls went to the local primary school at Pukekawa. Virtually all the local children went there, including the Thomas, Eyre, Stuckey and Tonga children. As she grew to high-school age, Jeannette, and her younger sister Heather, had admirers. One was Malcolm McArthur, who was so enamoured he gave up riding to school on his horse and detoured an extra 19 kilometres on the school bus just so he could sit next to Jeannette.[63] Another admirer was Arthur Thomas, the eldest son of Allan and Ivy Thomas. Because May Demler reputedly held stoutly Anglican views, the girls were chaperoned to local dances, but the attentions of local boys perhaps faded once the two girls started at St Cuthbert's College in Auckland.

After leaving school at the end of 1956, Jeannette spent the next year training at Ardmore Teachers' Training College. She qualified in 1958 and took up a position at Pukekohe North School. A friend, Edith Judge, told author David Yallop that Jeannette went home most weekends to Pukekawa, but it wasn't to renew those childhood crushes. 'She was unimpressed with the social life and male company of Pukekawa at that time . . . The only times I ever recall her mentioning Arthur Thomas's name was among others whom she listed as attending tennis club dance/socials that year. She also mentioned him, I vaguely recall, as somewhat of a nuisance in that he kept pestering her to go to "this and that" with him. She really thought the "local yokels" the absolute "last word", but nevertheless her references to them were still made with

38 THE CREWE MURDERS

a good-natured tolerance . . . her thoughts were chiefly occupied with planning her overseas trip.'[64]

After a year at Pukekohe, Jeannette landed a teaching position at Mangatangi School, in the north-east of Waikato. She lived in a teachers' hostel in nearby Maramarua, and was a hard-working and by all accounts successful teacher. When interviewed by Yallop, her friend and fellow teacher Grace Hessell recalled the hostel as having a very friendly atmosphere, with the young women living 'out of each other's pockets', cooking and socialising together. 'She was a very self-confident girl, typical of her age and generation. Very capable, very domesticated. A good cook, indeed the best cook amongst us. She had less contact with people in the locality than most of us mainly because she preferred to do extra preparation for her classes. She was very conscientious. She wasn't anti-social, just very occupied with her teaching, it consumed a great deal of her time.'[65]

As the 1960s rolled around, both Len and May Demler's daughters were settled into careers, Jeannette teaching and Heather as an air hostess. Len was probably looking forward to coasting into retirement and a chance to work on his bowls game. Unfortunately, that was not to be. He had underestimated his tax obligations and was fined by the Inland Revenue Department almost £10,000 — a huge sum in those days. He was advised by his accountant to sell half of the 450-acre farm to May, for £9450, to avoid further tax obligations.[66] But if her father's brush with the IRD bothered her, Jeannette did not seem to show it; that year, 1961, she embarked on her OE, travelling to Europe and North America with two friends.

Back in New Zealand, undeterred by the minimal encouragement he had received, Arthur Thomas had not forgotten Jeannette Demler. He wrote to her while she was overseas and sent her a writing compendium. With the good manners expected of a St Cuthbert's girl, Jeannette wrote back thanking him.[67]

Jeannette returned home in November 1962. A month later, Arthur Thomas visited her at her parents' farmhouse, where he gave her a Christmas present of a brush, comb and mirror set. He and Jeannette talked at the door for about 15 minutes but she didn't invite him in. She said she already had a boyfriend, which she didn't. When she later told her father that she didn't want to go out with Thomas, he said that in that case she should return the gift. It seems she did not; instead, she put the brush set away and forgot about it.

She had other things to look forward to. When the new year came around, she secured a relief teaching position at Maramarua District High School and Papakura Intermediate, but then her friend Beverley Ward encouraged her to apply for a job that had just come up in Whanganui. She did so, and got it.

Jeannette boarded in Whanganui with a young widow, Clare MacGee. They became close friends, and Jeannette stayed with her for the three years she would ultimately teach there. Jeannette told Clare she was happy to stay there for the rest of her life, that while she loved her mother, she did not get on very well with her father, and that there was no reason for her to return to Pukekawa. Arthur Thomas seemed to have given up pursuing her; MacGee said later she didn't know of him ever getting in touch during the time Jeannette stayed with her.[68]

MacGee thought Jeannette could have remained unmarried, but fate had other ideas. Jeannette's friend Beverley Ward had been dating a Tony Willis and was getting married, and Jeannette was her bridesmaid. The groomsman was a tall, powerfully built young farmer from Pahīatua named Harvey Crewe. By all accounts, the attraction was immediate, and intense.

CHAPTER TWO
RETURN TO PUKEKAWA

arvey Crewe always wanted to be a sheep farmer.[1] He had grown up on land owned by his father at Pahīatua, in the Wairarapa, but due to a rift in the family he wasn't to inherit it. Instead, he planned to work and save up to buy his own property. Marrying the wealthy Jeannette Demler fast-forwarded his plans, and in 1966, aged 25, he became co-owner of the 361 acres that had once belonged to Jeannette's grandparents. To do so, he used $9000 of his own money to secure a $31,000 loan, paying Jeannette's sister, Heather, $40,000 for her half-share of the farm.[2]

With no intention of resting on his good fortune, Crewe immediately set about improving the farm, which had been run by a manager following Howard Chennells' death, working long days and frequently arriving home after dark. His ambition was clear. 'Well, you won't see me for a few years,' he told a friend of Jeannette's shortly after the couple moved onto the land at Pukekawa. 'I'm going to get this farm into shape the way I want it.'[3]

David Harvey Crewe was born on 20 October 1941 to William David

Candy Crewe and Marie Lal Crewe. His sister, Beverly Elizabeth Turner, was born a year earlier. The children initially grew up in Pahīatua, a former timber town turned service centre, but before Harvey finished primary school his parents had separated and his mother had taken the children and left the farm. Marie Crewe filed in court for judicial separation, and William Crewe filed for a restitution of conjugal rights. Eventually, they abandoned the court action and agreed to separate, with William agreeing to pay Marie £450 for the upkeep of the children and £3000 so she could buy a house. In August 1952, William Crewe died. Harvey was just 11.

William left an estate of £26,000, but had largely cut his wife and children out of his will. 'I do not wish them to participate in my estate by reason of the fact that I have been deserted by them and that they have made statements concerning me which are untrue and harmful to me,' his will read. To ensure her children's future security and education, Marie Crewe had to twice take the issue to court. The first time, she was awarded £1000, and £3000 each for Beverley and Harvey. On appeal, this was increased to £4500 each.[4]

Like his future wife, Harvey was sent to boarding school, in his case to Scots College, the private Presbyterian boys' school in Wellington. Afterwards, he began to work the land, becoming a shepherd and then a stock agent in Hawke's Bay, Manawatū and Whanganui. At Kumeroa, near Woodville, he worked on a farm for his friend Graeme Hewson, whom he had met as a teenager when working on a farm near Whanganui. They shared an interest in dog trials; Hewson gave Harvey a couple of dogs to start him off when he moved to Pukekawa with Jeannette.[5] Harvey had lived with Hewson and his wife Mary at Kumeroa.

When she was interviewed by journalist Pat Booth in 1975, Mary Hewson described Harvey as a 'super fellow', wonderful to have in the house. 'I never had to ask for the wood to be cut when he was here.' Hewson, perhaps Harvey's closest friend, described him as a decent bloke, a 'great joker', who was quiet, hard-working and a good rugby player. Harvey, with his hefty 6-foot frame, played at lock. The friends also played a bit of golf, but they were both 'pretty rough', Hewson said.[6]

After Harvey met Jeannette at her friend Beverley's wedding they were together whenever possible. Harvey was living by himself in a shepherd's hut down country and came to stay for the weekend in Whanganui. Jeannette would bake biscuits for him to take back. Friends and family agreed that they were a great match.[7]

Harvey proposed at Easter 1966 and within three months the wedding was organised, the dress bought, and the plans to buy the farm from Heather finalised. On 18 June 1966, the couple was married at St George's Church in Epsom, Auckland. Photos show a bright, clear winter's day. Harvey wears a three-piece suit, a white carnation pinned to his left lapel. His hair is swept to the side, he is grinning, and there is a dimple in his right cheek. Jeannette's dress is simple, delicate, with a round neckline and slim sleeves. She wears a white headpiece on her dark curled hair, with her veil piled on top, creating a huge plume around her face. She is beaming in every photo.

The Crewes look overjoyed, and slightly overwhelmed.

Harvey and Jeannette moved to Pukekawa immediately after the wedding. Where Whanganui was a town of 35,000 people, Pukekawa had a population of just 600. There was no village centre. Shopping was done in Tūākau, 12 kilometres away, where there was a milk bar, clothing stores, a hotel, a grocer's, a post office and a telephone exchange. Pukekawa itself had little more than a school, a hall and a garage. The district's houses were scattered alongside Highway 22 in small clusters. The landscape was a rolling patchwork of green paddocks and red dirt fields sown with onions, potatoes and carrots, the main road snaking through it. The former Chennells property was number 1405, Highway 22, set at the point where the road curves up towards the crest of a hill. Due west, 30 kilometres away, was Port Waikato, with its black sand and crashing Tasman sea. To the east, the Waikato River.

The house the Crewes moved into was set 50 metres from the road, a single-storey, four-bedroom brick-and-tile box. There was no driveway and the garage was near the roadside, which meant that the family — and anyone visiting — had to trudge through two gates and a paddock to get to the front door. Behind the house was a collection of small sheds, and the woolshed was in another paddock to the right. Further back, the land sloped steeply into a gully.

Inside, the house was simple and functional, with a fire in the living room for winter, a small kitchen and a dedicated laundry. The Crewes furnished the main areas with a mismatched old-fashioned couch and chairs re-covered by Jeannette using her needlework skills. They didn't have any art to hang, so the walls were largely left bare. At first, the house was too big for the young couple. At least one of the spare bedrooms was used for storage.

Jeannette hadn't lived in Pukekawa since her childhood and she had only returned for holidays and for a brief time in 1962 after her trip overseas. At that point, she told Clare MacGee, Pukekawa felt very small after the excitement of Europe. Any close companions she might have had from her early years had drifted away or established new sets of friends.[8]

Yet, here she was, back in a village where everyone knew her, living next door to her parents, a farmer's wife. While the rest of the Western world was undergoing a sexual and cultural revolution, the most excitement Jeannette Crewe could hope for in her new home was a rugby club jubilee. According to Hewson, Harvey felt the same way about his new life, but the couple was pragmatic. It was a good farm and they were going to make the most of it, for the meantime.[9]

Life in Pukekawa in the late 1960s was much the same as in any New Zealand farming town: it revolved around stock prices and the weather. For sheep farmers like Harvey and Jeannette, the value of wool was also front of mind. The export prices that had boomed throughout the 1950s began to wane, and by the end of 1966 had dropped by 40 per cent. But drought had held off for the past few years, and while conflict waged overseas — in Egypt, Belfast, Cambodia and Vietnam — New Zealand's politics remained relatively stable.

In those first years in their home, Jeannette and Harvey Crewe settled in and worked. They bought a cat, a blue Persian that Jeannette adored. Jeannette planted a flower garden. They went to stock sales. They attended the odd local function. But, otherwise, the couple didn't really participate in community events. Jeannette would either decline to go to occasions or local meetings, or the couple would agree but then cancel at the last minute.

Some people began to gossip that she was a snob. They did have regular meals with Jeannette's parents, May and Len Demler, at the

Harvey and Jeannette Crewe on their wedding day in Auckland, 18 June 1966.

family farm next door.[10] Sometimes, Harvey would go to a rugby game with Demler, and afterwards to the pub.[11]

The Crewes didn't really entertain at home either, much to the puzzlement of their community. Nearby neighbour Ron Chitty and his wife, for example, invited the Crewes for dinner several times, but the hospitality went unreturned. 'One could never say that you got to know them very well. It's hard to explain. They were good neighbours, it was an ideal neighbour relationship. We felt you could borrow a bottle of gin or, as Carolyn my wife did on one occasion, a bag of potatoes. Harvey would come over and help me with the lambs or loan me a piece of equipment. But basically they kept themselves to themselves,' Chitty later told David Yallop.[12]

It wasn't that the Crewes were completely reclusive. Rather, they kept their circle of friends from outside the town, visiting MacGee, the Hewsons and the Willis family — although never for more than a few days as Harvey was reluctant to be away from the farm too long. There was some tension over this, particularly because Jeannette had been hoping for a honeymoon in Australia, and the inheritance generated tension over money.[13] She had told Clare MacGee it would have been better if she'd had nothing because she felt Harvey resented the fact she was wealthy, and that was why he worked so hard, to validate himself. But for the most part, they were devoted to each other.[14]

This quiet life was interrupted after just a year in their new home. On 29 July 1967, they returned home around nine o'clock, after dinner with Jeannette's parents, to discover the house had been broken into. Immediately they realised some of Jeannette's jewellery had been taken from the dressing-table drawer in their bedroom. Jeannette called her mother to tell her, and then took stock. Missing were Jeannette's sapphire and diamond engagement ring, a set of pearls with a diamond and sapphire clasp, a set of cultured pearls, some earrings, brooches, a watch and a brush and comb set. Jeannette's handbag containing her driver's licence had also been stolen.

It appeared the intruder had come in through the unlocked back door. There was no sign the rest of the house had been touched, and even then, other valuables, such as money, which were in the same room, were overlooked. The next day, Detective Len Johnston, based at Ōtāhuhu and with responsibility for rural investigations, attended the farmhouse in response to the couple's complaint. He took fingerprints from Jeannette, and some items for examination — a drawer, a comb and a photograph. But there were no matches. An offender was never identified, and the items were never recovered. The Crewes made an insurance claim to replace what was taken.

The Crewes and the Demlers discussed who might have been responsible for the burglary.[15] They came to the conclusion that it must have been someone who knew Harvey and Jeannette's movements and had watched them go out, as they had not been out of the house for very long.[16] Jeannette told her friend Beverley Willis that she was sure the property had been targeted. It was well known in the district that the Crewes were financially well-off and that Jeannette had inherited a significant share of her uncle Howard's estate.[17] Jeannette wasn't flashy, but her jewellery was of good quality. The person who took the jewellery must have known what she owned, Jeannette said; only the most valuable items were taken.[18]

Jeannette was not someone known to have a nervous disposition, but after this she began to feel anxious about being home alone and would go out on the farm with Harvey during the day.[19] Mary Hewson, who visited in early 1968 just after Jeannette had found out she was pregnant, described Jeannette as a 'very frightened woman'. On the day Mary Hewson visited them, Harvey and Jeannette invited her and her husband to stay the night, but they declined. 'Something in that house gave me the jibbers,' Hewson later said. 'It was not Jeannette or Harvey, but the whole atmosphere of the place. Jeannette was frightened all right, but we didn't pry, although I felt it was a family matter.'[20]

On 1 December 1968, Jeannette gave birth to a daughter, Rochelle Janeane Crewe, at the Pukekohe Maternity Annexe. Harvey visited his wife every day. But what should have been a happy occasion was ruined by a second unsettling incident at the farm. On 7 December, while Jeannette was still at the maternity home, Harvey returned home from dinner with his mother- and father-in-law to find the farmhouse on fire. The southern corner — the room that had been made ready for baby Rochelle — was ablaze. Harvey ran into the house and shut the bedroom door, then rushed next door to get Len Demler.

May Demler called the fire brigade, then the closest neighbours.

When Harvey got back to the house, the windows were breaking. He used a ladder to climb onto the roof and Demler passed up buckets of water in an attempt to contain the fire until the Tūākau volunteer fire brigade arrived. By the time the flames were extinguished, 20 per cent of the house was damaged, and clothing, linen and other items were also smoke damaged. A canteen of cutlery, which sat atop a dresser, was found to be missing from the house.[21]

The cause of the fire drew conflicting opinions. Chief Fire Officer Edward Wild visited the house the following day to find that the tiled roof had collapsed into the bedroom when the rafters had burned through, making reconstruction of the scene difficult. Despite this, Wild said he believed the fire had probably started on a bedroom dresser, burning it to the floor and then travelling up the wall. He stated that the fire could have been started by a cigarette that had been left on the dresser, but Harvey denied ever smoking in that room.

Eric Baron, a loss adjuster for State Insurance, said he thought the fire was caused by an electrical fault and had started in the ceiling. In his opinion, rats had chewed through electrical wiring, causing a short circuit that resulted in the fire. Electrician Peter Graham, however, did not agree. Harvey Crewe had asked him to restore power to the house and when he was replacing the cable he noted it was in good condition, and that nothing in the wiring could have caused the fire. He also said that rats would not have been able to chew the wire and start a fire.

Harvey Crewe, meanwhile, told Demler that someone had deliberately started the fire by setting alight 'a piece of rimu over one of the back windows'. He repeatedly argued with Wild, the fire chief, but Wild was not prepared to say the fire was arson, and the fire was not reported to police.[22]

With his wife and new baby due home, Christmas approaching and shearing imminent, the fire put Harvey under stress. He was anxious to get the repairs to the house sorted before Jeannette's return and began calling the insurance office two or three times a day, once even travelling to Auckland to see Baron, the assessor, to ask to have the repairs started immediately. But the work was held up by late quotes from builders and did not start until the following year. By then Jeannette was home, and also clearly under stress; the fire had not improved her nerves.

In January, the couple was due to attend the wedding of Harvey's good friend Anthony Eaton in Masterton. Harvey was to be the best man. But a couple of days before the wedding, Harvey telephoned to cancel, saying they would be unable to attend because of the fire. The repairs dragged on through February and March. Almost all the tradespeople who came to the house during this time reported difficulties with the Crewes. Some said they were asked to enter through the window rather than the door to get inside, even if the Crewes were home.

Builder Harold Reeve, who started work in March 1969, said he found Harvey difficult and almost obstructive. The builders could only work when Harvey gave approval and often he would say it wasn't possible to be on site because he was going out or because the shearers were there. When the bill arrived, Harvey refused to sign it off, saying the work wasn't finished.[23]

Harvey Crewe's apparent bad temper, his brusqueness and lack of tact soon became the topic of local gossip. A story circulated about two stock agents arriving 10 minutes early one morning, at which Harvey burst out of the house in his socks to angrily tell them they could wait while he finished his breakfast. In another story, Keith Christie, a pilot working for local topdressers, Barr Brothers, was confronted by an angry Harvey Crewe when he arrived to spray the farm. Harvey apparently thought Barr Brothers cheated on their spray, which explained their low prices.

Harvey also didn't like anyone shooting on his property, locals said. Other farmers in the district were more amenable, but anyone who came onto Harvey's land without permission would be ordered off and told not to come back.[24]

But others found him reasonable. Ronald Geoffrey Brown, who painted and wallpapered two rooms in the house in 1968, said that although Harvey seemed unapproachable, they 'got on', and Harvey paid the bill straight away. And the Yearburys, who were shearers, said Harvey was a good boss although he was particular about how the fleece was sorted.[25] Teenage neighbour Ross Eyre worked for Harvey, cutting hay. 'He was a good guy to work for, very strict, and very tough,' Eyre said. 'You had a job to do and you'd do the job properly. He expected quality workmanship.'[26]

And it was clear to friends that despite his strict business approach and sometimes dour demeanour, Harvey adored his daughter. 'Harvey was a real good father,' Graeme Hewson said. 'He loved that little girl.'[27]

The Crewes only had six months' reprieve before a third incident at the farm. Late in the evening of 28 May 1969, local resident David Fleming was driving past when something on the Crewe property caught his eye. The hay barn was on fire. Fleming pulled over, found Harvey in the woolshed and yelled at him that the barn was ablaze. But this time, nothing was salvageable. By the time Harvey got to the barn, the structure, along with the 800 bales of hay stored within it, was already well alight. 'Who would have done this to me?' Harvey lamented to Fleming.

An insurance report for L. M. Bernard & Son identified the cause as spontaneous combustion, given there was no other credible explanation available. Harvey told the assessors he didn't know how the fire started, and again did not report the incident to police.[28]

Jeannette was still suffering anxiety from the burglary and the first fire, and so in April, when Harvey had to go into hospital for a gallstone operation, she refused to stay alone in the house. Instead she took Rochelle to stay with her aunt in Auckland until he could come back to Pukekawa with her.[29] The second fire seemed to have made her even more fearful. When Owen Priest, their neighbour of four years and a good friend of her father's, visited the day after the hay barn had burned down to offer help, Jeannette wouldn't even open the fly-screen door to him.[30]

In February 1970, May Demler died. Heather flew back from California for the funeral. She had been somewhat estranged from her mother for a number of years after beginning a relationship with Robert Souter, a father of three and a divorcé. May had not agreed with Heather's choice, and before she died had amended her will to effectively cut Heather out. She left her share of the farm, and all her possessions, including her jewellery and her car, to Jeannette. Her granddaughter Rochelle inherited $2000, and $400 went to the Anglican Church. Jeannette and her father were to be joint trustees of the farm, while Len was allowed the house, its occupation and its income during his lifetime. He received $23,000 to satisfy the mortgage debt taken on after May had bought half the farm to pay his tax arrears in 1961; with the balance of the estate also going to Jeannette.[31]

Len Demler did not agree with his wife's decision to cut Heather out of her inheritance, but he had been unable to change her mind before she died. Under pressure from May, Demler had had little contact with Heather in recent years, but after his wife died, the two had begun writing letters, and Heather had recently sent Demler some pyjamas.[32]

While Heather was in New Zealand, she visited her sister at her home three times. Once, she babysat Rochelle, and another time she went into town with Jeannette. Heather also noticed that her sister was worried about being alone. Jeannette told her sister that she was sure 'someone must have had something in for them' but she didn't know who. Jeannette's behaviour was out of character, Heather said.[33]

Around this same time, Jeannette apparently told friends she believed she was being watched. There were no coverings on two of the windows in the lounge — the curtains had been damaged in the fire and not yet replaced — making it easy for someone to get close to their home, particularly at night when lights were on inside the house.[34] Jeannette never said who she thought might be watching, only that she was feeling increasingly unnerved about their home in Pukekawa.[35] 'It seems that the farm has got a jinx on it,' she told Clare MacGee during a visit to Whanganui in early 1970. 'So many things have happened there.'[36]

Despite the couple's creeping sense of unease, life in Pukekawa carried on. As the winter of 1970 set in, the Crewes were busy on the farm. The wet weather was making shearing difficult, Jeannette wrote in a letter to her mother-in-law, Marie Crewe. Some of the sheep had facial eczema and would need to be taken to the works. Harvey was considering buying a bull but didn't want to pay big money for it. Jeannette was knitting Harvey a jumper.[37] She had also ordered some material to finally get curtains on the living-room windows hung, but it had a flaw in it, so she had arranged to send it back to the Smith & Caughey department store in Auckland.[38]

On 16 June, Jeannette spent the morning running errands in Tūākau with Rochelle while Harvey was out on the farm. On their way into town, they saw Len Demler, who was collecting his mail at the gate, and tooted at him as they passed. Their first stop in town was Sturrock & Monteith Solicitors, where Jeannette had a meeting with her lawyer, Douglas Monteith, about the death duties on her mother's estate. After signing some paperwork, Jeannette was also handed a statement of the estate's assets and liabilities.

Although Jeannette had been aware of the contents of the will since March, this meeting was the first time she was aware of the exact value of her share. Jeannette was in good spirits at the meeting, laughing about the debacle over the shearing and how drawn out it had been. After saying goodbye to Monteith, Jeannette and Rochelle drove to Pukekohe, where they did the shopping and filled the car with petrol before returning to the farm.[39]

Earlier that morning, Jeannette had telephoned her father and invited him for dinner, a weekly routine they had developed since May's death.[40] Demler arrived around 6.30 p.m., after Rochelle had been put to bed. The timing was at Jeannette's request, so the baby didn't get excited by seeing her grandfather and would settle down to sleep. Demler sat with a whisky in front of the fire in the lounge, where he was joined by Harvey, who also had a whisky; Jeannette had a brandy. After a dinner of corned beef, potatoes, carrots and onion sauce, Jeannette cleared the table and made cups of tea, which they had with cake. All three then moved back into the lounge and watched television with more cups of tea. Harvey and Jeannette then got up and did the dishes.

At 9.30 p.m., Jeannette made another cup of tea, they switched off the television and sat talking while Jeannette knitted. The conversation was mainly about farming. Jeannette told Demler that she had gone to sign the papers at the lawyers' that day, but they didn't discuss the matter further. Jeannette and Harvey asked Demler what he would like for his upcoming birthday, pushing him until he agreed they could buy him some shoes. He left to drive home around 10 p.m.[41]

On Wednesday 17 June, the weather was once again atrocious. Len Demler was supposed to be going to Hamilton to watch a rugby game, but it was so wet he stayed home and listened to the game on the radio.[42] At the Crewe household, stock agent John Gracie called in for a cup of tea. He and Harvey discussed stock prices, while Jeannette played on the floor with Rochelle. Harvey and Gracie then left to look at a bull in Glen Murray. Jeannette was baking biscuits when another visitor arrived unexpectedly — a local woman called Thyrle Pirrett, who had brought her three-year-old daughter to play with Rochelle. Pirrett thought Jeannette seemed tense, and maybe even a little depressed. Her manner was abrupt, and when she invited Rochelle to visit them at their home, Jeannette didn't appear enthusiastic.[43]

After Pirrett and her daughter left, Harvey, Jeannette and Rochelle drove to a stock sale in Bombay. On the way there they stopped at a vegetable stall, another of Jeannette's weekly routines. It was still pouring with rain, so Jeannette stayed in the car with Rochelle until the sale finished, around 2.30 p.m. Then they drove home, and Harvey changed into his work clothes.

At 5 p.m., the empty Crewe car was seen by the side of the road 2 kilometres south of the house, near the cemetery. It was still raining. Alexander Irvine, a farmer from Glen Murray, didn't see Harvey but assumed he was nearby, shifting sheep.

It was the last day the Crewes were seen alive.

CHAPTER THREE
A TERRIBLE BLOODY MESS

For five days during that miserable week of weather, no one missed the Crewes. When they didn't arrive at the meeting of the Pukekawa Ratepayers' Association at the local hall on the evening of Wednesday 17 June, it wasn't regarded with any surprise. They weren't regular attendees anyway, and they weren't the only family missing. Local farmer Arthur Thomas and his wife Vivien didn't arrive either as a sick cow was due to calve. Len Demler also didn't turn up, but that wasn't out of character because he never did.[1]

The Pukekawa Hall was just off the main road. To get there, many local residents would have passed the Crewe farm. But no one noticed anything unusual. And no one travelling to indoor bowls at Glen Murray, or to a table tennis tournament at the Ōpuatia Hall that night, saw anything either.

The next day, Thursday, also passed without attention drawn to the Crewe farm. But on Friday 19 June, delivery man Emmett Shirley arrived at the Crewes' mailbox to find the bread and milk he had left there the day before untouched. Shirley paused and glanced up at the little brick house. Usually, he saw Jeannette giving Rochelle her bottle in the front room. On this day, however, the blinds in Rochelle's room were down, and there was no sign of the family, which he thought was a little odd. He left the family's weekend order of two and a half loaves of bread, three quarts of milk and the *New Zealand Herald* newspaper, and drove away.[2]

That weekend was a busy one in Pukekawa. The Onewhero Rugby Club was celebrating its fiftieth jubilee, with a party planned for Saturday night and a game between the Old Boys and the present players on Sunday. The whole town was excited. Len Demler had a double ticket (the tickets were only sold in doubles at a cost of $8) to the Saturday dinner at the Onewhero Hall. It started at 6 p.m., with speeches and dancing.

Demler drank heavily and didn't leave until 1.30 a.m. When he got home, he turned on the radio and listened to the All Blacks playing the first match of their South Africa tour, against Border in the Eastern Cape province. The game, which the All Blacks won 28–3, went into the small hours of the morning.[3]

Despite his late night, he was up early the next day spraying thistles before attending the jubilee match on the Sunday afternoon.[4] Harvey and Jeannette did not show up at either event, and Demler did not contact them or hear from them the whole weekend.[5]

On Monday, Demler's phone rang just before 7 a.m. It was local stock agent Joseph Moore, who said he had telephoned the Crewe house several times over the weekend, but there had been no answer. Did Demler know where they were? Was their phone working? Demler told Moore that as far as he knew the couple was at home, and he had no idea about the phone. Moore decided to visit instead, and arrived at the Crewe home with John Dagg, another stock agent, just before 9 a.m.

Dagg knocked on the back door. There was no answer. The men couldn't hear any movement inside the house, so they left. When delivery man Emmett Shirley arrived as usual at 9.30 a.m., he again could see no sign of anyone in the house. The milk and bread he'd delivered the previous week was still in the box. Wanting to avoid attracting rats, Shirley threw the old bread into the paddock. He decided the Crewes had gone away without notifying him, and this time he didn't leave anything further.

That Monday, Tuakau Transport Limited foreman Ronald Wright phoned the Crewe house several times. A truck was about to arrive to pick up some sheep Harvey was sending to the works, and Wright wanted to make sure the sheep would be ready. Again, there was no answer. Wright phoned Demler to ask if he would go and see Harvey. Concerned enough by now that something was amiss, Demler went outside, got into his red Cortina and drove down the hill. The couple's green Hillman Hunter car was in the garage when he arrived. There were about 10 sheep in the front paddock. Both gates, the one on the roadside and the small gate to the lawn, were shut.

As Demler approached the house, he could hear 18-month-old Rochelle talking, but couldn't see any sign of his daughter or son-in-law. The outside light was on, he noticed, and the key was in the back door. Stepping inside, he saw Harvey's slippers placed together on the floor.[6] Demler went into the kitchen. On the table were the remains of a meal of flounder. Most of the fish had been eaten but the dishes were on the table, uncleared. On the bench, he saw more dishes, and more food, including part of an apple and cooked potatoes.

And then he saw the blood. It was smeared lightly across the kitchen's lino floor. In the lounge there was more, with large stains seeping into the carpet and a trail of blood leading from a fireside armchair across the room, as if something had been dragged towards the hall.[7] He looked in the main bedroom, where the bed was still made. It was empty. Then Demler checked on Rochelle, who was in her cot. The room smelt rank and Rochelle seemed unable to stand up.[8] She looked very thin and her eyes were sunken, as if she had been crying. As her grandfather walked into the room she watched him, making no sound.[9]

Instead of taking Rochelle with him, Demler said later, he panicked and left the house, thinking someone might have been lurking nearby. He drove home and called Ronald Wright to tell him not to come for the sheep. Shortly afterwards, he got back in his car and drove to his neighbour, poultry farmer Owen Priest.

Priest was working in a paddock when he heard Demler's car pull up. Demler asked him to go to the Crewe farm with him. 'I don't know

A police photographer took this image of the Crewes' living room, showing the armchair in which Harvey was sitting when he was shot, the bloody drag marks on the carpet and Jeannette's abandoned knitting on the couch.

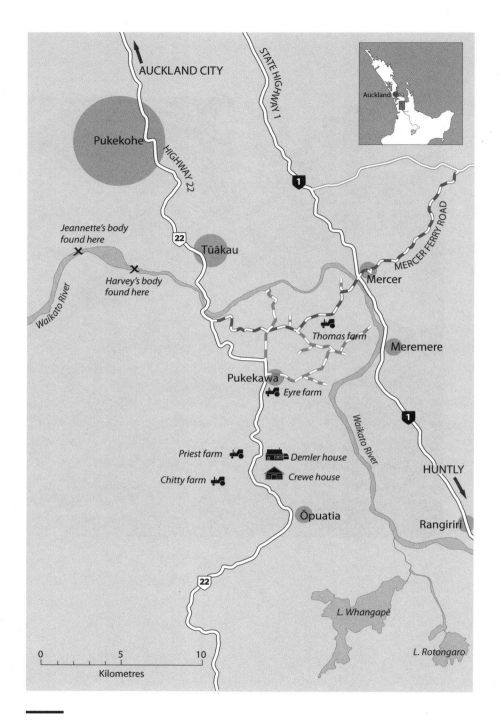

A map of the Pukekawa district showing the Crewes' neighbours and the locations of Jeannette and Harvey Crewe's bodies.

what's happened up there but there's a terrible bloody mess,' he said.[10] On the way to the house, Demler turned to Priest and said, 'They're not there. I wonder where the bloody hell they've gone to.'

When Priest walked into the house, the sight of the blood stopped him in his tracks. 'The bugger's killed her and done himself in,' Demler said to Priest. 'I tell you, Harvey's killed her.' Priest began to walk through the house, first entering Rochelle's room. She was lying propped on her elbow on her right side in the cot. She wasn't making any noise. She didn't sit up or move when he entered. Priest noticed the bedding and clothing was soiled, but not extremely so. He then went down the passage to the first room on the right, the master bedroom. The door was ajar. He walked in; he looked in the wardrobe. He walked out.

In the hall, he noticed the cord connecting the television set was disconnected. Then he looked through the rest of the rooms. In the kitchen he noticed a bottle of milk on the bench. He sniffed it, finding it had soured. When he got to the bathroom, he looked around for Demler, who was still standing by the front door. It struck him that he had gone through the entire house on his own, and that someone may have been in one of the rooms and could have attacked him.

Demler repeated that Harvey had done Jeannette in. Priest turned to him and said, 'Look Len, we don't know what's happened. It could have been a third party.'[11]

Together, Demler and Priest then searched the hay barn, the chicken coop, the dog pen and the woolshed. Nothing. Even the three dogs were quiet, although it was evident that they had had no food and no water for some time. The men went back inside through the back door, through the kitchen, into the lounge and out the front door. This time they noticed more blood — on the hearth, on an armchair, on the front door. There were smears on the porch and flecks on some bricks near the steps.

Having finished their search, the two men went back into Rochelle's room. Demler picked his granddaughter up from her cot and wrapped her in a blanket. She put an arm around his neck. Priest picked up a teddy bear from the cot. Outside, they put Rochelle in the car, with the teddy bear. It took some effort for Demler to get her to sit down because she didn't want to let go of him.[12] Demler dropped Priest at home, then drove a further 7 kilometres to the home of family friend Barbara Willis.

When Demler arrived, between 2.15 and 2.30 p.m., he parked the car in the driveway and went inside to ask for help. Willis came out to find Rochelle in the front seat, still wrapped in her blanket. Demler picked Rochelle up and gave her to Willis, and then promptly left, upset and in tears. Willis, who had three children of her own, took Rochelle straight inside, undressed her, and put her in a bath. She had been wearing night nappies — a cloth nappy with another folded inside it lengthways — and she had a nappy rash that had turned to blisters. The nappies were sodden with urine and caked with hard faeces. The smell was foetid. Willis concluded the nappies were beyond washing and threw them in the fire.[13]

Rochelle was cold and rigid. She shook, as if in shock, for hours. Her eyes were very sunken, with dark rings, and the whites were bloodshot. She was weak, and either couldn't, or wouldn't, stand up, and she clung to Willis desperately that day and for days afterwards. Willis couldn't put her down.

After the bath, Willis phoned the local doctor, John Lightbody, who arranged for the district nurse, Nancy Crawford, to deliver some cream for the rash. Willis told Lightbody that she didn't think the baby needed further medical attention. She fed Rochelle a boiled egg and some bread and butter, ice cream, peaches and a drink of milk, and then the child was sick. But she was still thirsty and kept wanting more milk. Willis noticed that any time the phone rang, Rochelle became very upset. Whenever Willis picked up the receiver to answer she would push it out of her hands.[14]

When Crawford arrived with the cream around 4.30 p.m., she too noticed that Rochelle was very upset, 'hollow-eyed' and very dehydrated. She also noticed that the tissue on Rochelle's legs was soft, as if she had rapidly lost weight, and that she was struggling to stand. Looking at the rash, Crawford concluded, as Willis had, that Rochelle's nappies hadn't been changed for a few days. She recommended Willis give Rochelle fluids with glucose for the following 12 hours, but didn't prescribe any further medical treatment.[15]

Meanwhile, the first police officers began to descend on the Crewe property. As soon as Len Demler dropped him home, Owen Priest telephoned the Tūākau police station to report the disappearance of Harvey and Jeannette Crewe. Constable Gerald Wyllie, the sole officer at the station, took the call about 2.20 p.m. Wyllie collected Priest on his way to the house. He made a cursory search, and then used the Crewes' telephone to call for more help. Then Wyllie noticed something strange. The clothes dryer in the kitchen was switched on, but the fan wasn't working, and it was emitting a huge amount of heat. Thinking it was unsafe to leave it on, Wyllie turned the dryer off at the wall.

Upon instructions from his superiors, Wyllie locked the back door and waited outside with Priest. By then, Demler had arrived back at his farm. He had some sheep in the yard that he wanted to draft while waiting for the police.[16] More and more cars began to pull up at the Crewes' farm gate as locals heard the news that something terrible had happened at the house.

Detective Inspector Bruce Hutton arrived at the farm from Auckland around 5 p.m. Hutton, 41, had been a farmer before joining the police in 1948. By the time of the Crewe case, he was the head of the Otahuhu Criminal Investigation Bureau, and was renowned as an efficient, energetic detective with experience of at least 30 homicide investigations. But none of those cases were as troubling as what he found when he stepped inside the Crewe home; it bore no relationship to any other investigation he had undertaken or any that he had read or studied — there were not just one but two persons missing and a child alive in a cot.[17] He was immediately horrified, he told David Yallop in 1977, that here was a crime scene and that cars were lining up, contaminating it. He ordered the vehicles and people out, but by that time the damage had been done.[18]

After working to secure the scene from further contamination — something of a lost cause given evidence such as any footprints in the mud at the gate had possibly already been destroyed by either visitors or sheep — Hutton went through the house with a pathologist, Dr Francis Cairns. They focused mainly on the bloodstains on the armchair in the living room, the blood patches on the carpet, and the drag mark. Hutton and Cairns decided that given the amount of blood, they were most likely dealing with a homicide, or perhaps even a double homicide.

As there were no signs of a gun having been used, the most likely weapon was either a sharp weapon causing wounds, or a heavy blunt weapon causing head injuries. It was thought likely that the drag mark indicated that one of the victims, probably Harvey, because he weighed 16 stone, had been dragged out of the house through the front door. They also decided that whatever had happened must have occurred on Wednesday, given that Thursday's *Herald* and the milk for 18 June were still in the letterbox.[19]

On these assumptions, Hutton began assigning his team their roles. Pat Gaines was put in charge of the search, which began that night, with 20 farmers and 10 police scouring the farm for the couple or the weapons. Other officers were put in charge of cataloguing the scene, interviewing witnesses, canvassing the area, and taking photographs and fingerprints. One of the detectives, Murray Jeffries, took a brief statement from Len Demler during the afternoon.[20]

At some point, Demler also spoke to the press, who had swiftly caught wind of a dramatic event unfolding in rural Auckland. By that evening, the first article was already on the news wire. 'Police fear for the safety of the parents of a starving baby found in a blood-spattered Pukekawa farmhouse this afternoon,' the opening line of the New Zealand Press Association bulletin that went out to a range of papers read.[21]

Demler told the reporters what he had told the police: he had found the house empty except for Rochelle in her cot. 'There were dinner dishes on the table,' he said. 'There was blood on the carpet and on the chair. But the house was not in disorder. The car was in the garage. The three dogs were in their kennels. They couldn't have been fed, but it was a mystery that they had survived for five days. I only live down the road but I didn't hear them bark,' he told the reporters.[22] After helping police to search the farm, Demler went home. The Crewe house was left empty, a police guard stationed outside.

CHAPTER FOUR
THE INVESTIGATION

On 22 June, Detective Bruce Parkes was on his honeymoon when he got a phone call from his boss at the Auckland Central police station. He needed to come back to work the following day; he was needed for a murder case south of Auckland. Parkes was one of dozens of extra police called in from across Auckland to help on the Crewe inquiry. His next day off wouldn't be until after Labour Weekend, four months later.[1]

When he got to Pukekawa on the cold, drizzly morning of 23 June, a search of the farm was already under way. The police and local farmers combing the paddocks and bush had been told to look for a blunt weapon or a knife, and for a body, or maybe two. By the end of that first day, nearly all the bush had been gone over. The searchers had found nothing.

Parkes, who had graduated from detective training earlier that year, was part of a group assigned to inspect the grounds immediately around the house.[2] Determined to do things by the book, he set out a grid of string across the lawn, and each square within it was inspected by police officers and the findings recorded at the end of the day. The first thing they found was the remnants of the fish-and-chip meal some officers had eaten and discarded across the grass the night before. When they reached the flowerbeds, Parkes instructed the officers to pull out the plants, shake the dirt from their roots, and toss them over the fence. It was gruelling work, with the officers on their knees, in suits, from early morning until afternoon. But again, they found nothing.[3]

Inside the house, two more of Hutton's detectives, Murray Jeffries and Graham Abbott, were making a meticulous record of the crime scene. A set of louvre windows in the kitchen was open, they noticed. The table was set for two, with a third plate in the middle. An unopened pile of mail was next to the plates, including bills and a letter from friends.[4] On the kitchen bench, either side of the sink, there were two bloodstained saucepans. The lino floor, the cupboard doors beneath the sink, the kitchen bench and the hot-water tap were also covered in diluted bloodstains. More drops of this watery blood were found on the hearth in the lounge.

There was also some evidence of a possible altercation in the lounge. Jeannette's knitting was on the couch; there were several dropped stitches, and a slightly bent knitting needle lay on the floor in front of the couch. Two women's slippers were found — one near a bloodstained armchair and the other across the room. A closer inspection of this armchair — which would come to be known as 'Harvey's chair' — revealed that blood had dripped right through the seat to the floor, indicating that a body may have been there for some time before it was moved.

In the afternoon Len Demler arrived to collect some clothes for Rochelle and was taken through the house by Detective John Hughes. He told police there were several items missing from the lounge, including a piece of carpet that was usually in front of the fireplace. Ash in the fireplace indicated that it had probably been burnt, as had a cushion from the armchair, and the fire screen had been replaced afterwards.

In the master bedroom, a brown bedspread had been taken off the bed. But nothing else was disturbed — Jeannette and Harvey's pyjamas were still neatly folded under the pillows, a pile of Jeannette's clothes was in the corner and Harvey's trousers, shirt and jersey were hanging over the door. The car keys to the green Hillman were in the drawer of a cocktail cabinet in the lounge. Jeannette's purse was in the kitchen, with change in it, as was her cheque-book; its last stub, dated 17 June, was made out to the Farmers department store for a pair of plastic Stardust pants for Rochelle.[5]

In Rochelle's room, the cot bedding was very badly urine-stained, the urine soaked deeply into the mattress. Inside the cot was a pair of pink pyjama pants and a wet nappy. The blinds in her room were closed. More dirty nappies were in the washhouse, two pairs on top of the refrigerator, and another on the lid of the washing machine. A bucket containing a fresh mix of NapiSan, but with no soaking nappies, was on the floor.

Harvey's shotgun was in the washhouse, in a canvas bag. Ammunition for the gun was in the spare bedroom the Crewes used for storage. An ironing board was set up in a fourth bedroom. In the clothes dryer, the one found running the day before, were a pair of men's underpants and a pair of men's socks.[6] Outside, rust flakes at the bottom of the steps looked as if they had come from the underside of the Crewes' wheelbarrow, which was not far from the steps and which appeared to have been washed. The officers surmised it was likely that the wheelbarrow had been used to transport a body — or maybe two — to a vehicle.[7]

That night, police held their first conference at Pukekawa, in their newly established makeshift headquarters in a cottage at neighbour Ron Chitty's farm. The detectives took turns to report their findings, before discussing their initial impressions of the scene. 'There has been some attempt to clean this mess up,' said Detective Stan Keith. 'Somebody got a cloth wet, lifted it up, drops have fallen off onto the carpet, they've gone back into the kitchen and water from the cloth has been dropped on the floor as they have been going.'[8]

From what police could tell, it seemed that until Wednesday 17 June, everything had been as normal at the farm. The detectives had already done a wide area canvass and had heard about the visit from the stock agent, the trip to the sale, and the sighting of the car down the road at the gate. But when it came to the couple themselves, police were having more trouble. They were known by so few people. Detective John Roberts said that, so far, Harvey had been described as dour and a hard businessman, but 'not a bad fellow'. Meanwhile, Jeannette was said to be 'a companionable woman' who was arty, liked sport and used to play golf. She was the less reserved of the two and might have socialised more if not for her conservative husband, Roberts summarised.

There were other differences: where Harvey was meticulously tidy, the officers concluded Jeannette had been a 'poor housekeeper' despite her polished personal appearance. They noted, for example, her clothes from the previous day lying on the floor and the food left out on the bench. The dirty nappies, in particular, drew the detectives' scorn. 'I would think it would be normal for the average woman to throw them into a bucket and let them soak but she was not a tidy and house-proud woman from the dirt and dust around the place,' Jeffries said.[9]

The officers wondered if this could provide a motive for the crime. 'There seemed to be some degree of incompatibility between them,' Roberts surmised. He was convinced the couple had had an argument that had soured. 'I think domestic at this stage is a fair assumption.'[10]

But Hutton was not convinced. He told the media gathered at the house that although the case was being treated as a double homicide, he had no theory yet. 'We have not come up with a definite reconstruction of what happened. We are not discounting that a third party is involved.'[11]

Hutton's attempt to solve the puzzle presented by the crime scene was complicated by three separate pieces of information. The first came from farm labourer Bruce Roddick, who had been working across the road at the Chitty farm on Friday 19 June. He was feeding out hay around nine in the morning when he saw a woman dressed in slacks standing outside the Crewe house, 'which was about 75 yards away', apparently watching him. 'She seemed to be looking in my direction,' he told police. 'She would be in her thirties, and about 5'10 to 5 foot 11. I am 5'10 and she looked very tall to me. Her hair was not blonde, but light brown, her hair was cut short but curled up at the bottom.' Nearby he saw a parked car which he described as being a dark green Hillman. Roddick was sure of his sighting, even saying the woman 'seemed good looking'.

Roddick had spoken to police at his parents' behest, after he heard

Detective Inspector Bruce Hutton was in charge of the Crewe murder investigation from the start. A former farmer, he had a reputation as a tough, shrewd investigator who got results.

on the radio that the Crewes had been killed on Wednesday. Police were wrong, he told his parents, because 'he had seen Mrs Crewe on the Friday'. It later eventuated that Roddick had only assumed the woman was Jeannette Crewe and didn't know her by sight.[12] After confirming Roddick's whereabouts with his employer, Detective Roberts said he thought it was likely an accurate sighting, despite describing Roddick as 'limited' intellectually.[13]

The second piece of information came from resident Queenie McConachie, who reported seeing a little fair-haired girl standing at the Crewes' roadside gate on Saturday 20 June, as she drove along State Highway 22 towards Tūākau around 1.30 p.m. McConachie and her husband were on the way to the rugby game when they saw the child, who was holding on to the wire fence near the delivery box and was wearing blue trousers with a bib at the front. As she watched, the child turned and toddled away towards the house. She also saw a light-coloured car parked outside the house gate.[14] Detective Sergeant James Tootill, who took the statement, said he had verified the existence of the rugby match.[15]

Later, McConachie's husband disagreed with her, saying he thought they'd seen the child on the way home, around 4.30 p.m.[16] But McConachie remained sure. She was about to have a baby herself, and thought the child looked a lovely little girl.[17]

The third piece of information came from paediatrician Dr Charles Fox. On Tuesday afternoon, the day after she had been found, police had taken Rochelle and Barbara Willis to his rooms in Auckland for an assessment. Rochelle had gone to bed the previous night with a bottle of milk and had woken at 7 a.m. She had refused toast but had drunk another 6 ounces of milk during the morning, Willis told Fox. When Fox examined Rochelle, he found her 'of good build' and well covered. The tone of her skin and muscles suggested she had recently lost one to two pounds in weight, but aside from nappy rash, no other abnormalities were found.

He couldn't find any literature on how many days a normal, healthy 18-month-old child could survive without food or water, but he said Rochelle was a robust child, and had probably conserved energy by sleeping and by being confined to her cot. The colder temperatures would also have helped prevent fluid loss, he said. Despite that, Fox doubted Rochelle had been alone since the previous Wednesday. 'A child such as Rochelle, living under the conditions outlined above, might survive five days, but she would be seriously ill at the end of that time,' he said. Taking the rashes into consideration as well, Fox said, Rochelle had most likely been without normal care for a maximum of 72 hours, and possibly only 48 hours.[18]

On 24 June, based on all of this information, Hutton issued a statement to the press saying police believed someone had been in the Crewe house as late as Friday 19 June — two days after the disappearance of Jeannette and Harvey — and that Rochelle may have been fed up to that time.[19] By then, police were relatively confident they were dealing with two deaths: tests had revealed the blood on the armchair was from the same blood group as Harvey, while the blood near the hearth belonged to the same group as Jeannette. Equally, it was likely the mat that had been burned in the fire had also been covered in Jeannette's blood, while the burnt cushion likely contained Harvey's blood.[20] Hutton told the press he was now 'almost certain' a third person was involved.[21]

Publicly, police didn't say who they thought the third person was, but behind the scenes, suspicions began to circle around one man: Jeannette's father, Len Demler. Just the day before, Detective John Hughes had told his colleagues at the daily debrief that he was convinced Demler was above board. 'I stake my reputation on him,' Hughes said. 'He is a good solid type of bloke, I would say. I don't think he has really realised what has happened yet, don't think the shock has hit him. Sort of putting on a bit of a front at the moment.'[22]

Yet by the evening of 25 June, Hughes' assessment seems to have been forgotten. Detective Inspector Hutton had interviewed Demler himself that afternoon, after going over his statement and taking fingerprints. He'd asked Demler about his movements, and whether he could have been involved in the disappearance of the Crewes. Demler denied this, but Hutton said he felt the usually taciturn farmer had made a slip-up while they were talking: 'I let him have a look at a photo . . . and he said "I can't see how she could have been killed".' Hutton thought this was suspicious since at no time had he told Demler that Jeannette was dead. 'He is either a real good liar or a psycho type,' Hutton told the other detectives at that night's conference.[23]

Other officers added what neighbours had to say about Demler: that he was hot-tempered, and that when his wife was dying he was somewhat callous. At first, they said, Demler had made regular trips to see May but as time wore on he went more and more to bowls instead. He had also tried to defraud Inland Revenue. One neighbour, who openly admitted to hating Demler because he was 'inclined to be mean', said outright they suspected him of the crime. 'They said that Demler contacted the Crewes every day,' Detective Roberts reported back. 'If Demler said he wasn't there for three or four days, he was telling lies.' Roberts concluded that Demler had killed the Crewes.[24]

The next day, police carried out a search of Demler's house. He willingly let them in. The home was tidy and beautifully furnished. From inside, Detective Seaman took Demler's pocket knife, a meat knife, some torn clothing and some brown shoes. The shoes appeared to have blood on them, but Demler told police the stains were spilled liquor from the party he'd been at on Saturday night. Outside, officers searched the garden, fowl house, barn and woolshed.

'We could not find anything there that looked the slightest bit suspicious. There was a bit of paddock turned up but it was only a rabbit burrow,' one of the searchers told his colleagues.[25] Officers returned and searched again the following day, taking blood samples from a stain in Demler's car and removing an assortment of other items from the farm. That afternoon, Hutton again took Demler to the Ōtāhuhu police station for questioning. Part way through the interview, Hutton asked Demler why he hadn't been helping with the police search.

Demler: 'You think I did this, don't you?'

Hutton: 'I think you are the person who removed Harvey Crewe's body from the Crewe household. In fact I'm quite certain you've done this.'

Demler didn't reply and looked at the floor, Hutton said.[26]

During the first three weeks of the investigation, the search team numbered more than 200. Police, army personnel and volunteers cut through bush, climbed into limestone caves, and even dived the swift, murky waters of the Waikato River to try to find the Crewes' bodies. Each day, the officer in charge of the search, Inspector

Above: Hundreds of people from the Pukekawa district joined the search for the Crewes in the days following their disappearance. *Below:* Police used then-new forensic methods such as grid- and sieve-searching the Crewe garden in the hunt for clues.

Pat Gaines, provided an update to the evening debrief on their progress, and then the team of detectives would report what they had found.

The bulk of the officers' work involved following up information provided to the inquiry team, or re-interviewing friends and neighbours spoken to only briefly in the initial rush of the inquiry. The slower pace of life in Pukekawa added extra time to their schedules, the detectives learned. Cups of tea and a biscuit were offered, or there'd be 10 minutes of chat before the interviews began. By the end of the day the team would be behind, rushing to transcribe the handwritten notebook entries into an official typewritten jobsheet in time to catch a car or a bus back to Auckland.

Given that all of the inquiry team were men and they had not been trained to type, the information recorded in their jobsheets tended to be as brief as possible.[27] At the daily meetings, however, the detectives would run through the most important findings in more detail as a minute-taker recorded it: the multiple sightings of cars near the Crewe property on the days the couple was missing, including a green-and-white Valiant seen parked in the Crewes' driveway at 7 a.m. on Saturday 20 June; and the tip-offs about people who might have had grievances against Harvey Crewe, particularly given the burglary and the fires.

Suggestions in this category included a painter, a mushroom picker and a former neighbour who let his lice-ridden sheep mix with Harvey's mob, causing the pair to fall out. John Hughes also followed up a tip from Beverley Willis about a 'persistent' former suitor of Jeannette's who she thought was called 'Murphy'.

But each suggested suspect was quickly ruled out. Police and scientists also investigated all fingerprints from the Crewe house, including a mystery fingerprint from the rear-view mirror of the couple's Hillman. Some of the information discovered was helpful in reconstructing what might have happened to the Crewes but some caused yet more confusion. For example, early on, detectives heard from a roadside vendor who said he'd sold Harvey six flounder in a packet on 14 June, and they decided those must have been the flounder on the dinner table. But just a few days later, a fishmonger in Pukekohe came forward saying he had sold two flounder and chips to a woman who resembled Jeannette on Wednesday 17 June, leaving police with a completely different scenario to contend with.[28]

By the end of June, at the urging of Dr Fox, who believed police should get a second opinion, Rochelle was taken to two more specialists, the children's physician Ronald Caughey and Dr Samuel Lundbrook of the Crippled Children's Society. These visits further frustrated the police team's attempts to reconstruct the scene. Separately, each doctor said Rochelle could have survived since Wednesday and, if necessary, even longer. 'They say that the physical decline in a baby of that age and height would be negligible,' Detective Roberts told the police conference that evening. 'They both say they have studied previous research . . . and find that four or five days is well within the possible limit.'[29]

While his team was scouring the countryside for clues, Bruce Hutton's focus remained on Len Demler. Every move Demler made was documented by the police, who erected a board in their headquarters on the Chitty farm to record where Demler went and who he talked to.[30] Graeme Hewson, Harvey's best friend, became the police 'eyes and ears' while staying at Demler's house. To Hewson, Hutton and Hughes continually spoke as if Demler was without doubt the murderer. 'As soon as we find a body we'll turn the key on Len Demler,' they told him.

Every morning when Hewson came up to the farm from Demler's house, they would ask him what had been said in the house the previous evening.[31] Suddenly, even innocuous events were viewed with suspicion, such as the terse way Demler responded when the police wished him 'good morning', or when he threw a clod of dirt at his farm dog for refusing to obey commands. His habit of referring to the police as 'the bastards' made the detectives' ears prick up, as did his nervous, high-pitched laugh.[32] Detectives wrote lines and lines of notes about his body language, goading him to get a reaction, as Detective Craig Duncan recorded after he struck up a conversation with Demler about Rochelle while he was working at the Crewe farm one day:

Duncan: 'Well, Len, it won't be long before she remembers who did it.'

Demler: 'She's not old enough.'

Duncan: 'Oh yes she is, she will remember it for the rest of her days.'

Demler: 'She's 18 months, I don't know, she might be.'

Duncan: 'She will, all right, it might be a while but she will be able to tell us.'

Demler: 'She's not talking yet, she was a slow talker. Another six months and she'll be right.'

Duncan: 'Oh no — it'll be sooner than that.'

Duncan recorded that Demler then turned away from him and that when he turned back, all the colour had drained from his face.[33]

When Jeannette's sister, Heather Souter, arrived from the United States on 26 June with her husband, Bob, she too was quizzed for clues about what might have happened. Heather told Detective Sergeant Mike Charles that the only explanation she could offer was that 'Harvey had a fit and has carted Jeannette out of the house'. But, she said, that didn't seem likely: as far as she knew, the couple had never had a cross word and were attached to each other in a way that was slightly 'unnormal'.

Charles believed it hadn't occurred to Heather Souter that Demler might have been involved. When Charles asked her about how Demler behaved when her mother was dying, she told him that at the beginning he had been a good loyal husband and had gone fairly regularly to hospital to see her, but as time went on he went less often. She thought he was a 'typical farmer' in his approach. 'He treated death in the way of animals the same as humans,' she said. 'And it may be on this occasion as well, that he apparently is accepting the fact that [Jeannette and Harvey] are both dead and if that is the case, that is the case.'[34]

Charles dismissed this interview as 'not much help', but Hutton seized on one detail: Heather said everyone had expected Jeannette to hand over the ownership of her mother's car to her father after she inherited it, but Jeannette was yet to do so.[35] The next day Hutton announced to his team that he believed the Crewes' deaths were somehow tied up with May Demler's will, which had left her half-share of the farm jointly to Len Demler and Jeannette.

Hutton said there was a suggestion from a witness that because of this, Demler had thought he might have to move from the farm. 'Therefore we think the likely motive is that Len Demler became upset over the terms of his wife's will, very likely as a result of these terms, Jeannette being able to interfere with the running of the farm and possibly wanting to put a manager on it, therefore necessitating Demler

74 THE CREWE MURDERS

Len Demler, Jeannette's father, lived on the farm next door. His behaviour after the murders made him the subject of intense police scrutiny.

to leave the farm.'[36] Hutton was so confident about this scenario that on 29 June he told the press he now had a theory and a motive, although he didn't elaborate on the details.[37]

The detectives worked quickly to find out more about the potential fracture within the Demler family, this time mapping Demler's visits to his lawyer and his accountants in the weeks before the Crewes disappeared.

They found out that May Demler had died in February 1970. In March, probate had been granted and her daughters had learned the contents of her will. On 11 June, the solicitors Sturrock & Monteith had written to Demler and Jeannette saying the papers to settle the estate were ready to sign. Demler visited the solicitors on Monday 15 June, and met with Colin Sturrock. While there, he learned that death duties on his wife's estate were higher than anticipated; however, they would be 'adequately' met by the cash in May Demler's savings account plus the value of her Morris car (about which, it turned out, Heather was wrong; Jeannette had agreed to sign it over after all).

Sturrock and Demler then discussed what to do about the inequities in May's will, an issue that clearly troubled Demler. Sturrock suggested Demler make a new will of his own that left Heather a larger share in order to balance what had been bequeathed to Jeannette by her mother. Demler thought about that for a bit, and then asked Sturrock to draw up another will, leaving Heather two-thirds of his estate and Jeannette one-third. Demler told police neither Harvey nor Jeannette knew about the planned changes before they died.

Immediately after leaving the solicitors', Demler drove to Hamilton to see his accountant, Thomas Hutchesson, to sign some tax documents. At the accountant's office, he questioned the ownership of some shares listed in his wife's estate, an issue he had just discovered at Sturrock's office. Demler had been under the impression that those shares were in his name only, but Hutchesson told him they were partnership assets. Hutchesson explained to Demler that he was neither losing nor gaining anything as a result of his wife's will.[38]

After police went to see Sturrock and Hutchesson to discuss the will, they were obliged to concede that what had been thought to be a strong motive did not stand up. Demler would not have gained financially by killing his daughter and son-in-law.[39] An officer also spoke to Demler's former farm manager, Jack Handcock, who had run the farm after Howard Chennells' death. 'He would probably know the two and Mr Demler as well as anybody else. He doesn't think Demler is capable of this,' he reported back.[40]

Then, just as it seemed Hutton's theory was flailing, a new piece of physical evidence arrived from the laboratory to bolster his case: blood found in Demler's Cortina belonged to the same rare group as Jeannette. Demler had previously said the stain, a mark about an inch long on the back of the car's front seat, was from a cut on his finger.[41]

Hutton waited five days and then once again brought Demler in for questioning. He left the first part of the interview to Detective Senior Sergeant Leslie Schultz, who repeatedly told Demler that police believed he was responsible for removing the bodies, attempting to clean the carpet, and burning the cushion and mat. Demler denied having any involvement, growing agitated, snapping matches, and continually pulling threads from his sports coat. When Schultz asked him about the blood in the Cortina, Demler said it was from his hand. Schultz said police had discovered it was Jeannette's blood.

Demler: 'You do not know the difference between my blood and Jeannette's.'

Schultz: 'We do.'

Demler didn't answer, then said, 'I did not kill them and did not remove them from the house . . . The first time I went into the house was on the Monday . . . You will not find the bodies on my farm . . . Harvey was too big for me to handle.' He said the last time Jeannette was in his car was at his wife's funeral. 'I would like to know as much as you would where the bodies are.'

After an hour and a half, Hutton took over the interview. He asked why Demler never mentioned anything about the wills. Demler said he didn't think to raise it. On the Tuesday night when he'd had dinner with Jeannette and Harvey — the last time he'd seen them alive — they'd only discussed the matter briefly. Mainly he and Harvey had talked about farm matters, Demler said. Hutton then asked him why he hadn't called Jeannette and Harvey for five days, and why he hadn't invited them to the Onewhero Rugby Club jubilee on Saturday 20 June, even though he had a double ticket to the dinner. 'I suppose I should have and all of this wouldn't have happened,' Demler replied.

Hutton also asked Demler about why, on the day he discovered the bloodstained house, he went home to draft his sheep after taking Rochelle to Barbara Willis, rather than heading straight back to the farm.

Hutton: 'Surely that's a strange thing to do while waiting for the police . . . why didn't you carry on having a look for them?'

Demler: 'I didn't see any sense in that. Besides I had the sheep in the yards and wanted to draft them.'

At the end of the interview, Hutton again asked about the bloodstain in the car. Demler had clearly lost patience: 'By Christ, I don't know how that got there. Mr Schultz asked me about this. I have nothing further to say on that.'[42]

Before he let Demler go home, Hutton made him strip off his jacket. In the top pocket he found an envelope with writing on it — a list of dates and what Demler was doing the week the Crewes disappeared. Demler would later tell police he wrote the note just after he was questioned the first time, so he could remember what he had said.[43] While Demler was undressed, Hutton also noticed a scratch on the left of his neck. Demler said he must have been scratched by a prickly vine when he had been cutting weeds on his farm about a fortnight earlier.[44]

The constant interrogation was plainly having an impact on Demler. During the interview, he was shaking and ill at ease, and when Hughes went to see him on 11 July, he found him 'very weary'. 'He would appear to be suffering from lack of sleep and looked very drawn,' Hutton recorded on the jobsheet.[45]

Rumours about Demler had begun to spread through the district, including that he was a voluntary patient at a nearby mental institution, and that Heather was firmly convinced of his guilt.[46] On 13 July, Demler told Hughes that when he arrived home from the pub at midnight on Saturday, he'd discovered that someone had wired his electric fence to his gate, electrifying it. 'His eyes were red . . . and he was very upset,' Hughes said. Shortly afterwards, Demler informed police that he had hired Auckland lawyers Brian Shenkin and Lloyd Brown QC to act for him, and that police were not to speak to him without them present.[47]

O n 15 July 1970, three weeks after Harvey and Jeannette Crewe were reported missing, Hutton and his team were called to the seventh-floor conference room of the Auckland Central police station to give an update on the case to police top brass. Among those present were Assistant Commissioner Robert Walton, Assistant Commissioner George Austing, Crown Prosecutor David Morris, pathologist Dr Francis Cairns, DSIR scientists and a handful of Hutton's detectives. Over four hours, Hutton presented what his men had learned so far.[48]

The theory that most appealed, he said, was that a third person had entered the Crewe house on the evening of Wednesday 17 June, killed Harvey and Jeannette and taken their bodies away that night before rigor mortis set in. Several factors led them to think the offender knew the couple: the possibility of the baby being fed, the attempts to clean up the house, and the removal of the bodies. 'The offender felt there was a need to remove all trace of something happening in that house so there's nothing to point towards him,' Hutton told the assembled group.

Therefore, he said, the most likely suspect, and the one person police found themselves coming back to even when they tried not to, was Len Demler. 'You have heard me consider other people who may have committed the crime, but you cannot convince me that any of those were going to clear up the scene — take pots of water back and forwards to the kitchen,' Hutton said. 'Demler, certainly. He is living on the adjoining farm, knowing that the evidence is here and that a third person committed this crime and that it can't have been a murder–suicide.'

He laid out the evidence the team had assembled: Demler leaving the baby in the cot then going home to ring the stock truck; his inability to account for where he had been on the Wednesday; his antipathy towards the police; the odd business with the wills; the scratch on his neck, which Hutton had decided came from a fingernail; the bloodstain in the car.

Hutton added that police also found it suspicious that Demler had not helped with the search since the first day. Inspector Pat Gaines said that despite not taking part, Demler was obviously taking a keen interest in what police were doing. They had realised this on day four of the search, when the men had been working shoulder-to-shoulder in heavy fog and

Crown Prosecutor David Morris (second from left), Detective Sergeant James Tootill (second from right) and Detective Inspector Bruce Hutton (right) at a meeting of scientific and legal advisors on 15 July 1970 to discuss progress on the investigation.

kept coming across fresh hoof marks in the mud. 'It subsequently turned out that Demler on his horse had been tracking us. He had been with us all day and in the fog we did not see him,' Gaines said.

The group went on to discuss, at length, the merits of Hutton's theory. They all agreed the reason for removing the bodies must have been to hide the way they were killed; that the offender must have used a weapon that would somehow lead back to them. The detectives also agreed that 61-year-old Demler would have been strong enough to lift the bodies, despite his age and his 'crook leg'. 'We have seen examples of this during inquiries, with full-grown sheep, hay bales and heavy farm gates not swung, whereas policemen, quite strong ones, have struggled with these — he handled them with ease,' Hutton said.

However, prosecutor David Morris, renowned at the time for his ability to find holes in police cases and working unusually closely with police on the Crewe case, said there was a weakness in Hutton's theory.

Morris: 'He must have surely had some bloodstains or brain tissue on him, on his hands or clothing?'

Hutton: 'No, we have gone over that. He is a very clean man, washes himself and keeps the house quite clean, fantastic for washing — and he has had five days.'

Morris: 'This is worrying me. No blood on him at all. Why wasn't that one in the car wiped away?'

Hutton: 'Always mistakes made. It is quite possible that he didn't immediately remove the bodies and . . . went home in his Cortina and washed the blood from his clothing.'

Not all the officers agreed with Hutton. Paddy Byrne, the chief superintendent, had a theory of his own. He believed it was more likely that Jeannette had killed Harvey and then gone to get her father. Byrne suggested that Demler had come around and had gotten rid of the body, to make it look as if Harvey had left her. 'She is filled with remorse, standing in the paddock as though she is half crazed, ultimately commits suicide — then the alibi is gone and he's got to get rid of the other body,' he said.

Hutton, however, had already said police had decided that Bruce Roddick's sighting of the woman in the little paddock in front of the Crewe house — to which Byrne was referring — was unreliable. They were also viewing the second sighting by Queenie McConachie of the child by the gate 'with suspicion', he said. Although he said there was one sighting they hadn't resolved: a stock agent had reported seeing the Crewe car parked by the little gate to the house on Sunday morning. When the bloodstained house was entered on Monday, the car was in the shed. If the sighting was correct, that meant the car had been moved by someone after the Crewes disappeared. The stock agent was considered 'very reliable', and this information was 'troubling' Hutton.

Part way through the conference, Cairns revealed for the first time that some of the tissue found on the arm of the bloodstained chair had been confirmed as brain tissue. Dr Donald Nelson, the DSIR scientist, asked whether this meant the couple might have been killed by a gun. Hutton said there was no sign of bullet holes, but they planned to do another examination.

Robert Walton raised the issue of Demler's newly hired lawyers, who had instructed police not to speak to their client without a legal advisor present. Morris suggested that in terms of formal interviews the demand should be obeyed, but that it was always possible for police to just 'bump into' Demler. At that, Hutton bristled. 'I am investigating the disappearance of his daughter and son-in-law and if I think he can help me in these inquiries I will see him any time of the day.' His main line of approach now, he said, was to try to get Demler to crack.

By 11 August 1970, police and the army had spent six weeks searching 320 square kilometres of land for signs of Jeannette and Harvey Crewe, and had found nothing. The decision was made to suspend the search.

Five days later, Pukekawa locals Joseph Adams and John Gerbowitz were whitebaiting from their boat on the Waikato River when they noticed what appeared to be a piece of cloth floating in the water near a bend called Devil's Elbow, 10 kilometres downstream from the Tūākau bridge and 20 kilometres from Pukekawa. The whitebaiters turned the boat around. As they got closer, the two men realised they were possibly looking at a corpse. It was clad in a yellow jersey, a black brassiere, pantyhose and what Adams said he thought was a tartan skirt.[49] They called the police.

When police arrived in another boat, they carefully steered the body downstream to a landing on the riverbank, and gently pulled it to shore. Once they got it out of the water, they saw that a length of copper wire was wrapped around the body's knees, binding it to a dragging bedspread, a blanket, a cotton cover and some green tape. Most of the hair was missing from the body's head. There was a wound in the area of the right eye and nose. It was clear some teeth were missing from the lower jaw. And in the skull, a bullet wound.

Hutton, who had made little headway with Demler since the meeting with his superiors a few weeks earlier, now seized his chance. Hughes was sent to retrieve Demler from his home. He arrived at the farm around 2 p.m. Heather was in the house and Demler was out the back working. He was not happy to see the police. 'Don't come down here disturbing my sheep,' he yelled at Hughes.

When Hughes told him they believed they'd found the body of his daughter and needed him to identify her, Demler agreed to go. They arrived at the riverbank and Demler was led to the body, Hutton and Hughes watching him like hawks. Demler walked over to the body and took a long look. From her appearance, her height and build, her teeth, and from the skirt she had been wearing the night he'd gone to her home for dinner, Demler was able to identify his daughter. He showed no emotion, nor had he from the time Hughes told him in the paddock that they had found a body, nor during the 20-minute drive to the scene.[50] That evening, Hughes interviewed Demler at the Auckland police station for nearly four hours. At times, Demler got angry but he stuck to his story — he had nothing to do with the murders.[51]

That same day, Dr Francis Cairns performed an autopsy at the Auckland morgue. He found the injuries to Jeannette's eye, nose and right side of her face were probably caused before death. The bullet had entered her head on the right side above the ear, and there was an exit wound in front of the left ear. Cairns also noted that her clothing was not torn. He concluded that Jeannette Crewe had been hit with a heavy weapon, knocking out six teeth, and had then been shot with a .22 calibre bullet, at close range, probably while lying on the mat in front of the fire, where she had bled to death.[52]

Police began collecting all .22 rifles within an 8-kilometre radius of the Crewe house. The collection yielded 64 rifles. When Hughes went to see Demler on 18 August to ask if he had a rifle, Demler told him he had never owned a gun of any sort. 'He raved on about his eyes being bad and he wouldn't be able to see anyway,' Hughes reported back. Demler, despite being an excellent bowler, was well known to be short-sighted, friends and family confirmed. Demler said Harvey also didn't own a rifle, and neither had Jeannette's uncle, Howard Chennells.[53]

When the news broke that Jeannette Crewe had been killed by a bullet and not a blunt instrument as first thought, Julie Priest, who lived about 500 metres from the Crewe farm with husband Owen, approached police with some new information. She said that one night, around the date of the murders, she had heard three gunshots in quick succession. Priest couldn't remember the exact day, but she thought it must have been 17 June because she had been out late at a ball in Auckland the night before and therefore had gone to bed early the following evening, around 8.30 p.m. She was lying in bed alone when she heard the shots, so it must have been before her husband had come to bed, which was after television shut down for the night at 11 p.m. Priest had not come forward earlier because she didn't realise it was relevant.

In a bid to establish the time the Crewes died, the police decided to test whether shots fired at the Crewe property could be heard from the Priests' house. Hutton stood at the Priests' house and Detective Sergeant James Tootill fired two shots near the back steps of the Crewes' house. Hutton stated he couldn't hear them, even in mild weather.[54]

Meanwhile, a group of officers, including Murray Jeffries and Constable Ross Meurant, again searched around the Crewe house, looking for wire, bullet lead and cartridge casings. All the gardens were cleared once more, the weeds pulled and the soil sifted and examined.[55] This time police used a rotary mower to cut the grass in the front paddock so it could be searched, too, and the grass clippings were dug through. But other than finding a small piece of copper wire by the gate to the house, they came up empty-handed.[56]

A week after her body was found, police began to wonder whether Len Demler was going to make plans for Jeannette's funeral. He seemed more intent on finding Harvey Crewe's body, Detective Parkes noted.[57] The funeral was finally held on 7 September. Afterwards, Jeannette's body was interred at the tree-lined Tūākau cemetery, near the grave of her mother.

As gun-testing progressed, DSIR scientists found that only two of the 64 guns collected could not be ruled out as having fired the bullets found in Jeannette's head. One belonged to the Eyre family of Pukekawa and the other to local farmer Arthur Thomas. The Eyres were visited and found to be at home the night of the murders, and were subsequently left alone.[58] Thomas, however, was brought in for a formal interview. This was the third time detectives had spoken to Thomas, who lived with his wife, Vivien, about 14 kilometres from the Crewe farm.

During the first visit, after he'd recovered from getting a shock when the door of his car caught on the electric fence, Hughes had found Thomas friendly when he questioned him about his relationship with the elder Demler daughter.[59] Hughes had looked into the tip-off that Jeannette had a persistent suitor called 'Murphy', and after talking to Demler and Heather Souter, had decided that her friend had the name wrong, and the man was actually Arthur Thomas. Thomas admitted to Hughes he had once been 'fond' of Jeannette and he used to 'chase her along a bit' when they were both at the local school and later when she came home in the holidays, but he said that he was now happily married. After that visit Hughes had reported that Thomas was 'not implicated in any way' in the disappearance of the Crewes.[60]

The second visit to Thomas was made by Bruce Parkes on 12 August. During the search of the Crewe house, police had found a brush and comb gift set in the wardrobe, still in its wrapping paper, with a gift card saying 'from Arthur'. Parkes showed Thomas the card and asked whether he was the writer. Thomas confirmed he was, and that he had given it to Jeannette when he wanted to court her in the early 1960s. Parkes left without further comment.[61]

For the third interview, on 7 September, Parkes and Detective Phil Seaman drove Thomas to the Tūākau police station. This time the atmosphere was quite different. The officers quizzed him about his whereabouts on 17 June, the night the Crewes were killed. Thomas told them he had been at home, looking after a sick cow that was about to calve. He and Vivien had missed the ratepayers' association meeting, and instead had a night in with his cousin Peter Thomas, who lived with them. When Parkes told Thomas that it was his .22 Browning rifle that had been used to kill the Crewes, Thomas replied: 'Is it? If you say it was my gun it must have been, but I didn't do it.' Thomas later described the interview as a 'grilling'.[62]

Parkes and Seaman were pushing to get a confession, but Thomas continually denied involvement in the crime.[63] Eventually, the officers relented, telling Thomas they had just been 'trying him out'. Recalling these events in 2022, Parkes said he ended that interview with a gut feeling that Thomas was not their killer, and that Seaman, who was relatively new to the role but known for sifting out the truth, felt the same.[64]

The next day, Detective Sergeant Mike Charles gave Thomas back his rifle, retaining the test-fired bullets and cartridge cases.[65] It wasn't the one they had been looking for, Charles told Thomas. He also returned the other rifle to the Eyre family.[66]

O nce Jeannette Crewe's body had been pulled from the muddy waters of the swollen Waikato, police resumed searching the river as often as the weather allowed. Just before lunchtime on 16 September, Constable Gerald Wyllie located a body on the river's northern bank, amid a patch of overhanging trees, 4 kilometres upstream from where Jeannette had been found a month earlier. Wyllie, who was using his own boat to search, called in the find on the radio. When his colleagues, including Detective Inspector Bruce Hutton and a police photographer, arrived in a jetboat soon afterwards, they found the badly decomposed corpse was caught on a dangling tree branch.

Hutton was worried that if they hauled it in, it could disintegrate and disappear. A cradle designed for getting bodies from the water was rushed down from Auckland. Two police divers slid into the cold water to manoeuvre it into place. But as the divers and the police pushed and pulled at it, the body wouldn't move. Hutton leaned over the side of the boat and felt a heavy object under the body. As he strained to get hold of it, police diver Paul Spence noticed a piece of wire around the body leading down into the water like an anchor. Hutton grasped for it but the wire snapped and the body bobbed up. It was then moved easily into the cradle.

Spence dived again and this time, immediately below the spot where the body had been found and in less than 2 metres of water, he saw a car axle. He surfaced with it. Hutton grabbed it and hauled its 17-kilogram weight into the boat. A brown bedspread wrapped with galvanised wire was also snagged in the tree near the body. The remnants of a greenish blanket were wrapped around the body's waist, together with a piece of galvanised 16-gauge wire, and another piece of galvanised 16-gauge wire was wrapped around its chest. The socks, blue woollen pullover, trousers, singlet, underpants and green checked shirt on the corpse were all eaten away.[67] After holding the axle up for a photograph, Hutton immediately examined it and discovered there was a kingpin in one end, which he said he had felt under the water prior to the wire breaking. There were also scratch marks on the axle, which made it obvious to Hutton that at one point wire had probably been attached to it.

Once again the investigation team required Len Demler to identify the body. By the time Detective Sergeant John Hughes and Detective Sergeant Mike Charles arrived at the Demler farm at 6.25 that evening, Demler had already heard the news that a body had been found from a radio report. On the way to the Auckland mortuary, Hutton sat in the rear of the police car with Demler. As they drove onto the Tūākau bridge, Hutton noticed Demler shake his head repeatedly and rub the back of his neck but he did not speak.

At 7.30 p.m., Demler walked into the mortuary room with his hands in his pockets and looked closely at the body. Even decomposed, the face resembled his son-in-law, and he recognised the socks and pullover, he said. He said he felt satisfied that the body recovered was that of David Harvey Crewe.[68]

When Harvey Crewe's body was examined by Cairns at the Auckland mortuary later that evening, it was discovered that he had also died as a result of a bullet wound through the left side of his head. Small fragments of the bullet were recovered around the entrance to the skull and brain, and a large fragment of bullet was found beneath the skin in front of the left ear.[69]

The discovery of the second body gave police fresh evidence to trace. Detectives immediately began collecting more wire samples from properties in Pukekawa, hoping to find a match to the galvanised wire found on Harvey Crewe's body and around the bedspread.[70] And after further investigation on the wire that had been wrapped around Jeannette's body, they decided it was likely a weight had been attached

Above: Bruce Hutton holds up the axle found under Harvey Crewe's body in the Waikato River on 16 September 1970. *Below:* Harvey Crewe's body is brought to the riverbank.

to her, too. Using a large electro-magnet made for them by a local steel firm, police searched the river for anything that might have been used as an anchor.[71]

Hutton began to attempt to identify the axle. He placed a picture of it in national newspapers, calling for help from experts who might know its model by sight. Murray Jeffries also appeared on television with the heavy rusty axle, pointing out its unique features: the stainless-steel welding and signs of gas cutting, and the lone kingpin from the right-hand end.

The task of following up any leads was assigned to Detective Len Johnston, who had joined the inquiry team in mid-September.[72] Johnston had investigated the burglary at the Crewe house three years earlier, but had been busy on another job over the previous months.[73] Johnston's first task was to attempt to match the type of axle and to discover where it might have come from.[74]

Meanwhile, Hutton instructed Mike Charles to begin compiling a brief of evidence against Demler, a process undertaken before police arrest and charge a suspect. While Charles worked on the file, Hutton interviewed Demler yet again, pushing for that elusive confession. Hutton accused Demler of showing no concern at all over Jeannette and Harvey going missing. He pressed Demler repeatedly on why he hadn't helped with the search or contacted Hutton about progress on the case. Demler replied that he didn't want to when he knew the police began to consider him a suspect. 'I got my back up,' he said. 'I got my back up and I didn't want anything more to do with you.' He once again denied having anything to do with the murders.[75]

W ith two bodies now, and no arrests, Hutton was clearly under pressure to make progress. The Crewe homicides were extremely high-profile, ironically due in no small part to Hutton's knack for keeping the case on the front page of the national newspapers. Some of the stories' keenest readers were Auckland's wealthy residents, who saw Jeannette Crewe, a former pupil of St Cuthbert's College, as one of their own. 'I think that's what drove the story, the elite of Remuera all talking about it,' said Parkes in 2022. 'Amongst the St Cuthbert's alumnae there was a strong interest in the case and perhaps even a determination to get a result.' This included prosecutor David Morris, whose daughters attended the same school.[76]

But there was also pressure coming from the police hierarchy itself. The police had a reputational issue on their hands. When the Crewes went missing, the police were already dealing with three other unsolved murders that year, an extremely rare scenario for New Zealand at the time, and a fact the newspapers began to tally with increasing regularity.[77]

Tasmanian schoolteacher Jennifer Mary Beard, 25, had gone missing from Fox Glacier while hitchhiking on New Year's Eve. She had last been seen with a middle-aged man in a green Vauxhall. Police had mounted a huge, difficult search through dense native bush for Beard before finding her body under a bridge after a tip-off 19 days later. But they hadn't found the man in the green Vauxhall, even after tracing almost 29,000 cars during the investigation.[78]

Betty McKay, a 34-year-old mother of three from the small Bay of Plenty village of Awakaponga, had disappeared in April. Just two days earlier, she had moved to her brother's home in Thornton, near Whakatāne. The last sighting of McKay had been at 12.30 a.m. on 12 April, when she was dropped at the Thornton bridge by a male friend after they had attended a function. It was less than a mile's walk to her brother's home but she did not ever arrive there. Investigations centred on a blue-and-white Chrysler and a saloon car parked in the area at the time. Despite extensive searches and more than 1000 interviews conducted by a 40-strong inquiry team, no sign of McKay was found.[79]

Olive Walker, 18, had been killed when she left her home on Leslie Street in Rotorua to walk to her sister's house on a Friday evening in May, a month before the Crewe murders. Her beaten and bloodied body was found on the side of the road 5 kilometres south of the township the next day. She had been raped before being killed. There had been few leads and no arrest.[80]

During a police conference on the Crewe case two months earlier, Assistant Commissioner Robert Walton had made it clear to Hutton that police needed to work hard to close at least one of the homicides: 'You have got to drive for evidence and we leave it to you. If you have got enough to bring a prima facie case — you go as hard as you can. From my point of view, with the Beard one, the Walker one and this one — we have to get one. We leave it to you and if you have any ideas or need any further help, you call out for it. Evidence is what we want.'[81]

But despite Hutton's assurances that they were getting closer, Walton was clearly concerned about the direction of the Crewe inquiry. After reading the briefs of evidence completed by Charles in early October, he travelled to Christchurch and gave the documents to Detective Patrick O'Donovan, who held a special interest in the way police ran major crime cases. O'Donovan read the briefs overnight and told Walton bluntly the following morning that there was no evidence to justify arresting Demler. Walton decided to send O'Donovan and Wellington detective Wally Baker to Auckland to carry out an overview of the Crewe case. Their instructions were to read the files to establish whether they considered the investigation team was keeping an open mind to all possibilities, or whether the lines of inquiry were too confined.[82]

It quickly became apparent to Baker and O'Donovan that Walton's concerns were justified: the whole thrust of the investigation was directed towards establishing the guilt of Len Demler. The police reconstruction was that Demler had come through the back door with a rifle, had shot Harvey Crewe from the doorway between the kitchen and lounge and had then shot Jeannette after hitting her in the face with the butt of the rifle. But after reading carefully through all the files, and visiting Demler themselves, Baker and O'Donovan were not convinced.

First, they said, the only physical evidence against Demler was the bloodstain in the car. The police had found no evidence of an axle on Demler's farm. Tests on the wire, carried out by DSIR scientist Harry Todd, had found that none of the wire samples collected from either Demler's farm or other Pukekawa properties matched any of the wire found wrapped around the bodies. Second, police could not prove that Demler had ever used or owned a gun. Third, unlike the inquiry team, Baker and O'Donovan were certain that the earlier burglaries and the fires must have been connected with the murders, particularly because the offender had stolen only items personal to Jeannette while leaving money untouched. Therefore, if the previous crimes were connected, Demler could not have been involved as he had been with the Crewes during the burglary at least.

In short, while Demler's emotionless demeanour was disconcerting and his reticence in discussing the murders was frustrating, Baker and O'Donovan concluded he was not the killer. Rather, the Crewes were murdered in anger by someone with a grudge, who had possibly had help from a second person to clean their mess up.[83]

At a conference on 19 October, O'Donovan and Baker met with the remaining inquiry team, now reduced to just Bruce Hutton, Leslie Schultz, James Tootill, Len Johnston, Bruce Parkes and Stan Keith, to discuss the state of the case. Their views on Demler were 'not well received' by the investigators.[84]

Schultz pushed back about the significance of the burglary and fires, saying they were too long ago. Tootill argued that if Harvey Crewe had thought there was danger, he would have acted. Hutton was also sceptical. Surely, he said, the Crewes would have known if someone had a grudge against them and would have mentioned who the person was. Baker pointed out that the family had discussed possible suspects — including the former neighbour with the lice-ridden sheep, whom the inquiry team had visited in August and had discounted without even asking him about the burglaries.

Surprisingly, although he refused to accept their opinions about the burglary and fires, Hutton did not disagree with the rest of O'Donovan and Baker's critiques. The supposed motive — May Demler's will — was weak, he admitted, and there was no link between Demler and the axle, the wire or the gun. But he did announce there was a second suspect, and that evidence suggested this man was the only person besides Demler who could be responsible for the crimes. He said they would now discuss the case against Jeannette's one-time suitor, Arthur Allan Thomas.[85]

CHAPTER FIVE
THE ARREST

rthur Allan Thomas was what people called a 'country boy'. Uncomplicated and unworldly, with a laconic attitude, it was said Arthur took the general view that everything in life would work out all right.[1] He was born in 1938, the second child of Allan and Ivy Thomas, and raised on the family's 272-acre farm on the banks of the Waikato River. He spent his childhood running barefoot, hunting rabbits and overseeing the cattle. The Thomases' three-bedroom house was at the northern tip of the Pukekawa district, on Mercer Ferry Road, the last farm before the ferry landing itself.

The bus didn't come all the way to the Thomas house, so the kids walked a mile across paddocks and gravel roads to get to the bus stop for Pukekawa School each day. Popular and polite though he was, school was not for Arthur. When he was eight years old he was held back a year after failing standard one, and ended up sharing a classroom with pupils two years his junior, including Jeannette Demler. But while Jeannette finished form two and went off to boarding school, Arthur's father pulled him out of school on his fourteenth birthday to work on the farm. For the next five years he cut scrub and fixed fences, working alongside his brother Ray. It was hard labour, and all unpaid.[2]

At 19, seeking a change and a pay packet, he got a job with the Roose Shipping Company at Mercer, repairing the cranes and barges used to freight sand along the river. He worked his way up to driving the ferry across to Mercer township and back. The ferry, the fastest way across the river until the Mercer ferry bridge was built in 1972, opened Arthur Thomas's eyes to the world. He saved money and bought a car. He developed a love for country music crooner Johnny Cash. He began to take more of an interest in girls, but he was too shy to ask them to dance so he signed up for dance classes with his friend Mervyn Cathcart to build up confidence. To his dismay, there were no girls at the classes, and instead the young men were paired up with the stern female instructors.[3]

In 1960, Arthur moved out of Pukekawa for the first time, for a stint in forestry at Maramarua, a small town 40 kilometres north-east of his home where, by chance, Jeannette Demler was living at the teachers' hostel. Arthur phoned her several times, and twice visited the hostel, but she rebuffed his advances. During this time Arthur went out with several other women until he quit forestry to become a loader for the topdressing company Barr Brothers, a job that would see him based at different locations across the North Island over the next five years.

In 1961, he discovered that Jeannette had gone overseas and he visited her father to get her address in London. Arthur wrote several letters to her, sending her a gift of a writing compendium via the Overseas Visitors Club. Jeannette wrote back to thank him. Arthur continued to date other women, but at Christmas 1962 he once again tried his luck. She was in New Zealand and he bought a brush and comb set and delivered it to Jeannette at her family home. He later said he did not visit her again and did not harbour a grudge, and that she had let him down kindly.[4]

In January 1964, he and one of the Barr Brothers pilots visited signwriter Pat Vesey to arrange to paint the pilot's name on his aircraft. As they were talking, a young woman walked past them and up the stairs. 'Who's that?' Arthur asked. 'That's my niece, Vivien,' Vesey replied.

Vivien Carter, the only child of truckie Nick Carter and his wife Edna, had emigrated from England just a few months earlier and had celebrated her twenty-first birthday on the ship on the way out. Vesey and his wife Joyce had sponsored her visa, and found her work at a farm accountant's in Wellsford, where Vivien put her bookkeeper skills to use. 'Gosh, she's a looker,' Arthur had said to Vesey.[5]

Soon after, Arthur called again, asking if Vivien would go to the movies with him. They bonded over a shared interest in dancing and country music, and that November they were married at the Wellsford Presbyterian church. Vivien was 22 and Arthur was 26. Vivien was a city girl with an office job and had never lived on a farm, but suddenly she was immersed in rural life, shifting from place to place for Arthur's work across rural Auckland, from Hūnua, to Clevedon, to Kingseat.

They found a permanent home in June 1966, when Arthur's father Allan asked him if he wished to lease the family farm. Thomas senior wanted to move to Matakana, to farm pigs, and Arthur had just been let go from a farming job he'd taken after leaving Barr Brothers. He and Vivien moved back to Pukekawa just two weeks before Jeannette and Harvey Crewe also returned to the district.

The two couples could not have been more different. Where the Crewes kept to themselves, the Thomases formed a tight circle of friends who visited each other regularly. They loved to entertain at home. Vivien took up cooking and threw dinner parties to put her new skills to use. Arthur made homebrew and wine, and while he didn't drink much himself, he was generous to his guests.[6] Vivien was soon keeping the books and learning about milking, calf rearing and herd management. They did not have children, as a result of apparent infertility, yet the marriage seemed happy. Their shared love of dancing was a regular activity, and in her spare time Vivien bred Siamese cats, and took them to shows.[7]

Filling spare time wasn't an issue for Arthur either. Running the farm and building up the dairy herd was a seven-day-a-week job, and not always a smooth one. In early 1970, the couple was $3000 in debt, having borrowed money to get through a drought. The debt was a source of stress, but they were confident everything would 'come right' once the farm picked up again.[8]

A couple of times after he and Vivien returned to Pukekawa, Arthur saw Jeannette in the street. Once he spoke to her at a stock agent's in Tūākau, but other than that chance meeting, during those four years that the Crewes and the Thomases both lived in the Pukekawa district, they never socialised, and they never saw each other at local events. Whether Jeannette was deliberately avoiding Arthur and his wife

Above: Worried that with two other unsolved murders that year New Zealanders were losing confidence in the police, Police Commissioner Robert Walton (left) took a close interest in the Crewe murder investigation. Here he confers with detectives Len Johnston (centre) and Bruce Hutton outside the Crewe house. *Below:* The paddock in front of the Crewe house where Bruce Roddick claimed he saw the woman the police believed had fed Rochelle after her parents were killed.

is unknown. On one occasion, Jeannette was invited to a cosmetics demonstration run by the Tūākau Young Wives Association. When she was told it would be hosted by Vivien Thomas, she cancelled. One neighbour considered there was no way Jeannette Crewe would go near the Thomases' home.[9]

Vivien Thomas had certainly never been to the Crewe farm. When news broke that the Crewes were missing, she baked scones and took them up to the house for the search team, but she had to ask for directions to get there.[10] Arthur Thomas had first heard that something awful had happened at Pukekawa from a stock agent, who told him on the afternoon of 17 June that there was 'a bloodstained farm four miles from Tūākau bridge'.[11] It wasn't until the next day that he and Vivien learned that Harvey and Jeannette Crewe were the victims.

When the police first visited his farm in July, it was recorded that Arthur was only too happy to speak to them. He answered the officers' questions, offering any extra information he could think of. When they took his gun away with them, he told Vivien not to worry about it, telling her they had to do everything they could to help. Even after Bruce Parkes and Phil Seaman grilled him at the Tūākau police station, accusing him of committing the crime, he held no malice, believing they were just doing their job.[12]

As the investigation began to wither and Hutton needed another target, the evidence kept bringing police back to Arthur. First, it was his association with Jeannette, and the accusations he had 'persistently' gone after her when he was a young man. Second, it was the gun and the fact it couldn't be ruled out as having fired the bullets. And third, in October, Detective Len Johnston discovered that the axle used to weigh down Harvey Crewe's body appeared to have links to the Thomas farm.

On 19 September, Hutton placed a picture of the axle in national newspapers, calling for information about it, and Johnston visited a vintage car enthusiast in Birkdale, Auckland, named David Keruse, who was restoring a Nash Standard 6 420 series car. The axle from Keruse's car and the one tied to Harvey's body were found to be identical and had matching part numbers. That same day, Charles Shirtcliffe from

Te Puke saw the newspaper article, and contacted police to say that in 1956 he had bought the front assembly of a 1928 Nash to build a trailer. He had since sold it but he thought the axle looked similar to the one he had used.

Len Johnston and Bruce Parkes met Shirtcliffe and showed him the axle; however, he was unable to say with certainty whether it was the same. Regardless, Johnston began trying to track down the man who had bought the trailer from Shirtcliffe, resorting to publishing a photo of it supplied by Shirtcliffe in the *New Zealand Herald* on 10 October. Eventually, Johnston found out that Shirtcliffe had sold the trailer to a Gordon Whyte, who had worked at the Meremere power station in the mid-1950s. In 1959, Whyte had sold the trailer to Arthur Thomas's father, Allan Thomas.

Johnston went to see Arthur Thomas at his farm on 13 October and showed him the axle. Arthur didn't recognise it, but he did recognise the photo Johnston showed him of Shirtcliffe's trailer and agreed it was similar to one that used to be on the farm, which belonged to his father. He'd seen the photo in the *Herald* three days earlier, he said, and assumed his father would have already been in touch. The only other axle on his farm was in the farm tip, he said, and had wheels attached to it. Arthur took Johnston to one of the farm tips to show him, but it had no relevance to the case, Johnston said.[13]

While he was at the farm, Johnston also took some samples of wire and a box of .22 ammunition. Before leaving, he asked Arthur more questions, including about the brush and comb set he had given Jeannette. Did he know what she had done with it? 'It could still be wrapped up for all I know,' Arthur replied.

The next day, Johnston and Parkes visited Allan Thomas in Matakana, where Thomas senior showed police the trailer, dug out its certificate of ownership, and took Parkes out the back to a cottage where he kept his cheque-books to find the stub that covered the purchase of the trailer. They went through stub after stub until they found it, and Allan Thomas also suggested where to look for the axle parts on his old farm.[14]

The following day Johnston returned to Arthur's farm and searched around the old cowshed, along the fence line, under hedges and in the woolshed. He and Arthur then searched the three dumps. Arthur crawled through the piles of rubbish, including metal and wood and the occasional animal carcass, looking for parts of the axle. Whenever he found any car parts, he threw them from the dump up on to the grass for Johnston to assess. It was dirty work, but Arthur appeared happy to help. He found Johnston an 'obliging sort of a guy', and Vivien offered cups of tea and they chatted away during the visit.[15]

But Johnston knew something Arthur didn't. He had been speaking with local welder Roderick Rasmussen, who made trailers in his own workshop in his spare time. On Johnston's first visit, on 12 October, Rasmussen was unable to recall the axle when Johnston showed it to him, but said the method used to cut the right-hand end of the axle was similar to the way he removed stub axles (the two parts which join to an axle to allow the wheels to swivel independently) from the axle beam itself. When Allan Thomas told Johnston that Rasmussen had done some work on his trailer, Johnston returned to see him on 15 October.

Rasmussen remembered replacing the trailer axle beam with a new piece of steel for Thomas. That meant that the old Nash axle and the axle stubs were now superfluous. Rasmussen said his memory was that those parts had been returned to the Thomas family when Allan's son Richard came to pick the trailer up. Johnston, therefore, was certain the parts were on the farm.[16]

During the month since joining the Crewe inquiry, Johnston had been working hard to catch up on the case, going through the thousands of documents that made up the file. In early October, his set of fresh eyes proved useful. While examining a photo of the crime scene, Johnston began thinking again about the open louvre windows in the kitchen, and wondered whether the shot that had killed Harvey Crewe could have been fired from outside, through the gap in the parallel panes of glass.[17]

In Johnston's scenario, the bullet could have passed through the open sliding door between the kitchen and lounge and entered Harvey's skull while he was sitting in the chair by the fire. Up until that point, the police had considered that the shots that killed Harvey and Jeannette must have come from inside the house, most likely from the doorway between the lounge and kitchen.

The prosecution team reconstructs the way they believed the killer had shot Harvey Crewe through the kitchen's open louvre windows.

Detective Patrick O'Donovan, the expert recruited from Christchurch, and Detective Inspector Wally Baker were still in Auckland, so Johnston came to see them to discuss this new scenario. Baker then approached Hutton and they all went down to the Crewe farm on the evening of 13 October to test the theory, with DSIR scientists Rory Shanahan and Donald Nelson, and a DSIR technician.[18]

Baker, who was a similar build to Harvey Crewe, sat in the armchair in the position they believed it was in when Harvey was shot. Then the police arranged a target, made of two telephone books and a piece of paper, at head height. While standing with one foot on the wall next to the back steps and the other foot on the windowsill, Nelson used a .22 rifle to fire two shots at the target while another shot was fired by Johnston. Both men hit their mark. Johnston's scenario was plausible, they decided. During the tests, the ejection of the bullets was watched carefully, and each spent cartridge was retrieved.[19]

Six days later, when O'Donovan and Baker and the inquiry team met to discuss their views on the case against Demler, Hutton now had the sketchy outline of an alternate reconstruction of the night of 17 June, repurposed in a case pointing towards Arthur Thomas and bolstered by the louvre theory. Thomas, he told the detectives, was their only option. There was no other evidence suggesting any other person as a possible suspect.

He advanced a list of motives: jealousy, Thomas's previous possible infatuation with Jeannette Crewe, his knowledge of the Crewe farm from topdressing there, his proximity and access to transport to remove the bodies, his firearm, the axle, and the possibility that, if the fires and burglary were connected, they appeared to have been done by someone local.

The points that would rule Thomas out as being the killer were his alibi that he was home with Vivien and the sick cow, that he was well regarded in the district, that he was happily married, and the long time lapse since his association with Jeannette. There was also the question of his temperament — whether he had the makings of a killer.

Bruce Parkes was asked to give his impressions of Thomas, taken from their previous interviews. He told the meeting that Thomas was fit and strong, 6 foot tall, perhaps 13 stone, and would have the strength to move the bodies. He appeared to have lower than average intelligence,

Parkes said, but he wasn't stupid, more 'slow'. He described Vivien Thomas as 'very astute'.[20]

Some of the other officers were hesitant about the focus shifting to Thomas. After Parkes had finished speaking, Detective Leslie Schultz asked him, 'Do you think his wife would support him if he had done this murder?' 'I don't think she would. I don't think she is covering up for them,' Parkes replied. But he also said that since being questioned at length at the Ōtāhuhu police station, Arthur was now more guarded. 'I have since seen him again and have spoken with him three or four times and we have never got through to him as much as before when it was put to him that he was the offender. He is more cagey now, expecting to get his face slapped.' Nonetheless, Parkes seemed unconvinced of Thomas's guilt, and pointed out that his association with Jeannette was 10 years in the past.

During the conference, Hutton explained the science behind the firearms and the bullets gathered so far. Of the 70 guns tested, only two could not be ruled out: the Eyre family's Remington pump-action and the Browning pump-action belonging to Arthur Thomas. Donald Nelson was able to rule out the other rifles by comparing the marks on the bullets found with the Crewes against the design of the guns' individual barrels. Every rifle has spiralling grooves cut into the interior of its barrel to help the bullet spin. The direction of the spiral can be left or right. The metal ridges between the grooves are called 'lands'. As the bullet scrapes along the barrel, these lands leave marks on the bullet which Nelson called 'land markings'.

The remains of the bullet found in Jeannette Crewe had four clear land marks and most of a fifth. The sixth was badly scored, very likely as a result of coming into contact with bone. 'These five land marks indicated quite clearly to me that this bullet had been fired from a weapon with six fairly broad right-hand twist lands,' Nelson said at the conference.[21]

When Harvey Crewe's body was recovered from the river, the bullet from his head was found to be significantly more damaged than the one from Jeannette's body. It had only three lands visible and just one of good quality. Nonetheless, Nelson said, the width of the marking was consistent with the bullet found with Jeannette Crewe and therefore could have been fired from the same weapon.[22]

In an attempt to match the rifles more specifically to the bullets, Nelson examined the characteristics of the grooves and lands of each rifle. When inspecting the Eyre firearm, he found it had no individual groove marks that would help identify it as the firearm. The Thomas firearm, however, while having five lands with no individual markings, had a sixth land that revealed two slight marks. Hutton said that although these marks existed, they would be unlikely to be sufficient to identify it as the rifle that fired a particular bullet. However, he said, on one of the three lands visible from the bullet found on Harvey Crewe, there were two small marks 'which may or may not be similar to the marks revealed on the sixth land of a test-fired bullet from the rifle of Thomas'.

Further, Nelson said, it was possible the marks may have been caused by something other than the rifle barrel, such as contact with Harvey Crewe's skull. But, he also pointed out, it was possible that similar individual marks may have been on the sixth land of the bullet recovered from the skull of Jeannette Crewe but the mark was badly scored.[23]

A t this point, the investigation team drew up a list of what they needed to do next. This included looking into Thomas's finances, searching for more wire and doing more work on the bullets. Hutton wanted Thomas's movements for all of 17 June verified, including whether he went to the stock sale at Bombay or the ratepayers' meeting at Glen Murray, and who else was at the meeting. Detectives would also check out his whereabouts during the previous fires and burglary and ask his reasons for not taking part in the search for the Crewes' bodies. Even his reading material would be investigated. 'Every effort must be made to immediately either confirm Thomas as a suspect or exclude him altogether from the inquiry,' the conference notes concluded.[24]

Len Johnston wasted no time following his boss's instructions. The next day, he and Bruce Parkes went to visit Thomas again at the farm to advise that they wanted to take some more wire samples. Thomas agreed. Then they asked if they could see his rifle again, having given it back to him in September. 'But the gun's been tested and it wasn't the one,' he said to them. Nevertheless, Vivien went to fetch it from the laundry.[25]

Next, Johnston asked for a spade and headed for one of the farm tips, still wearing his suit, with Parkes hard on his heels. They returned after a few minutes, got in their car and left. Johnston had made another discovery: an axle stub. Digging a bit further, Johnston then found a second axle stub, and a wooden drawbar, the shaft that connects the trailer to a car.[26]

When Johnston and Parkes arrived back at the Ōtāhuhu station, Patrick O'Donovan and Wally Baker were leaving for the airport, having concluded their review the day before. Johnston was keen to show them his find. He placed the two stubs against the axle and they fitted perfectly.[27]

The next day at 8 a.m., police, armed with a search warrant, descended on the Thomas farm. They seized scrap metal from the farm tip near where Johnston had found the stub axles and took bits of wood and spare car parts from other areas of the farm. From a jar in the scullery that also contained screws, nuts and bolts, police found 14 old .22 bullets. In a drawer they found letters written to Arthur by former girlfriends, and they took those, too. Detective Stan Keith was assigned to search the garage.

While he was sifting through boxes of odds and ends, Keith noticed Arthur and Vivien talking outside. Through a crack in the garage wall, he watched them. Vivien was extremely unhappy — the police had already ruined her freshly mopped floor, and her cat had a litter of new kittens inside that she didn't want disturbed. As they talked, Keith couldn't quite catch what Vivien was saying, but he heard Arthur reply: 'If they think I am guilty, I am, and that is that.' Keith dutifully wrote this exchange down in his notebook.

In an old apple box full of nuts and bolts, Keith found another .22 bullet. When it was separated from its cartridge case later that day, and the cartridge case fired to get rid of any remaining powder, on the base of the bullet was the same number 8 discovered on the bullets that had killed the Crewes.[28]

On 22 October, exactly four months after the murders, Bruce Hutton made two visits. For the first time, he went to see Arthur Thomas. And for the last time, he interviewed Len Demler. It had been a month since Hutton had seen Demler, their last encounter a tense discussion about why Demler didn't help with the search for his daughter and son-in-law. This time, the tone was different. Instead of grilling Demler about his own movements or motives, Hutton wanted to know about Arthur Thomas and his relationship with Jeannette. Demler told him Arthur was 'persistent' with Jeannette. He knew about the visit at Christmas time and the gift of the brush and comb set. He said Jeannette had gone out with Arthur, but only once.[29]

When he met Thomas for the first time, Hutton kept the interaction short. He asked for permission to inspect his legal papers held by his solicitors, which Thomas granted. They had a brief discussion about his father's trailer. Thomas was chatty. 'Now they found the wheels I suppose that's it,' he said.[30] Hutton did not record a response.

That weekend was Labour Weekend, a public holiday. Arthur and Vivien Thomas attended a fancy-dress function at the rugby club on Saturday night, getting home late, but still waking early for milking. Just as they were finishing up, the police arrived, announcing they were taking the couple to Ōtāhuhu for questioning. At the station, Johnston questioned Vivien Thomas in one room, while Hutton questioned Arthur Thomas in another.

In the room chosen for Thomas, evidence including the brush and comb set and the card, some galvanised wire, and Thomas's rifle with a packet of bullets tied to the trigger, was on display. Hutton opened the interview by asking Thomas if his marriage was a happy one. Thomas told him he thought so, but it would be better if they were able to have children. Hutton went on to ask about Jeannette Crewe, Thomas repeating what he had already told police, that he'd had a crush on her at primary school and later became very fond of her.

To Hutton's surprise, Arthur then produced a letter from Jeannette, sent from London on 14 February 1961, thanking him for sending a 'beautiful writing compendium and pen' while she was overseas. The detectives had missed it during the search of his house, Arthur said, and he thought Hutton might like to see it. Hutton took the letter and continued his questioning.

Hutton: 'What did Jeannette think of the present?'

Thomas: 'I think she got the idea that I was attempting to hang around. She told me she had a steady boyfriend.'

Hutton: 'If you had married Jeannette how do you think you would stand today?'

Thomas: 'Well, of course if that had happened I would be a wealthy man today.'

Next Hutton took Thomas into an adjoining room and showed him the axle found in the river tied to Harvey Crewe, and the stub axles found in the Thomas tip. 'What do you make of that?' Hutton asked.

'They must go together,' Thomas replied.

After viewing the evidence, Hutton took Thomas back to his office. He asked Thomas: 'How is it that the axle has got off your farm and then been wired to the body of Harvey Crewe without you being involved?'

Thomas looked at Hutton and said: 'I have no real answer to that, other than to say someone must have come on to my farm at night and taken it.'

'Do you mean you've been framed?' Hutton asked.

'If that's the word you used that's what I mean, I have been framed,' Thomas replied.[31]

'I've got a good mind to lock you up but, Arthur, I'm going to give you a chance,' Hutton said. Then he began to take Arthur's formal statement.[32]

Late in the afternoon, with no charges having been laid, Vivien and Arthur Thomas were allowed to go home.

While Hutton and Johnston were busy interviewing the Thomases, the rest of the inquiry team had been testing for holes in Arthur Thomas's alibi. They visited David Payne, the chair of the Pukekawa Ratepayers' Association, and established that Thomas had not been at the meeting on 17 June, and then visited Brian Murray, a neighbour, who gave the same answer as Payne.

After Parkes left, Murray grew concerned. Until that point in the investigation, he hadn't spoken to police. He had a .22 and they hadn't bothered to ask about it or test-fire it, and suddenly they were at his house on a public holiday weekend asking about Arthur Thomas's attendance at a meeting four months ago. That night, he went to the

Thomas farm, where Thomas, Vivien and Peter were sitting watching television. 'You're in a spot of trouble,' Murray told him.[33]

Thomas tried to brush it off, but Murray sat down and over the course of two hours got the full story from him: the searches, the interviews, the repeat inspections of the gun. 'My God, Arthur, they're trying to pin this on you,' he said.

Thomas was still unfazed. 'It's all right, Brian, I've got nothing to worry about. I've done nothing wrong. Inspector Hutton knows that, he's helping me to find out who's trying to frame me,' he said.

Brian Murray was horrified. He refused to leave until Arthur reluctantly promised to get a solicitor, someone to give him advice. Arthur Thomas phoned Murray a few days later to say he had hired lawyer Paul Temm, who had instructed the Thomases not to speak to police. Murray felt relieved; he saw Thomas as 'too trusting, too honest, too naive to take care of himself'.[34]

Try as they might, by the end of that weekend the police still didn't have enough evidence to charge Arthur Thomas with the two murders. A particular sticking point was the axle — they still had no proof it had been on the Thomas farm. Previously, Johnston had spoken to two of Arthur's brothers, Richard and Lloyd, but even though Richard was the one who supposedly brought the axle back from Rasmussen's workshop, neither man remembered it being on their father's property. Johnston then spoke to Arthur's youngest brother, Desmond, with the same result.

In late October, Hutton and Johnston also interviewed the third member of the Thomas household, Arthur's younger cousin Peter Thomas, then 18, who lived with the couple while working for Roose Shipping. Peter remembers being out in the yards crutching sheep with Arthur when he smelled tobacco smoke, and looked up. Behind the shed door were Hutton and Johnston, smoking a pipe, and quietly watching the two men work. Peter agreed to go with them to the Tūākau police station.

He had already been questioned by detectives twice before and had given them the same information that Arthur and Vivien Thomas had: they had all been home the night of the murders. Police had also been keen to know what Thomas's reaction had been when he heard the news that Harvey and Jeannette Crewe were missing. Peter told them Arthur was shocked, just as everyone else in Pukekawa had been.[35]

This time when they arrived at the station, Hutton and Johnston showed Peter the axle in the back of the police car. Did he recognise it? they asked. Peter said he didn't. The detectives pushed him, asking if he was sure. Peter repeated that he had never seen the axle in his life.

On Monday 26 October, Hutton gathered the investigation team together to discuss progress. They went over the evidence and the facts surrounding the new reconstruction. The discussion turned to Johnston's theory and, if the shot had indeed been fired from outside and the killer had then reloaded, where the spent cartridge case might have ended up. The trajectory should have seen it land in the flower garden along the fence line behind the house, police surmised, but they had already searched there and had found nothing. Then, one of the officers pointed out that the flower garden had never been sieved, only searched by digging. Hutton told Parkes and Detective Mike Charles to search the fence line the next day.[36]

Once again, the detectives found themselves on their knees in the Pukekawa mud. First they weeded the garden, which had regrown since the last search. Then Parkes picked up a rake and began to free up the soil. Charles used a sieve, and then his fingers, to sift through the damp earth bit by bit. After about two hours digging in silence, Charles called out to Parkes, 'Have a look at this.' In a clump of earth, Charles had found a .22 brass cartridge case, no bigger than a large oblong pill, buried in about 2 or 3 inches of soil.[37]

Parkes and Charles's first thought was that the find was too good to be true. But when they examined the case to find it had dried dirt inside it, they thought it must have been in the ground for some time. 'It had been raining and the topsoil was all wet and yet it had dry dirt inside,' Parkes said.[38]

They called Hutton on the radio and went to the Priests' house next door to have a cup of tea while they waited for him to arrive from the Thomas farm, where he had again been questioning Thomas about the sick cow.

Owen Priest could see that Parkes and Charles were excited, although they didn't say what about. Charles put on one of the Priests'

The back door of the Crewe house, showing the area of the garden where the cartridge case from Arthur Thomas's rifle was found.

daughter's hats and a pair of sunglasses and danced around the room. Priest suspected that they had found something.

When Charles took the case to the DSIR the next day, Rory Shanahan compared the cartridge to the others fired from the Thomas rifle during their earlier tests and was certain: this case had been fired from Arthur Thomas's rifle.[39]

On 30 October, police took Vivien Thomas to Pukekohe for an identification parade. She was asked to stand in line next to several other women who had been recruited from a nearby factory and look straight ahead. Then police entered with Bruce Roddick, the young labourer who had told the police back in June that he had seen a woman at the Crewe house from the neighbour's paddock on the morning of the murders. Roddick walked up and down several times, before declaring that the woman he had seen was not in the line-up. Afterwards, police tried to get Roddick to identify the car he'd seen next to the mystery woman. They parked Thomas's car on a side street and drove past several times, but Roddick didn't pick it.[40]

The next time Vivien Thomas saw police was the morning of 11 November. She was about to leave the house to take one of her Siamese cats to the vet in Pukekohe when Bruce Hutton and Len Johnston arrived at the farm, looking for Thomas. He was at the back of the farm, she told them. 'Don't worry,' the detectives said, 'we'll find him.' The officers found Arthur Thomas about to climb onto his tractor and asked him to come with them to the Ōtāhuhu police station.

Ignoring lawyer Paul Temm's instructions not to speak to police, he changed out of his farm clothes and willingly got in the car.[41] At 12.30 p.m., they arrived at the station. Inside, Johnston spoke first. He laid out all the evidence once again — Thomas's relationship with Jeannette Crewe, the axle, the gun.

'I've been framed,' Arthur told him. 'Someone must have known I was writing to Jeannette.' But, Johnston said, how did they get the gun? 'They must have cased my house the weekend before the murder,' Thomas replied.

Then Hutton spoke. 'Look, Arthur, a .22 shell was found near the back door of the Crewe house by the police. Scientists say that shell was fired by your rifle.'

Again Thomas said that the murderer must have got his rifle out of the house somehow. 'I'm not a fortune teller, I can't help you with that one. I wouldn't leave it there if I had shot them as I know shells can be identified by the firing pin markings. I have been framed and that's all there is to it,' he said.

'You must have done it, Arthur,' Hutton said.

But Thomas insisted, once again, that he had been home that night. 'I know I am sitting on rocks but I have got to stick to what I have already told you otherwise I am a goner,' he said.[42]

At 1.40 p.m., Hutton informed Arthur Allan Thomas that he would be arrested and charged with murdering Jeannette Lenore Crewe and David Harvey Crewe on or about 17 June, at Pukekawa.

'But I was at home,' Thomas said. 'I told you where I was when it happened.'

Hutton shrugged. 'We don't believe you.'[43]

Arthur Thomas was put in a police car with Stan Keith and Bruce Parkes. He was taken to Oakley Hospital in Auckland for a psychiatric assessment as to whether he was fit to be charged, then back to Ōtāhuhu for a brief remand appearance, then to Mount Eden Prison.

In the car, his mind began to race. He kept going over and over his alibi, telling the officers driving him that he was at home, he was at home the night of the murders.[44]

Parkes, the member of the inquiry team who felt most uneasy about Arthur's guilt, was still struggling to reconcile his personal views with the weight of evidence pointing towards the Thomas farm.[45]

The visit to Oakley didn't help. Thomas was seen by Dr Pat Savage, a forensic psychiatrist and the head of Oakley for many years. When the examination was over, and Arthur was getting back into the police car, Savage had a quiet word with the two detectives. 'Are you sure you've got the right man?' he asked.[46]

CHAPTER SIX
THE FIRST TRIAL

The day Arthur Thomas was charged with murder, Vivien Thomas arrived home from her appointment with the vet to find their farmhouse empty. Assuming her husband was still at the police station, she called to check if he would be home in time for evening milking. 'Probably,' she was told by the officer who answered the phone at the station. Less than two hours later, a car pulled up to the Thomas house. But it wasn't Arthur. It was Detective Sergeant Mike Charles, and he was alone. 'I have been sent personally by Inspector Hutton to tell you that your husband has been arrested and charged with the murders of Harvey and Jeannette Crewe,' he said.

'You must be bloody mad,' she replied. Charles told her he admired her loyalty to her husband. 'It's not loyalty,' she said. 'He's innocent.'[1]

The depositions hearing was set down for 14 December 1970 at the Otahuhu Magistrates Court. Arthur Thomas arrived, keeping his head down to try to avoid the newspaper photographers and onlookers. He was shackled and in handcuffs. The courtroom was full of local farmers, keen to hear what had really happened that night of 17 June, when someone had killed two of their own. From the dock, Arthur was able to catch glimpses of his wife and family. In the breaks, he was led back to the court cells.[2]

The purpose of a depositions hearing is to decide whether there is enough evidence to bring a case against the defendant. Usually, it is also the first time the defence counsel learns the narrative that the Crown is planning to present to the jury, via the prosecutor's opening statement to the court. But Crown counsel David Morris chose not to show his hand. Morris didn't open the case at all, instead forcing defence lawyers Paul Temm and Brian Webb — and the public — to piece together the Crown's case themselves as each of the 84 witnesses was examined.[3]

The Crown called so many witnesses, and the hearing moved so fast, that the reporters from the *Auckland Star* took turns to take notes in 20-minute bursts. At the end of his stint, Jim Tully, a young reporter newly assigned to the court beat, would run out of the hearing to the foyer and phone the newsroom with an update, improvising the story straight from his notebook to a copy-taker at the other end. Depositions were normally reported in a low-key way, if at all. But this was different: each day, the *Star*'s reporting on the case took up more than half of its broadsheet page.[4]

Over seven days, the court heard how Jeannette knew Arthur as a child, and how she had lived and worked in Maramarua as a young woman, while Arthur lived nearby. A friend from her teenage years, Beverley Batkin, told the court how Arthur had 'pestered' Jeannette at dances in the mid-1950s, that she found this uncomfortable and that his attention 'distressed' Jeannette. Batkin also said Arthur was 'usually rather untidy in general appearance and his shoes were particularly dirty'. Her evidence made sensational headlines in the newspapers. The *Star* seized upon her quote that Arthur had held a 'passion' for Jeannette and ran with it in bold type.[5]

Arthur's letter to Jeannette while she was overseas and the gift of the brush and comb set was also advanced as evidence of this infatuation. Then, the court heard about the burglary and the fires in the years before the murders, and their impact on the Crewes. It heard how Arthur had been in the Crewe house for a cup of tea and to use the toilet while working for the aerial topdressers Barr Brothers. It heard that the Crewes were wealthy while the Thomases were in debt.

THE FIRST TRIAL   113

The doctor who had examined Rochelle, Thomas Fox, gave evidence that it was likely Rochelle had been fed during the five days before the bloodied farmhouse was discovered by Len Demler. (The other doctors, who thought Rochelle might have survived without food, were not called.)

Labourer Bruce Roddick told the court about seeing the woman at the front of the Crewe house next to a dark green Hillman car on the Friday; and Pukekawa local Queenie McConachie described the child next to the light-coloured car she had seen the next day. Delivery man Emmett Shirley testified that when he had delivered the bread, milk and mail to the Crewe house on the Thursday morning, the curtains at the left-hand side of the lounge were open. On the Monday, they were closed, he said.[6]

Len Demler — once the main suspect — gave evidence for the Crown. He described his arrival at the house on the Monday, and seeing the bloody marks on the floor. Demler explained why he hadn't taken Rochelle with him when he left the house the first time. 'I didn't know what to do exactly so I thought I had better go home to stop these trucks coming for the sheep,' he said. Demler also told the court about how Arthur had once called at the house while Jeannette was overseas, asking for her address. He'd been back a second time, he said, before Christmas in 1962, with a gift for Jeannette. He'd left the pair talking on the doorstep.

Next, the scientists and the police presented their evidence: that Harvey Crewe was shot from behind while seated in his armchair; that Jeannette was likely knocked over and then shot. They laid out evidence about the bullets, the wire and the axle, all of which they said had ties to Arthur or the Thomas farm. Hutton went last, describing his conversations with Arthur when he arrested him, including Arthur's line that he had been framed.[7]

Even without a narrative from the Crown, the inference by the end of the hearing was clear: the murders of Harvey and Jeannette Crewe were a crime driven by jealousy, committed in the dead of night, then covered up by the faithful Vivien, who fed the baby in the days before the bloodied house was uncovered.

It was a compelling story. But the evidence was entirely circumstantial. There were no fingerprints directly linking Arthur Thomas to

114 **THE CREWE MURDERS**

the Crewe house, no hair, no blood. There was no eyewitness putting Arthur at the scene that night. At the end of the hearing, Arthur's lawyer, Paul Temm, made that point, and told the court there was no case to answer.

The magistrate disagreed with him. On 22 December 1970, Arthur Allan Thomas was committed to trial.[8]

Vivien Thomas, who had packed a suitcase full of clothes for her husband to wear in the car on his way home, was shocked to see Arthur led back to the cells. She had resolutely believed the court would see that the police had made a mistake. In this, she wasn't alone. Even before they heard the evidence police had against him, Arthur had unwavering support from both his and Vivien's families. After hearing about the arrest, his younger brother Lloyd had come to help on the farm. His sister, Lyrice, returned from Australia soon after. Vivien's aunt and uncle, Pat and Joyce Vesey, vowed to help her as soon as Vivien told them she knew Arthur was innocent.

Neighbours and friends including Brian Murray also stood by the Thomas family, citing Allan Thomas's high standing in the community and Arthur's good nature as reasons why they simply did not believe he was capable of such a crime. Arthur's parents were so confident their son would be released that his mother, Ivy, had been planning a Christmas party to celebrate.[9]

When the family went to visit Arthur in jail after the depositions hearing, he was in shock. While Ivy sobbed, he groped for words, asking about the farm, before blurting out to Vivien a secret: he had fathered a baby before he met her. He wanted to tell her himself, Arthur said, because he felt it would come out at trial. Vivien, reeling internally, reassured him. 'There are more important things to worry about.'[10]

Defence lawyer Paul Temm had two months following depositions to prepare for the trial proper. Outwardly, Temm remained confident, but behind the scenes he was struggling to get the information he needed to run a decent defence case. Under the rules of disclosure, Temm should have been able to see the evidence collected against Thomas by police. Disclosure is enshrined as part of New Zealand's laws on the 'right to a fair trial', as it allows a defendant's lawyer to assess the case against their client and test any gaps or errors in court.

But ever since Thomas's arrest, Temm had hit a brick wall. Before the depositions hearing, he couldn't access the records of the Crewes' estate or their personal accounts. He was unable to get some witness statements from the police file. Inquiries about the cartridge case went unanswered, and a question about a stain on the carpet was replied to with incorrect information. While some of those questions were answered when he cross-examined witnesses in the depositions hearing, there was still significant information on the police file — much of it stemming from their inquiries into Demler — that Temm had not seen.[11]

On the positive side, his own client was more forthcoming. Inside Mount Eden Prison, Arthur began to write down his life story for his lawyers. He used toilet paper, putting down anything he believed might possibly count against him, including the illegitimate child. He also began to settle into a routine, and to make acquaintances with the other inmates. He reported that when he had told his fellow inmates that Justice Trevor Henry had been appointed to hear the case, they had winced. Henry was a 'hanging judge', they told him, who would no doubt find him guilty.[12] Temm, more circumspectly, described Henry as a 'strong' judge, and told Arthur he remained confident.[13]

The trial began on 15 February 1971 at what was then the Auckland Supreme Court (now the High Court), a brick building in the gothic style on Waterloo Quadrant. In courtroom one, Justice Henry sat at an ornate desk under a carved canopy. The press were seated facing the jury bench, and the lawyers, in their wigs and black gowns, faced the judge. The public were crammed into the gallery's mezzanine. At the registrar's signal, Thomas was brought up from the cells beneath the court. The public could hear him before they saw him, his footsteps echoing on the steep, curved stairwell before he appeared, in suit and tie, through the trapdoor.

Justice Henry's first move was to sequester the jury, and so the eight men and four women who had been sworn in would spend the duration of the trial at the Station Hotel on Anzac Avenue, a short walk from the court. The rationale was that the separation would ensure

116   THE CREWE MURDERS

the jury couldn't be tampered with or influenced by family and friends after going home each night. It was a rare step, given that mandatory jury isolation had ended in New Zealand in 1966.[14] The defence team objected, saying it would place extra pressure on the jury. The Crown supported the judge, who was not persuaded by the defence. That night the jury moved into the hotel. On weekends, when the jury members still weren't allowed home to see their families, bailiffs would take them on trips to local hot pools, the movies, and once to a sailing race, the One Ton Cup.[15]

On 16 February, Arthur Thomas finally got to hear the full details of the Crown case against him. David Morris told the jury that on the night of Wednesday 17 June 1970, Arthur had left his home, with his rifle, and had driven to the home of Jeannette and Harvey Crewe. He had crept up to the house, balanced on the windowsill, and aimed his rifle through the open louvre window.

He had shot Harvey Crewe while he was sitting in his armchair in front of the fire, then had burst into the house, knocked Jeannette down and shot her. Later, he had wrapped their bodies in bedspreads and weighted them with the axle before depositing them in the Waikato River. Between the time the Crewes were murdered and Demler's arrival at the farmhouse five days later, there was a 'very distinct possibility' that baby Rochelle had been fed, Morris said.[16]

The Crown argued that three physical pieces of evidence linked Arthur Thomas to the murders: the gun, the axle and the wire. Further, Arthur had motive, Morris argued: his unrequited passion for Jeannette and jealousy over her money. He had the opportunity, as he could have snuck out after his wife was asleep. Other small details counted against him — mysteriously, Arthur had known that the brush and comb set he had given Jeannette eight years before was still wrapped up. And he had given two contradictory statements about previously meeting Harvey Crewe, Morris said. Arthur had first told Detective Sergeant John Hughes that Harvey was a 'decent kind of chap', but then later told Detective Inspector Bruce Hutton that he had never spoken to Harvey at all.

The defence case was simple: Arthur Thomas was not the killer. He was at home the night the Crewes were murdered looking after a sick cow, watching television, and was in bed with his wife by 9 p.m.

Vivien would confirm his alibi, Temm said, as would his cousin Peter Thomas. He told the jury the Crown's evidence was 'circumstance piled on guesswork' and that the question they should ask themselves was, 'If Arthur didn't do it, then who did?'[17]

The first blow to Temm's defence came when the Crown called Peter Thomas as its own witness. Morris had subpoenaed Peter soon after Arthur's arrest, meaning he wasn't even allowed to speak to Temm outside the court hearings even though he was part of Arthur's alibi. Peter told the court that Arthur owned a rifle, which he used to shoot rabbits and possums, and that it was normally kept in the room where Peter slept. He said he had been home on the night of 17 June with Arthur and Vivien. They'd watched TV and gone to bed around 9 p.m. Arthur didn't leave the house at all. At the time, there was something going on with a sick cow, Peter said, but he couldn't remember whether he'd helped Arthur that night, specifically. He remembered that week, though, because it had been Arthur's sister's twenty-first birthday party on the Friday night, and so when he and the Thomases had discussed what they were doing the night the Crewes died, he was able to recall it clearly.

Morris focused on these discussions. How many times did they discuss what they were doing the night of the murders? What did they say? When? How did this come up? The inference was that these conversations were somehow suspicious, and the effect was to draw attention away from the evidence that provided Arthur an alibi.

Temm was able to regain some ground when he cross-examined Len Demler. During questioning, Demler revealed he had been under police suspicion for a time, partially because of a bloodstain on the front seat of his car. Temm's questions revealed that the police interest in Demler was more than just a passing interest.

Temm: 'Did the police question you as to your movements on Wednesday 17 June?'

Demler: 'Yes they did.'

Temm: 'How long was spent in that questioning altogether?'

Demler: 'Quite a fair period . . .'

Temm: 'How many times altogether were you questioned?'

Demler: 'Two or three times.'[18]

Temm then planted the idea that Demler might have access to a rifle by asking about the gun belonging to the Chennells estate. Demler first denied that the gun existed, then confirmed there had been another broken-down rifle that was missing. It was a real win for Temm, particularly given his lack of access to the police investigation files. By presenting Demler as an alternate suspect, he was hoping to sow doubt about Arthur's guilt.

But the Crown case wasn't solely about Arthur. Someone had clearly fed the baby, and although she wasn't on trial, as Morris told the jury, Vivien — a determined, resourceful and loyal wife — could have been that person. The evidence in the Crown's favour piled up: Thomas Fox's evidence about Rochelle's medical condition, the dirty nappies left in the cot, the sighting of a woman, the changing position of the curtains.

When Bruce Roddick gave his evidence, Temm had a chance to undermine the Crown's conjecture. He asked Roddick to confirm whether the woman he'd seen standing in the Crewe paddock had fair hair. Yes, Roddick answered.

Temm then asked him: 'Do you know Mrs Thomas, the accused's wife?'

Roddick: 'I have met her before.'

Temm: 'What colour hair does she have?'

Roddick: 'Dark hair.'

Temm: 'Is it black in fact?'

Roddick: 'Yes.'

But Temm, who had been unable to speak to Roddick before the trial because he was a Crown witness, didn't ask Roddick directly whether the woman he'd seen was Vivien, leaving the door to speculation wide open.[19]

The more technical evidence came in the second half of the trial. By then, the Crown had worked hard to lay the groundwork for its theory that Arthur Thomas had shot Harvey and Jeannette through the louvre window, calling witnesses to describe the layout of furniture in the house, the Crewes' normal habit of watching TV after dinner, and the injuries to the bodies.

Francis Cairns, the pathologist, bolstered the Crown's argument when he said he believed the shot that killed Harvey had come from the direction of the kitchen. Temm spent significant time trying to undermine that theory, eking out small details about the movement of the couch, and pushing Cairns to say the injuries to Jeannette's face could have been caused by almost any blunt instrument, not just the butt of Arthur Thomas's gun.

Morris next called the senior police officers to give their evidence. Stan Keith described finding the solitary round of ammunition in Arthur's garage and taking it apart to find the number 8 on the base of the bullet. He recounted the conversation between Arthur and Vivien that he had overheard while in the garage, during which Arthur had said, 'If they think I am guilty, I am, and that's that.'

Bruce Parkes gave evidence about finding the brush and comb set in a cupboard in the Crewes' spare room, and the small card attached to it that said 'from Arthur'. Len Johnston then described how he'd questioned Thomas about the brush and comb gift. 'I asked the accused whether he knew if Jeannette had used the brush and comb set that he had given her. He said he didn't know, "it could still be wrapped up for all he knew".[20]

Johnston also told the court how he'd pieced together the axle's history, and detailed finding the stub axles in the Thomas tip. Mike Charles described finding the 'dark brown' cartridge case in the flower garden, with its bone-dry dirt inside. The officers said they took wire samples from Arthur's farm. Under questioning, Charles revealed he also collected wire from other farms, including Demler's property.

DSIR scientist Harry Todd was called to speak to the wire evidence. He said he had compared the wire samples from the farms with the wire found with Harvey and Jeannette's bodies. Todd was examined by Morris's junior, David Baragwanath. Baragwanath was meticulous, but the science was almost too overwhelming to follow. For starters, each piece of wire was labelled in three different ways: with an exhibit number, a wire number, and a snip number, i.e., exhibit 288(2) was also known as sample X6626(2), or simply, wire 2.

Then there were two types of wire — copper and galvanised 16-gauge steel. Baragwanath established from Todd that the copper wires were identical, but there was no match found for the copper wire among the wire collected by police. Two samples of galvanised wire taken from Harvey's body didn't match each other, or a sample from the bedspread found floating in the water nearby, or a first lot of samples collected from a number of Pukekawa farms.

However, Todd said, the samples from Harvey's body were the same chemical composition as some of the 11 wire samples from Arthur's farm. One of the wires from Harvey's body in particular was in 'excellent agreement' with, and therefore 'indistinguishable' from, four samples from Arthur's farm. A second wire from his body was in 'good agreement' with a sample from Arthur's farm.[21]

In his opening address, Morris had pointed to Arthur's .22 Browning rifle being the most important piece of evidence before the court. The gun could be linked to the crime in two ways, he argued: first, the bullets found in the bodies of Jeannette and Harvey could have been fired by Arthur's rifle; second, the cartridge case found in the flowerbed was also from his rifle. Most of the evidence about the bullets came from DSIR scientist Donald Nelson, who told the court that the bullets found in the bodies of the Crewes were .22 calibre, with an 8 stamped on the base, and were fired from a rifle with six right-hand lands.

Both the number 8 and the land marks were important: the Crown told the court that bullets with an '8' symbol were rare, having gone out of production in 1963. But, as evidence given by Detective Stan Keith revealed, Arthur was known to have such bullets because Keith had found one in an apple box in his shed. In regard to the land marks, Nelson told the court the marks on the murder bullets were 'identical' in spacing to marks found on bullets test-fired by Arthur's rifle.

Under cross-examination by Temm, however, Nelson acknowledged that parts of the bullets were missing, so he could not prove definitively where they came from. He was forced to admit they also matched one of the other 64 guns tested by police, a Remington rifle owned by the Eyre family.

Temm: 'And these bullets might or might not have been fired . . . from the Browning of the accused?'

Nelson: 'Yes, sir.'

Temm: 'Might have been fired from that Remington?'

Nelson: 'Yes, sir.'

Temm: 'And might have been fired by another weapon altogether that you have not tested?'

Nelson: 'Yes, sir.'[22]

Nelson and his colleague, Rory Shanahan, both gave evidence about exhibit 350, the cartridge case found in the garden. The marks on the case showed it came from Arthur's rifle, they said. But again, under cross-examination from Temm, Nelson was pushed to make a concession. Although his tests linked the cartridge to the crime scene, it wasn't linked to the bullets found with the Crewes.

Temm: 'Turning to the cartridge case found by Mr Charles, are you able to say that the bullet that killed Jeannette Crewe came from that cartridge case?'

Nelson: 'No, sir.'

Temm: 'From your examination of the two objects you can't say that the one came from the other?'

Nelson: 'No, sir.'

Temm: 'From your examination of the cartridge case and the bullet that killed Harvey Crewe can you say the bullet came from that cartridge case?'

Nelson: 'No, sir.'[23]

Temm's cross-examination of Rory Shanahan also served as an attempt to undermine the evidence about the cartridge case. He pushed him on two points: the marks on the case that the scientists said unequivocally linked the case to Arthur's rifle; and the level of corrosion it had sustained in the garden. However, Temm's argument about the marks was based on a comparison of photographs of the case in the flowerbed and those test-fired from Arthur's rifle. This was proved futile after Shanahan said the photos couldn't possibly reproduce what he'd seen through his microscope.

Temm's argument that the cartridge case should have had more corrosion after four months outside also fell flat: though Shanahan said the flowerbed case was somewhat duller than the other cartridge cases he'd fired from the rifle, he didn't know what four months of corrosion looked like, so he couldn't answer Temm's questions.

Bruce Hutton was the seventy-sixth Crown witness to give evidence. He told the jury a gripping detective story in which the police had methodically followed a trail of clues to arrest Arthur Thomas. Every decision, including searching the garden a third time, finding the cartridge case, and creating the louvre window reconstruction, was recounted for the court in detail. Hutton also re-created each of his interviews with Thomas for the court, from the conversations about the intricacies of the Thomas marriage to his assertion that someone had framed him for the murders. He even supplied photos of himself sitting in Harvey's chair while a photographer took a photo through the window, to show the angle the shooter would have taken. In his retelling, the four months the police spent pursuing Len Demler were totally erased.

Temm's first strategy in cross-examination was to undercut Hutton's story by revealing his reconstruction as a series of jumps in logic, made without proof. An example was the Crewes' time of death. Hutton said he had deduced that Harvey and Jeannette were killed after television programming had finished for the night at 11 p.m., because the TV was switched off at the wall and unplugged. Hutton also concluded they'd had a fire going because it was cold. Jeannette must have been knitting on the couch, he said: a bloodstain with her blood was found on its castor.

Temm then pointed out some discrepancies in the Crewes' bank accounts: the couple had a joint account of $1667, but where Harvey had a combined $34 in savings, Jeannette had more than $4500 in her three accounts. Hutton dismissed this as 'nothing unusual'. Then Temm turned to the reconstruction of the shot through the window. He picked through every detail — the height of the chair, whether the sliding door had been open, the angle of the shot. Temm suggested that if a marksman had taken the shot through the louvres as Hutton suggested, he would have hit the cocktail cabinet, rather than Harvey's head. At this, Hutton lost his temper. 'This is ridiculous. One knows with photos you can completely alter angles and position of door handles.'

Calmly, Temm then moved on to try to undermine the police theory regarding the angle of the bullets in relation to the position of Harvey, and Harvey's chair. When he asked Hutton whether he agreed with Francis Cairns' theory that Harvey's weight was at the front of the chair when he was shot, Hutton admitted it was pure guesswork. 'He could have been in any position. One would be a brave man to say the way he would be. So many theories have been proved wrong.'

Next Temm switched to the evidence about the axle. Hutton had told the court that he had first felt the axle while trying to get a cradle under Harvey's body in the Waikato River. It was stuck, so he reached underneath to find what was there and caught hold of the end of an object that appeared to be iron. Just as he did so, the wire connecting it to the body snapped. The axle was then found on the riverbed by the diving crew, and later matched to the stub axles found on the Thomas farm.

Temm put it to Hutton that the wire hadn't been attached to the axle, but rather to the bedspread found in the branches of a bush nearby. Hutton said he was sure of his evidence: the axle had been connected to the wire on Harvey's body.[24]

Hutton was supposed to be the Crown's star final witness, but after his cross-examination, Morris called one more: Pukekohe jeweller William Eggleton. Part way through the trial, Eggleton had approached police to say that a big man who was wearing a black singlet underneath a white shirt had come into his store with a broken watch, about a week after the Crewes went missing. The watch, which was gold and had a leather strap, was covered in blood and mucus.

Eggleton had replaced the glass and then thought nothing more of it until he saw a photo of Arthur Thomas in a local paper in November and 'knew it was the person who had brought the watch into me'. Because he had left it until after the trial had started to come forward, the Crown had to ask Justice Henry whether the evidence could be admitted. To Henry's surprise, Temm did not object and Eggleton was approved to give evidence.[25]

In court, Eggleton was shown a watch, and a newspaper photograph. He said the picture was the one he'd seen in November, but he didn't recognise the watch, which belonged to Arthur Thomas. In cross-examination, Temm asked him why he had come forward so late?

It had been worrying him, Eggleton said.

Temm: 'Are you also nagged by the doubt that you might be mistaken?'

Eggleton: 'No.'[26]

vidence for the Crown concluded at 2.53 p.m. on 25 February. The judge gave the defence a short adjournment to prepare themselves, during which Paul Temm and Brian Webb, the lawyer assisting him as his junior, had one final discussion about whether they should call Arthur Thomas as a witness. By law, he had the right to silence. But eventually Temm decided to let Thomas tell his story to the jury for himself.[27] He stepped into the witness box at 3.06 p.m.

Gently, Temm stepped him through his evidence. Arthur was clearly nervous, giving short, almost reluctant, answers. They made their way slowly through Arthur's upbringing, his association with Jeannette at school, and the last time he'd spoken to her, which he said was a friendly chat at a shop in Tūākau six months earlier. Then Temm turned to Cow No. 4. The cow had been sick for two weeks, Thomas said, and he had kept her in the implement shed, where she was given mineral water and hay, and helped to stand with the aid of a hoist and sling. During the late afternoon and early evening of 17 June, Cow No. 4 had calved. Vivien had helped Arthur with the birth, their work finishing after dark.

Temm: 'What did you do after you finished attending to the cow in the implement shed?'

Arthur: 'I had to clean everything up and my wife had gone to prepare tea and I cleaned up. Then I went back to the house when we had finished for the day.'

Temm: 'Did you go out again at any time that night?'

Arthur: 'No we did not.'

Temm: 'Did you?'

Arthur: 'No we did not.'

Guided by Temm, Thomas also put on record his early work life, including time in Maramarua, his marriage, and his history of going to dances, refuting Beverley Batkin's claim that he'd been at these events in the mid-1950s. He didn't attend a dance until 1959, he said, after he and a friend took lessons in Auckland. His dance lesson card from April that year was entered as an exhibit.

He recalled his interactions with police during the Crewe inquiry — including telling the story about John Hughes getting stuck in his electric fence — the interviews, and the searches on his farm. He said he had never seen the axle before. He said he had never seen the jeweller William Eggleton before. When Temm asked what help he'd given police with their inquiries, Thomas replied, 'I have given them every assistance that I can give them.'

Temm: 'Did you have anything to do with the things that happened in the Crewe house on 17 June?'

Thomas: 'I certainly did not.'

David Morris used his cross-examination to highlight the number of witnesses who, he argued, must have been wrong for Thomas's story to be true. This included, firstly, evidence given by John Hughes, who said that during his first visit to the farm he'd asked Thomas how he knew he was home the night of 17 June.

Hughes had not asked him that, Thomas replied.

Morris: 'So if he did not ask you that question, then he is lying, is that what you say?'

Thomas: 'I suppose so.'

Morris then pointed to the evidence of Detective Stan Keith, who had reported overhearing Thomas say 'If they think I am guilty I am and that's that'. Keith was mistaken, Thomas said; he didn't say anything like that. Then Morris asked Thomas about Beverley Batkin's assertion that he had been at dances in the mid-1950s. She was wrong, too, he replied.

Lastly, Morris asked about William Eggleton. Thomas said Eggleton was mistaken in his identification of him as the man in a black singlet under a white shirt who brought in a bloodied gold watch. But Morris was laying a trap, and Thomas walked right in.

Morris: 'Do you normally wear a black singlet when you go to town?'

Arthur: 'Not when I go to town.'

Morris: 'When you dress to go out do you wear a black singlet?'

Arthur: 'No, never.'

Morris: 'With an open-necked shirt when you go to Tūākau, would you wear a black singlet?'

Arthur: 'No, never.'

Then Morris pulled out a newspaper photo to show the court. It was the newspaper William Eggleton had seen in November 1970. Arthur and Vivien Thomas are together at a dress-up party, grinning at the camera. Arthur is wearing a pyjama top. A black singlet can be seen clearly underneath.[28]

ivien Thomas was called to the stand at 10 a.m. the next day. Before her turn, *Star* reporter Jim Tully saw her sitting outside, swotting up on her notes, when he went to file his copy.[29] This time, Temm's junior, Brian Webb, asked the questions for the defence. Webb spent an hour and a half asking Vivien Thomas about the intricacies of herd management and cowshed record-keeping before turning to the Crewe murders. Vivien said they'd heard the news from a stock agent and had then seen it on the television news that night. Arthur had told her the missing woman was a girl he'd gone to school with, she said.

Webb asked Vivien to step through her movements on the week of 17 June. Referring Vivien to the calving records, Webb established that Cow No. 4 calved on 17 June. It was shot six days later, on 23 June. Then Webb turned to the police investigation — the searches at her home that upset her because the floors were clean — and her participation in the identification parade. Vivien told the court that at one point she was questioned by Len Johnston for five hours. Webb saved the most important question until the end:

Webb: 'You and your husband occupy one room in the house?'

Vivien: 'The bedroom on the left of the hall as you go in the front door.'

Webb: 'How do you sleep?'

Vivien: 'In a double bed.'

Webb: 'Are you a light sleeper?'

Vivien: 'Reasonably light, yes.'

Webb: 'If your husband were to leave the bed, would you know?'

Vivien: 'Yes I would.'

Vivien had answered Webb's questions competently, but under cross-examination by David Baragwanath, she fell apart. Baragwanath immediately began grilling Vivien about the discussion Arthur, Peter and Vivien had held about what they were doing on the day of the murders. He wanted to know the date of this conversation. Vivien told him she couldn't remember. Was it an hour, a day or a week afterwards? Vivien again said she couldn't remember. Who brought it up? Vivien couldn't tell him.

Baragwanath applied the same pressure when asking about the cowshed records, and whether they were complete at the time Hutton first visited. (In his evidence, Hutton had said they were not.) 'I just can't remember,' Vivien repeated over and over. At one point she apologised: 'I am sorry I have been through so much since my husband has been in prison, I just can't remember now.'

Baragwanath's questioning cast doubt on Arthur and Vivien's story about Cow No. 4. By the end of the session, he had managed to suggest that the dates in the records had been filled out belatedly, or were altered, and that Vivien was actually mistaken and the cow could have calved up to four days after 17 June, weakening Thomas's alibi.

He also managed to imply that Vivien, who wore slacks, had dark brown hair and drove a light green Hillman car, could have been the woman who fed the baby because she was unable to give definite answers about where she was when Bruce Roddick saw the brown-haired woman wearing slacks in the paddock the day after the murders, or when Queenie McConachie saw the light-coloured car outside the Crewe house on Saturday 20 June. She would have been at home, Vivien said, or with her husband on the farm.

In re-examination, Temm tried to undo some of the damage. 'Have you ever been to the Crewe farm at any time?' he asked.

'Never,' Vivien said.[30]

But it was too late. Vivien Thomas, usually so strong and determined in her support of her husband, had instead come across as brittle and unconvincing, her memory vague.

The defence called another 20 witnesses, mainly friends and family of Arthur and Vivien, who could testify to Arthur's character, his movements leading up to that week, and further evidence that there definitely was a sick cow, including from the vet who treated it. Brian Murray, the Thomases' neighbour, gave evidence there were .22 shells everywhere on the Thomas farm, implying that anyone could have picked one up and planted it in the Crewe garden.

Mervyn Cathcart, Arthur's school friend, helped refute the story about Arthur 'pestering' Jeannette at dances. He was the shy teenager who had taken dance lessons with Arthur in 1959. But Cathcart also told the jury another useful piece of information. To leave his place and go anywhere, Arthur would have to pass Cathcart's house, as the other end of the road finished at the Waikato River. Living close to the road, Cathcart said, they heard any traffic going past. He knew Arthur's car by sound, because of its noisy 'rear end' — a fault in its differential, but

Cathcart heard nothing distinctive the night of 17 June, he said.

The final three witnesses were a photographer, a marksman and a firearms expert. They told how, earlier that week, they had tried to re-create the shot through the louvres just as police had described. In their evidence to the court, they each explained the findings of their experiment. Percy Brant, the firearms expert, who had spent 30 years in the army, told the court the shot was challenging, both because of the awkward way he had to balance on the ledge outside and because taking the shot without hitting the cocktail cabinet meant the gun had to be held at a very specific angle.

'I found that the position . . . for one, my size was quite uncomfortable and I could not guarantee a steady sight in that position. The eave was close to my head, my knees were bent and I found it quite difficult,' Brant said. 'I suppose a shot could be fired. There was a certain amount of restriction with both top and bottom louvre . . . and the limited angle at which to get an offhand shot.'[31]

Temm then called evidence from psychiatrist Kenneth Newton, from whom he wanted to hear that Arthur did not have an obsessive personality, to undermine the Crown's alleged motive. But Justice Henry said he could not hear such evidence, ruling it inadmissible. Newton was able to tell the court he had conducted psychological tests on Thomas, but he was stopped before he could list his findings. This infuriated Temm.[32]

With the defence case concluded, the court adjourned for lunch, and then the closing arguments began. David Morris went first. His speech was confident and deft, and his recap of how the Crown viewed the events of the night held no new surprises. He contended that Thomas shot Jeannette and Harvey Crewe on Wednesday 17 June, after their evening meal. Television had finished for the night and Jeannette was sitting on the couch knitting.

Thomas fired a shot through the open louvre window, killing Harvey in his chair. He reloaded, ejecting the shell case into the garden, then burst into the house, knocking Jeannette down and shooting her. She jumped up, dropping her knitting, using one needle to defend herself, leaving it bent. Thomas wrapped the bodies in bedspreads and then weighted them with the axle, before depositing them into the Waikato River.

The axle came from the Thomas farm and there was no doubt whatsoever that the cartridge case was ejected from the accused's rifle, he said. Morris, standing in front of the jury, gestured to it. 'This case was from the bullet which killed Harvey Crewe. This rifle on the desk in front of me fired it.' Taken together, the evidence led to the conclusion that Arthur Thomas killed the Crewes.

Morris said the Crown was not suggesting that Vivien Thomas knew anything about the murder. But she may have visited the Crewe farm on the Friday to feed the child, to minimise the tragedy. 'This would explain the apparent inconsistency of the careful and meticulous planning by the murderer and the seemingly foolhardy behaviour in feeding the baby and attempting to clean up.'

Paul Temm told the jury that the Crown's case rested only on circumstantial evidence. He began critiquing that evidence: Eggleton was honest but mistaken; Harvey wasn't shot through the window because it wasn't possible; and anyway, it was cold and raining that night, the louvres would have been closed; the axle hadn't been wired to the body, it was found nearby by chance. Temm said Arthur hadn't 'pestered' Jeannette, and she wasn't scared of him.

As evidence of this, he read from the thank-you letter Jeannette sent after she received Arthur's gift while overseas. 'Thank you for your very kind thought in sending me that beautiful writing compendium and pen,' she had written, before giving details of her travels, and her plans to work in London for a while.

Thomas had not been in touch with Jeannette after Christmas 1962, Temm said, and was now happily married. 'There's no proof at all for any reason why this man should do the monstrous thing he is accused of.' Instead, Temm put a different theory to the jury. 'There is a distinct possibility that this was a case of murder–suicide,' he said. 'It's hard to know sometimes what goes on inside a marriage. Very little is known of this couple. Any disagreements would not be heard because of the loneliness of the house. We know their financial positions were very different. From her savings account she had a substantial amount, but Harvey Crewe had an account of only $34. This was a wealthy young woman. Isn't it strange that there were no curtains in the living room, baby's room or main bedroom?' he said. 'Perhaps there was some discussion and sharp words. The injury to Jeannette's face might have come from her husband's fist.'

Temm suggested Jeannette might have shot her husband, and then herself. 'Did someone with the interests of the family at heart, to conceal what had taken place and in the hope it would remain unknown, put the bodies into the Waikato? Perhaps so that Rochelle would not know what had happened? Can you say that's impossible?'

Temm used the rest of his closing speech to attack the quality of the police investigation and its evidence. There was no firm evidence linking the wire and the bullets to Arthur Thomas, Temm said. 'Nobody has been able to, or dared to, say that the bullets in the bodies came from this rifle and no other.' He said Hutton's theory on the time of deaths could be wrong, arguing it was most likely the Crewes were killed soon after dinner, rather than late at night.

Then he turned to the cartridge case found in the garden. 'How did it get where it was found? Three thorough searches of the area. Would you expect it to be buried under the surface? If it fell from the rifle of a marksman and was ejected and flung out as suggested, it would be there to be seen by the police.' However, he didn't overtly say he thought the case was planted.

Finally, Temm advanced his defence of Arthur and Vivien Thomas. Arthur was a man of almost guileless simplicity, he said. 'A less honest man would have hedged with the police. Instead he has been completely truthful in his dealings with the police.' Equally, he said, Vivien was not the kind of woman to support a murderer. 'Do you think that woman, if she had known her husband had been out, do you think that woman, if she had known her husband had done that, would go back and lie alongside that man?'

Arthur Thomas was innocent, Temm said. 'And if he is convicted he will be done [a] wrong, in my submission, which can never, never be put right.'[33]

When the court adjourned, Temm's closing was the talk of the court. It was the first time he had raised the murder–suicide theory, delaying it until his closing argument so the Crown experts were unable to have the opportunity to shoot it down. It is a well-known tactic of defence counsel, but on this occasion, some of the lawyers and journalists following the case felt it was a mistake. By presenting a second option, Temm had given the jury a choice of theories — distracting them from his arguments about the weakness of the Crown case.[34]

Justice Trevor Henry began summing up before lunch and continued into the afternoon of 2 March. As he spoke, the Thomas supporters in the gallery felt their hearts sink. Amid his lengthy summary of the Crown evidence, Henry effectively wrote off most of the defence case by giving his opinion on each of Temm's points, then qualifying it as simply 'one point of view'. For example, when it came to the cartridge case found in the garden, he said: 'Please do not think I am suggesting it, but you may well think that any suggestion of the planting of a shell has little merit of validity.' On the axle: 'I am suggesting to you — although it is a matter for you . . . that the axle was in fact the weight used.' On the evidence about the dances: 'You may think that that has gone into the background and may be of little importance now. That is a matter for you.'

Henry also used this same phrase to highlight particular parts of the Crown case. On whether Arthur had lied about meeting Harvey Crewe, he said: 'You may think — it is a matter for you — that the accused has not always given consistent accounts on this.' Six times, Henry returned to Thomas's comment about the wrapping on the brush and comb when he had been questioned by Detective Johnston. 'Was that remark — and the accused did not really deny it — pure coincidence?' Henry asked. 'Is it possible that the accused has, in some unguarded moment, given himself away?'[35]

The jury retired in the late afternoon. The media and the observers from the public gallery drifted away. The Thomas family, including Vivien, lingered at the court. Jim Tully, who'd gone back to the *Star* office to file his story for the day, thought he still had hours and hours left to wait and was walking slowly back to court when people began coming towards him shouting, 'You'd better run, Jim, the jury is coming back.' They had reached a decision in less than two hours. As he rushed up the hill, a crowd of onlookers was hurrying, too, trying to get one of the few seats inside.[36]

The verdict was guilty on both counts of murder. The packed courtroom was stunned into near silence. Arthur Thomas was reeling. 'What's happened? Where are we going?' he asked his lawyers. Temm assured him they would appeal the conviction, and the sentence of life imprisonment that came with it.

But Arthur Thomas didn't really hear him. The guards were already leading him away.[37] His sentence would be served at Auckland Prison at Pāremoremo, home to a specialist maximum security unit and notorious as the country's toughest jail.

CHAPTER SEVEN
THE BACKLASH

The verdict was a terrible shock for the Thomas family. They had been told by Temm that the case against Arthur was not strong, and he would get off.

After the initial hammer blow of the conviction had eased, Thomas's supporters began to gather their thoughts. It was clear something had to be done. But how? Some encouraging signs started to emerge. The weekend tabloid *8 O'clock* headlined its story after the verdict: 'PUKEKAWA BACKS MRS THOMAS: MY MAN'S INNOCENT'. Angry calls came into local radio stations from members of the public. It was clear there was a lurking undercurrent of unease, but as yet it had no channel through which to run. And there was the appeal to be heard first. Surely that would remedy the obvious injustices and mistakes and clear bias of the trial?[1]

The appeal was heard in May 1971. Paul Temm appealed on three grounds: firstly, that Justice Henry had failed to put the defence case adequately (he had allowed only five lines in his summing-up); secondly, he had failed to direct the jury on the standard of proof to be applied to circumstantial evidence; and thirdly, that he should not have ruled the evidence of psychiatrist Kenneth Newton, that Arthur had no obsession for Jeannette, as inadmissible. All three were rejected. This was not only a blow for Arthur Thomas. Temm now wanted to take the case to the Privy Council in London, but by then the Thomas family had lost faith in him.[2]

Among those who attended the trial and who watched Arthur Thomas being driven off to begin his sentence was a man who was to become perhaps Arthur's second-greatest ally, his de facto father-in-law, Pat Vesey. A signwriter by trade, Vesey was one of the many who gathered around the Thomas cause. He had no university education or elite connections, but he had some important qualities which, as it turned out, were worth more. For one, he was not a Kiwi. He was Australian by birth and had no fear of New Zealand's social hierarchy. He loved his niece Vivien and was determined to stand by her. And he believed Arthur was innocent.

In July, shortly after the failed appeal, Vesey formed what was to become known as the retrial committee. Led by him, and with unstinting support from the Thomas family, it was to become a formidable public relations machine.

In an interview in 2022, Vesey recalled: 'We were all stunned because the lawyer Arthur had, he kept saying, "It won't get past [depositions]" and then when it came to the trial, he said, "Don't worry about it, [it's] cut and dry, I don't lose cases."'[3]

One of Vesey's first decisions was to dump Temm. Temm was hurt and frustrated by the rejection because new evidence was coming in which backed Thomas. In particular, there was new evidence from a man who had been continually phoning his secretary and demanding to see Temm but who refused to give his name. This was Graeme Hewson, Harvey Crewe's best friend.

A few days after hearing of the disappearance of the Crewes, Hewson had driven the 400 kilometres from Woodville to Pukekawa, where he stayed with Len Demler and helped in the search for the bodies. The Crewe family asked him to run the farm until a manager could be found. Once one had been appointed, he went back to Woodville, only to return again when he heard about the discovery of Jeannette Crewe's body. He kept helping with the search. Crucially, he helped, or so he claimed, in a search of the garden where exhibit 350, the cartridge case, was later to be found.

Temm agreed to see Hewson and took a sworn affidavit from him that in August 1970 he had helped police sieve-search the flowerbed where the case was found two months later. Temm passed on the affidavit to his replacement, Kevin Ryan.[4]

The current of unease after the trial verdict now burst into the open. The Sunday papers, the closest thing New Zealand had to a tabloid press, picked up the vibrations. The retrial committee, with nowhere else to turn, took full advantage of the newspaper interest and Vivien became the face of Arthur's campaign. She was a natural with the media. Whether being interviewed on the farm in gumboots, or speaking at a lunchtime forum for students at the University of Auckland, she was convincing and down to earth.

'VIV'S FIGHTING FOR HER MAN' (*Truth*, 29 June 1971), 'ARTHUR WAS "GOOD BLOKE"' (*Dominion Sunday Times*, 20 June 1971), some of the headlines ran. The *Weekly News* ran a double-page spread: 'VIVIEN THOMAS: "MY HUSBAND IS INNOCENT".[5] 'If you think I'm annoyed now,' she told one journalist, 'you should have heard me when a policeman told me he admired my loyalty. I hated him for that. As if I would be loyal to a murderer. If I thought for one moment Arthur had done that, he could rot in prison and I wouldn't care . . . I know it is nine months since my husband's freedom was taken away but I haven't got time to think about what his absence is doing to me. You can't dwell on yourself.'[6]

These were not just small local newspapers: they were the national papers, the equivalent, in those days, of Stuff or NZME. Suddenly, the spectacular case of the local farmer jailed for the killing of his neighbours was the talk of the country. Everywhere, people took sides: there were those who backed the police, and those who thought Thomas was innocent. The law did its best to shut it down, with the solicitor-general, Richard Savage, threatening journalists with prosecution for contempt of court when they tried to interview jurors.[7]

In Pukekawa, the debate took an uglier turn. The murders had made the area a minor tourist attraction. TV teams, journalists and sightseers roamed up and down Highway 22, slowing as they passed the Crewe house. Among the locals, divisions that had appeared during the investigation widened. Thomas family members were spat on in the street in Tūākau.

Witnesses who had appeared for the Crown also felt harassed and intimidated. William Eggleton, the jeweller, said he had been physically threatened. Cars slowed down outside Owen Priest's house, then drove away. His wife, Julie, believed she was followed when shopping.

Vivien Thomas became the face of the Thomas campaign; her unwavering support for her husband and her down-to-earth, straight-from-the-farm manner won many over to the Thomas cause.

Someone fired shots up the driveway of local farmer Ian Spratt; someone else shot at the home of Thomas supporter Ted Smith.[8]

Meanwhile, the retrial committee was busy trying to challenge the evidence against Arthur Thomas. Members of the committee crept onto the Crewe property and buried .22 shell cases to test how corroded they would be after four months in the ground. They also measured how far a shell case would be ejected from a rifle at the kitchen window and found it could not have flown the nearly 5 metres to reach the garden where the shell case had been found.

Public concern continued to mount. Petitions were being signed all over the country calling for a new trial. As *Sunday News* columnist Odette Leather noted in September 1971: 'The trial of Arthur Thomas has ended but in its stead a strange new trial has begun. The defendant in this instance is "the system".'[9]

By October, the petition had over 20,000 signatures and the retrial committee presented it to Governor-General Arthur Porritt. In December, the government announced the case would be reviewed by former Supreme Court judge Sir George McGregor. However, when his report was released in February 1972, it concluded that there had been no miscarriage of justice. The minister of justice, Sir Roy Jack, told the nation in late 1971: 'Justice had been done.' The *New Zealand Herald*, taking the establishment line, considered McGregor 'one of the finest legal minds in the country'.[10]

Many thought otherwise. Among them was the shadow minister of justice, Martyn Finlay. In an interview with investigative journalist David Yallop, he said he became uneasy after reading the notes of the first trial. 'The theory of the louvre shooting worried me. From this very unsteady and strained position he had to shoot with the absolute requirement that the shot be fatal. That seemed to me to be stretching a possibility to breaking point. That was the first flaw I saw in the Crown's case. Logic pointed to the murders having been committed inside the house.'[11] Finlay was soon to have his part to play.

Meanwhile, Vesey tried the personal approach: he went to Wellington and knocked on George McGregor's door. He could vividly recall the audacity of the decision when he told us about it 50 years later: 'His wife came and opened the door, and it was Victoriana personified, there was an aspidistra plant, it was like stepping back, you know, and she said, "Come in, His Honour will be here in a moment." I sat down in the sitting room, and she ushered in this . . . shuffling old man. I just couldn't believe it. And I looked at him and I thought, hell . . . As far as I was concerned, the government had paid a lot of money to have a cover for their actions.'[12]

Frustrated, Vesey tried to raise interest from every MP he could. He also wrote to then Minister of Justice Sir Roy Jack, outlining his concerns about McGregor, and he received an appointment. 'I went in and he was behind the desk. He said, "I must admit I haven't had time to read your letter, I don't remember getting it" and his secretary — if you wanted to go as a secretary to a fancy dress, she had on lisle stockings, a plaid tweed suit and horn-rimmed glasses — she turned around and said, "I beg your pardon, his letter has been on your desk for the past fortnight." You could see in his eyes he could have killed her.' But despite the unexpected support from Jack's secretary, the meeting failed to produce any change in the government's stance.[13]

Vesey also sought an appointment with Robert Muldoon, then deputy prime minister and minister of finance. Muldoon has become something of a notorious figure in New Zealand for his later actions as prime minister, but in 1971 he was at his peak, a vigorous, astute politician with solid support in the rural wing of the conservative National Party. His boss was Jack Marshall, a lawyer who had supported the reintroduction of capital punishment in the 1950s. With that sort of background, Muldoon might have shown Vesey the door. But Vesey was to find an ally in this most unexpected of places.

'So, I had an appointment with Muldoon,' Vesey told us in 2022. '[He said] "So what do you want to see me for?" I said, "This report, it's just wrong", to which he said, "That's your opinion", and I said, "Yeah, it is." I asked him had he met Judge McGregor? He said he hadn't. I said, "Well, if you do nothing else, give me your word that you'll go and see him." Now he was a pretty gruff speaker, he didn't want to be bothered too much, I think he wanted to go to the races, but he agreed.

'Anyway, he promised, and he did, and I got a phone call from him, and he said, "It's Rob here. I did what you said, and I agree entirely. I went to see [McGregor], and I'd been talking to him for about 20

Pat Vesey, Vivien Thomas's uncle, had introduced her to Arthur Thomas. His determination and his ability to get the ear of politicians was crucial to the Thomas campaign.

minutes, and he turned round to me and asked "What newspaper do you represent?" And to do that to Rob Muldoon summed it up. So Muldoon then became interested in the case.'[14]

By now, mid-1972, talk of the Arthur Thomas case was everywhere. Vesey's own demands for justice were greatly aided by the first book to analyse the case. Written by former *Auckland Star* journalist Terry Bell, *Bitter Hill* outlined inconsistencies in the prosecution's case and the theory advanced by the committee that argued for a retrial. Meanwhile, the public meetings called by the committee were attracting hundreds of people.

The committee's new legal advisor, Kevin Ryan, had also been busy. Ryan was a vigorous, young, former West Coaster who had gained a reputation as a 'streetfighter' who could win tough cases. He had arranged for the forensic evidence, including the bullet fragments, cartridge cases and Thomas rifle, to be flown to the UK for testing by the Home Office. The tests established that the rifle could have fired the fatal bullets, but so could 15 other rifles in the Home Office collection.[15]

The retrial committee was working to undermine what they saw as the three weak areas in the prosecution case. It now had Hewson's affidavit that the garden had been sieve-searched (which strongly suggested the cartridge case had been planted), it had Bruce Roddick saying the woman he saw was not Vivien Thomas, and evidence that a cartridge case buried for four months should have shown more corrosion than exhibit 350 displayed. They also attacked the evidence of the Pukekohe jeweller, William Eggleton, presenting affidavits that Thomas had never owned a gold watch.

With an election looming at the end of 1972, and the case clearly becoming an issue, the National government buckled. Following a further petition dated 2 June 1972, it announced that the verdict would be referred back to the Court of Appeal. But this announcement wasn't enough to counteract its loss of popularity: Labour swept into power in December that year, led by the charismatic Norman Kirk.

Three Court of Appeal judges heard the case in Wellington in February 1973. Chief Justice Richard Wild chaired the court, with justices Thaddeus McCarthy and Clifford Richmond alongside him. David Morris and David Baragwanath again led the prosecution team; against them was Kevin Ryan.

Morris did his best to undermine Graeme Hewson, cross-examining him about his failing marriage and difficult financial situation, and managing to extract an admission that Marie Crewe, Harvey's mother, had loaned him some money.

He suggested Hewson had stolen the Crewe dogs. Hewson replied that Len Demler and Marie Crewe had asked him to take them. Hewson stuck to his story: the gardens had been sieve-searched in August 1970. Bruce Roddick was also a strong witness, and the three judges were clearly impressed.

William Eggleton was brought back and his evidence began to crumble. A couple who were friends of his, Tūākau mayor George McGuire and his wife, Ella, said they had been in his shop in December 1970. They'd discussed the recent newspaper photo of Arthur and Vivien and Eggleton had said he didn't know them and had never seen them. They were shocked when he later gave evidence that Arthur had brought in a bloodstained watch.

Cross-examined, Eggleton told the court he had lied to the McGuires about not knowing Arthur and Vivien Thomas because he did not want them to know he was to be a Crown witness. But Kevin Ryan managed to get Eggleton to admit that an uncle of Arthur's, who bore a strong resemblance, had been in and out of his shop at that time.

The court announced its decision on 26 February 1973: there was to be another trial. The judges made it clear they were not saying there had been a miscarriage of justice; simply, they could not be sure that if the evidence they heard was put to a new jury, the same decision made in the first trial would remain.[16]

The Thomas camp rejoiced; it was by any measure a remarkable achievement. Thomas was moved from Pāremoremo to the remand wing of Mount Eden. Many felt his freedom was only weeks away, after what would surely just be the formality of a second trial.

But behind the scenes, Chief Justice Sir Richard Wild, who had been outvoted by his fellow judges at the Court of Appeal, was disturbed by the attacks on the legal system the case had invoked.[17] The police were also worried about damage to their credibility from the constant claims that the cartridge case had been planted, among other insinuations.

They saw the upcoming trial as their opportunity to snap the prison doors closed on Arthur Thomas forever.

This time, nothing, not even the jury, would be left to chance.

If there had not yet been a miscarriage of justice, there soon would be. The infamous second trial of Arthur Thomas was about to begin.

CHAPTER EIGHT
THE SECOND TRIAL

After two years working night and day on winning Arthur Thomas a new trial, barrister Kevin Ryan was exhausted. The case had completely taken over both his personal and working life, and Ryan was now so emotionally involved that he even briefly considered asking another lawyer to defend Arthur Thomas at the new trial, fearing he was too close to the case. But he decided the Thomas case was too important and too big not to carry on. Ryan wanted to win, not only to prove Thomas's innocence but also to highlight how the justice system many considered infallible could lead to the conviction of an innocent man.[1]

Despite his confidence in their case, Ryan was on the back foot before the trial even began. For example, the trial was to be heard just four weeks after the Court of Appeal verdict, giving the defence team almost no time to prepare. Ryan also felt that the judge appointed to lead the trial, Justice Clifford Perry, had previously been more hostile to him than any other judge in Auckland. And third, unbeknown to Ryan, the police had managed to get an advance copy of the jury panel from

Above: Queues form outside the Auckland Supreme Court in March 1973 as the second trial of Arthur Thomas opens. *Below:* Kevin Ryan (left) and his twin brother Gerald were confident of freeing Arthur Thomas at the start of the retrial. They did not then know how the police had skewed the jury against them.

the Auckland Supreme Court. Staff had then spent weeks checking the backgrounds of every person on the list. Anyone who held political views or had family connections that might cause them to be even slightly anti-police was highlighted to be challenged when the jury was called.

The defence, meanwhile, received the jury list just two days before the trial, and had to work around the clock to decide which six jurors they would object to. Unlike the Crown, the defence do not have an unlimited number of challenges; they have only six.[2]

When jury empanelling began on the morning of 26 March 1973, there was yet another surprise for the defence team. Justice Perry announced that the jurors would be isolated, as they had been in the first trial. Ryan objected, saying this would limit the demographics of the jurors to those who could afford to be away from their jobs and families for two weeks, but Perry said the decision was made to ensure a fair trial. Ryan was proved right, however. More than a third of the jurors applied to be excused because of the inconvenience of the isolation. Eight were excused; another 13 had their requests denied.

As their names were read out, the Crown challenged a further seven potential jurors. The defence objected to six. Taxi driver Bob Rock, one of those whose application to be excused was denied, was appointed foreman. A day later, Rock tried again to be excused when he heard that Detective John Hughes was a witness in the case. Rock had been in the Royal New Zealand Navy with Hughes, he told the deputy registrar. The registrar took this information to the judge, but he still refused to excuse Rock, even directing the registrar not to tell Kevin Ryan about it. Consequently, Ryan did not know about Rock's connection to Hughes or the judge's decision.[3]

The next day the trial opened at the Auckland Supreme Court amid a frenzy of anticipation. During the Court of Appeal hearing at Wellington there had been a total press ban on proceedings to avoid prejudicing a potential jury were another trial to be ordered. That 'secret' hearing had only served to heighten the interest in the case, to the point that the queues for a spot in the public gallery snaked from the court out to the footpath on Waterloo Quadrant and around the corner towards Parliament Street.

There were few reserved seats and even Arthur's mother, who

by then was very unwell, had to line up to get inside. At breaks, the lawyers and witnesses had to push their way through the crowds if they wanted to go for a walk or to have a quiet cigarette on the courthouse lawn. Meanwhile, Arthur Thomas spent his time between sessions in the stone cells below, traipsing the steep stairs from the dock to the cells and back.[4]

Crown solicitor David Morris didn't disappoint the voyeurs in the gallery with his opening speech. The deaths of Harvey and Jeannette Crewe were 'most horrible killings', he said. He urged the jury to put aside any sympathies they might have for Arthur Thomas: no matter what they'd read about him, he was charged as the defendant in a murder case. Over the next two and a half hours, aided by a map of the Pukekawa district and a floor plan of the Crewe house, Morris methodically laid out the Crown's well-practised argument: a wealthy young woman was murdered alongside her husband by her one-time suitor, who attacked by stealth on a rainy winter's night.

The case he outlined was almost identical to that presented at the first trial, but for a few subtle shifts. Morris told the jury they would hear evidence from two doctors, one who said baby Rochelle had been fed in the days between the murders and the discovery of the bloodied farmhouse, and one who believed she was strong enough to survive alone the whole time. Morris made no mention of Bruce Roddick's sighting of the woman in the paddock.

Clearly, the Crown was wanting to back away from overtly implying that the woman who fed the baby must have been Vivien Thomas, knowing from the evidence at the appeal hearing that this time Roddick would surely be asked if the woman he'd seen was Arthur's wife, and that his answer would be no.[5]

After lunch on that first day, the jury, prosecutors, the judge and Bruce Hutton were driven to Pukekohe by bus to inspect the crime scene for themselves — the judge and lawyers without their wigs and gowns. They took a tour of the Thomas farm and were shown the places along the Waikato River where Harvey and Jeannette's bodies were found. Afterwards, they all had lunch at the Tūākau Hotel. No such arrangements were made for the defence counsel. Kevin Ryan and his twin brother Gerald, who was assisting him, had to take a taxi for the hour's drive south to join the crime-scene visit and they were not

David Morris (right), shown here with David Baragwanath, was the brilliant young prosecutor who led the case against Arthur Thomas. He was masterful in court, but later made one mistake which ultimately undid the whole Crown case against Thomas.

invited to the lunch. Ryan believed the incident was another example of favouritism towards the prosecution by justice department officials.[6]

Ryan was also keenly aware of the disparity in resources between the defence and the Crown; on the defence side, Ryan had Gerald, his secretary and Pat Vesey, who acted as a runner for most of the trial.[7] Meanwhile, Hutton had set up a mini police headquarters in a caravan in the Supreme Court carpark. His officers could come and go from the court hearing and report back on any new information entered into evidence, or on any particularly interesting lines of questioning by the defence. Hutton also had officers stationed at Pukekawa, ready to make checks in real time. Any information gathered could then be fed back to the Crown in the courtroom.[8]

The first witnesses entered the courtroom to find the atmosphere brittle with hostility. From both sides, the lawyers were tense, quick to interrupt each other with objections to the judge. Morris and Baragwanath began to whisk each witness through their evidence with clinical precision. It was clear that some of the witnesses had changed their answers since the first trial. This included small details such as the temperature of the Crewes' living room, or the date a witness said they first spoke to police, for example.

But in some instances, witnesses suddenly remembered extra information that had significant bearing on the trial. Jeannette's friend Beverley Batkin now recalled that she had seen Arthur Thomas in the streets of Tūākau wearing a black singlet; and rather than only attending local dances in the mid-1950s, she and Jeannette had also danced together right up until she was married in December 1960. In cross-examination, Ryan accused Batkin of obtaining her evidence from newspapers, and reminded the jury that she had not named Thomas as the man accused of 'pestering' Jeannette until after he was arrested.

Ryan: 'You actually hate Arthur Thomas don't you?'

Batkin: 'No I don't.'

Ryan: 'Don't you?'

Batkin: 'No I don't.'

Ryan: 'Sure?'

Batkin: 'I feel rather sorry for him.'

Ryan: 'How sorry for yourself?'

Batkin: 'I don't feel sorry for myself.'

Ryan: 'You have told lies in court?'

Batkin: 'That is very unkind to say to anyone. I have told not one lie in this court. I could not live with my conscience if I told a lie.'

Ryan: 'If you had a conscience.'[9]

Batkin was left visibly rattled by Ryan's accusations. Justice Perry reprimanded Ryan for his comment, a pattern that would continue throughout the trial as Ryan's frustrations with the witnesses and the prosecution continually boiled over.

But the Crown had a plan to shore up Batkin's credibility. They called Beverley Willis, Jeannette's best friend from Whanganui, to the stand. Willis said Jeannette had also told her about a man being very persistent with her at dances in Pukekawa. Willis said Jeannette had told her she had gone to primary school with the man, and said his name was Thomas.

The Crown then called Jeannette's landlady in Whanganui, Clare MacGee, who gave similar evidence about a man who had been giving Jeannette trouble. Jeannette didn't appreciate the man's attention, MacGee said. MacGee initially had not remembered the man's name, but knew he was the same person who gave Jeannette a brush set, she said.[10]

When Len Demler got on the stand, he, too, had new recollections to offer. He told the court that Jeannette had moved from Maramarua to Whanganui to get away from Arthur Thomas. Ryan immediately picked up on this point in cross-examination. 'You have given information on oath on two prior occasions, have you not?' he asked.

'I have,' Demler replied.

'Did you make any mention on either of those prior occasions that your daughter had gone to Wanganui to get away from Thomas?'

Demler said, no he didn't mention it at the time, that he didn't have to.

Ryan also tried to push Demler on the matter of the bloodstain in his car. He'd managed to get photographs that showed it was larger than police had described. Demler said Jeannette had left it there when she hurt her finger one day when they were going to see May Demler in hospital.

'It must have been in January when they were put there?' Ryan said.

'Yes, in January,' Demler replied.

'No one washed them off?' Ryan said.

'There wasn't much to wipe off; I never touched them.'

'Did anybody else sit in the passenger seat after Jeannette?' Ryan asked.

'That's hard to say,' Demler said.

Eventually, Ryan brought the questioning to a head: 'Did you take the bodies of Jeannette and Harvey Crewe to the Waikato River after 17 June 1970?'

'I didn't do anything of the sort,' Demler replied.[11]

As the various detectives were called, Ryan pressed them about the search of the Crewe gardens in mid-August, after Jeannette's body was found. The defence wanted to make the argument that the cartridge case hadn't been there during the earlier search, and to imply it must have been planted. He asked four of the officers involved — Murray Jeffries, Kevin Gee, Ross Meurant and Leslie Higgins — whether Graeme Hewson had been at the Crewe house while they'd mowed the lawns and sifted through the dirt, and if he'd gone with them to pick up a mower and a sieve.

But none of the four policemen remembered Hewson helping with the search, and they said they definitely hadn't sieve-searched the garden bed where the shell was found. They'd only pulled up weeds and looked through the dirt.

In his 1997 book *Justice Without Fear or Favour*, Ryan remembered being gutted — he thought there was no way the jury would believe Hewson over the four police. He was given brief hope when former Chennells estate manager Jack Handcock was called. Handcock remembered Hewson being at the farm during the August search, he said, and that he held something in his hand. 'It could have been a fork or something like that, he might have been loosening the soil. He appeared to be working with the police party or close by.'[12]

However, he said the garden where the shell was found had not been sieve-searched. Neighbouring farmer Ron Chitty said he remembered Graeme Hewson coming to borrow the mower, to clear the grass at that time. But his wife then said she thought it was a different date; a further blow to the defence.

THE SECOND TRIAL 151

One witness Kevin Ryan had been relying on to further the defence case was Peter Thomas. When they had been in Wellington for the Court of Appeal hearing in February, Ryan had spoken to Peter afterwards, at Hotel DeBrett on Lambton Quay. Peter mentioned that on the night of 17 June his car had been parked right behind Arthur's, so even if he'd wanted to, Arthur wouldn't have been able to get out to drive anywhere. However, during the second trial, when Peter was on the stand and Ryan was ready to shock the Crown with this new evidence, for some reason Peter Thomas didn't repeat what he'd apparently said in Wellington. Instead he said he felt Arthur would have been able to get his car out from where it was parked at the Thomas home.[13]

During the questioning of Detective Len Johnston, Ryan worked to cast doubt on Bruce Roddick's sighting of the woman in the paddock. Johnston said he had been to the neighbouring farm where Roddick had been working that day and had re-created the scene, but had found it difficult to make out the facial features of a person standing at the Crewe house, where Roddick said the woman had been. He produced photographs, designed to emphasise the distance. Once Roddick had been a star Crown witness, but he was now painted as vague, unreliable, and making claims that couldn't be verified.

Then Ryan managed a small win. When Detective Bruce Parkes took the stand, Ryan put it to him that, when visiting Arthur Thomas on 12 August 1970, during a conversation in which Parkes asked about the brush and comb set, Parkes had actually told Arthur it was still wrapped up. After some back-and-forth, Parkes agreed — he had mentioned the gift was wrapped up.[14]

More new witnesses emerged as the days ground on. To add weight to the assertion of Thomas's alleged obsession with Jeannette Crewe, the Crown called one of Thomas's former workmates, Charles Liddell, who had worked for Barr Brothers at the same time as Arthur. He told the court that during early 1963, he and Thomas and two women had been to see a fortune-teller because Arthur wanted to know whether he had a future with Jeannette. Before the visit, Thomas had spoken highly of Jeannette. 'My impressions were he thought a lot of her. I would even say he was probably very much in love with her,' he said. However, when further questioned, Liddell told the court Arthur had also mentioned other girls around that time. The story about the fortune-teller made for more eye-catching newspaper copy, despite lacking any corroboration.

The Crown called a second doctor to give evidence on whether Rochelle Crewe had been fed during the five days after her parents were killed. Dr Thomas Fox held to the opinion that she had been fed, but Dr Ronald Caughey, a consulting children's physician, disagreed: 'Her clinical state was, I believe, consistent with her not having been fed.' He said she could have survived for four or five days or longer without being fed, given her healthy condition. But Fox had seen Rochelle within a day of her being found in the cot; Caughey had not seen her until nine days after. He based his assessment on records of her weight loss, and her rapid recovery from what he called 'moderately severe dehydration', he told the court.[15]

A large part of the Crown's time was once again devoted to experts' opinions about the wire and the bullets. The court heard that 158 million rounds of bullets with the number 8 had been manufactured in New Zealand between 1949 and 1963, meaning the rounds that killed Jeannette and Harvey were common. There was also significant evidence about the level of corrosion, or lack of, on the cartridge case found in the garden.

Rory Shanahan from DSIR said he had been conducting tests to determine the effect of wet soil on cartridge cases. He had buried cases at 21 locations across the North Island. These produced similar results to the amount of corrosion observed on the original case. The Crown called two further experts on soil and corrosion, who essentially agreed with Shanahan — but, it was discovered, had not conducted any such tests themselves.

On Monday 9 April, two weeks after the trial began, Bruce Hutton was called as the final Crown witness. Coaxed by Morris, he walked the jury through the investigation. He had been going for two hours, and was describing the day Arthur Thomas was charged with murder, when Thomas groaned a loud 'no' and collapsed in the dock. Kevin Ryan heard the deputy registrar say 'what a Hollywood'.[16] A doctor was called, and decided Thomas was clearly not well, although he had recovered quickly. The trial was adjourned to the following morning.

As Hutton continued his evidence the next day, the defence team received yet another surprise: Hutton, too, had remembered some new information. Morris asked if Hutton had noticed anything missing from Harvey Crewe's body when it was removed from the Waikato River. Yes, Hutton said, a watch. And, he continued, there were no men's watches found at the Crewe farm. It appears Hutton was attempting to suggest that the mysterious watch allegedly brought into the jewellery shop by Arthur Thomas could have belonged to Harvey Crewe instead, as it had been established that Thomas did not own such a watch.

Throughout the hearing, Ryan had been blunt, almost rude, to the Crown witnesses, badgering their evidence from them. But he knew Hutton was too clever for those tactics. He needed to keep his cool. Hutton had faced Ryan in court before and knew how to get under Ryan's skin. During cross-examination about the police failure to provide Ryan with documents — specifically, a list of cars seen near the Crewe farm — Hutton told the court the reason Ryan hadn't got the information he asked for from police was because he failed to show up for appointments.

Ryan said it wasn't true; rather, he felt the police had deliberately obstructed his requests. 'I put it to you that you are a liar,' he snapped.

Hutton: 'I am not lying.'[17]

Hutton's evidence-in-chief had the same tone as the first hearing: the police investigation was thorough, logical and showed common sense. But under cross-examination, he shifted gears slightly, undermining the credibility of any witness who might damage the prosecution case. Graeme Hewson, Harvey's best friend, was a dog thief; Ella McGuire was a 'nasty woman' who wanted to put William Eggleton out of business; Bruce Roddick, the labourer, was unreliable.

Ryan's final question to Hutton was about the number of other unsolved murders in New Zealand at the time the Crewes were killed. Hutton told him there were three: Jennifer Beard, Betty McKay and Olive Walker.[18] The question was designed to frame Hutton as a man under pressure. But Hutton would not bite. 'I think that's it,' he said, after listing the names.

Once Ryan was finished with Hutton, the Crown case closed. It had taken nearly two weeks.

espite criticism from some in the legal community that Paul Temm had made a mistake in putting Arthur Thomas on the stand in the first trial, Kevin Ryan chose to do the same. On the afternoon of 10 April, Thomas entered the witness box. This time, he was better prepared. When Ryan asked him outright whether he was guilty, Thomas answered, 'I did not sir, as God is my witness, I did not murder either of the Crewes.'[19]

David Morris took two full days to cross-examine Thomas but he did not break under the pressure. He said he hadn't contacted Jeannette after 1962, and that he wasn't the reason she had moved to Whanganui, even when Morris said this put him in conflict with the evidence of three other people. 'I am telling you that from 1962 onwards I had not pestered her, that's what I'm telling you; if you can say asking her out three times is pestering.'

At one point, Morris showed Thomas pictures of Harvey Crewe's dead body. Thomas did not flinch. 'I was framed,' he told Morris emphatically at the end of his questioning. 'All I know is I did not do that crime and I was home with my wife on the evening of 17 June.'

Vivien Thomas was also a better witness the second time around. She gave clear, firm answers to endless questions about farming records, about Cow No. 4, about the conversations between herself and Arthur after the Crewes died. She even answered extremely personal questions about her health.

'You have been back to England last year,' Ryan asked.

'That's correct,' Vivien said.

'Did you have an abortion in England?'

'No Mr Ryan, I did not.'[20]

The topic must have seemed out of place to the jury — Ryan slipped it in between asking about axles and bodies — but it was a moment of public relations from the defence. Ryan was seeking to address the rumour that had been spread through the press that Vivien had become pregnant to a lover and had gone to England to have an abortion. The alternative had been to have Vivien undergo an examination and put out a media statement, which no one, least of all Vivien, wanted to do.[21]

Allan Thomas then gave his evidence, which largely focused on the origin of the axle found with Harvey Crewe's body, which the Crown argued had come from the Thomas trailer after it was refurbished

THE SECOND TRIAL 155

and no longer needed. Allan Thomas said he couldn't remember what happened to the original axle after engineer Roderick Rasmussen had replaced it but he didn't remember seeing it anywhere on his property afterwards. And in any case, Allan Thomas said, around that time a group of young men, including his son Richard, were working on a vintage car left on the property. When the car was moved, the group also took car parts and other miscellaneous items from the farm, such as iron and wood.

Ryan called two of those young men to the stand. They confirmed Allan Thomas's account of fixing up the car before Allan got sick of it lying around and asked them to get rid of it. One of the men, John Martin, said he remembered picking up an axle from under a hedge to take with them. The other, Bruce Eyre, said he did not recall an axle. Ryan also called up a group of vintage car enthusiasts who said they'd thoroughly searched the tips on the Thomas farm for car parts at the beginning of 1970. They said they hadn't seen an axle like the one found in the river, even though they had searched at least some of the tips quite thoroughly.

Pat Vesey, Graeme Hewson and Bruce Roddick were next in line for the defence. Vesey, who had spent a significant amount of time at the Thomas property after Vivien and Arthur moved there, again told the court there were empty cartridge cases lying all over the place, implying it would have been easy to take one and plant it in the Crewe garden.

Hewson described how he had been with police after Jeannette's body was found in August, and said they had definitely sieve-searched the flowerbed where the cartridge was later found. Hewson also had a chance to address Hutton's allegations against him. He said he had been urged by Harvey's mother and the estate solicitors to take the Crewe dogs — he hadn't stolen them.

When Bruce Roddick gave evidence, he was asked for the first time in court if the woman he'd seen in the paddock was Vivien Thomas. Roddick said he knew Vivien, and that the woman definitely wasn't her. In cross-examination, the Crown questioned Roddick's memory, asking if he had been confused. Roddick repeated that he was sure — it hadn't been Vivien at the house.

Bruce Roddick also gave evidence about John Eyre. Roddick said when they had been working for a farmer at Glen Murray, he had seen John Eyre 'grab a lamb and throttle it' when it wouldn't sit still during crutching. Earlier, Ryan had called three other witnesses to give evidence about Eyre, in an ongoing attempt to paint him as a possible suspect. One man said he had found John on his porch one night with a rifle in his hand. His wife also gave evidence. They thought the date was some time in 1959. The second man, who had been working in the Pukekawa area just before the murders, said he had seen John Eyre in October 1969 alone on the main road with a rifle.[22]

During cross-examination, as he was unable to call her as a witness, Ryan asked Ruth Eyre, who was giving evidence in place of her son, John, about his whereabouts. She told the court that she and John were home on the night of 17 June, and that because of his disabilities — he was deaf and had a speech impediment — John didn't go out at night alone. In cross-examination, Ryan grilled Ruth about whether this was true, and whether John was a good shot. 'I should say so,' she said. 'He is a duck shooter.' Ryan also asked Ruth Eyre whether John had ever assaulted someone, whether he had been ordered off the Crewe property, whether he had killed sheep by breaking their backs with his hands. He had not, Ruth said. 'My son John Michael is an extremely kind person.'[23]

Towards the end of their evidence, the defence intended to call forensic scientist Dr Jim Sprott. Ryan planned on Sprott arguing that the cartridge case found in the garden wasn't as corroded as it should have been after four months in soil, but now he had something even better to show the jury. Two days earlier, on Wednesday 11 April, while waiting to take his turn on the stand, Pat Vesey had been staring at the trees outside the court window when he felt a strange sensation. His hands and feet began to sweat, and he felt faint. 'I've got to go home,' he suddenly said to the others in the room. He then knocked on the door to the court and whispered to Gerald Ryan that he was going to leave.[24]

'What do you mean?' Gerald Ryan asked. Vesey was due to give evidence next. He couldn't leave, Ryan said.

'I'm sorry but I've got to go,' Vesey replied.

Compelled by some impulse, Vesey drove to his house in Balmoral, where he felt guided to go straight to a drawer that held a stack of containers of .22 cartridges. Back in 1972, in an effort to prove the Crown was wrong about the rarity of the bullets with the number 8 on them, the retrial committee had posted advertisements calling on the public to send in their ammunition. He'd been sent so many packages that by the time of the second trial, a pile of them were yet to be opened.

The box Vesey reached for was one of the unopened parcels. It was a box that had previously held fish hooks; the price was still attached. Inside were a series of envelopes full of cartridge cases, and a letter. The sender was Jack Ritchie, a sports shop owner and former policeman from Dannevirke. He'd been reading about the case and thought he'd discovered something that might clear up the mystery of the cartridge case found in the garden.

The letter instructed Vesey to open the envelopes in a certain order, while making notes about the characteristics of the cartridges inside. He duly did so, and then, still following Ritchie's instructions, began to use pliers to extract the bullets from the cases. The significance of Ritchie's discovery became clear: according to the type of case a bullet came from, it was possible to predict whether or not it would carry the number 8.

Immediately, Vesey rushed back to court, found Kevin Ryan during a break, then went to see Jim Sprott at his laboratory in Parnell. As Sprott watched, Vesey pulled out the final envelope, which Ritchie's letter specified must be opened in front of someone. Sprott looked at the five bullets inside and his face lit up. 'This is vital, thank you very much for coming,' he said. In an interview with us in 2022, Vesey said his heart leapt. He knew at that moment that they were going to win.[25]

That night, Jim Sprott called Kevin Ryan at home. He needed to see the bullets that were held by the court as exhibits as he wanted to check something. The exhibits were in the care of Deputy Court Registrar Ian Miller, in a glass vial, locked in the court safe.

The next morning, Ryan and Sprott approached Miller before court started for the day. Sprott was peering at the so-called Keith case — the cartridge found in the apple box in the Thomas shed — through the microscope when Bruce Hutton walked past and saw him. 'You are interfering with a police exhibit,' Hutton shouted. 'You have no right.' He argued that Ryan had conned the registrar; the exhibits were not to be inspected without police present. But Sprott already had what he needed, and the cartridges were placed back in the safe.[26]

On Friday 13 April, Sprott gave his evidence. He had worked quickly. He produced a sketch showing there were four categories of cartridge cases. On the base, each was stamped with the manufacturer's name: ICI. Sprott focused the jury's attention on categories three and four. The difference between the categories was the height of the C on the stamp, he said. Category three, which had a smaller C, would reliably produce a bullet with the number 8 on it. Category four, which had a larger C, would not.

For example, the so-called Keith case, the cartridge found in the apple box, was a category three, and correspondingly had a number 8 bullet with it. But exhibit 350, the case found in the garden, was a category four. Therefore, it was impossible for the number 8 bullet found in the skull of Jeannette Crewe to have come from the cartridge case in the garden — the case the Crown had unequivocally linked to Arthur Thomas's gun.

Morris cross-examined Sprott. The scientist told the court how he had only just discovered the categories the day before, and therefore had not checked his findings with ICI Australia, the bullet manufacturers. Morris asked the judge whether the Crown could examine the evidence and call experts in rebuttal. The defence counsel agreed, certain they would make the same findings. DSIR scientist Donald Nelson was called to examine the cartridge cases during a three-hour adjournment. During this time, the prosecution also called John Shea, a former employee of ICI's New Zealand subsidiary, the Colonial Ammunition Company (CAC), who had been involved in the manufacture of .22 bullets, to come to the court and give evidence.

When the hearing resumed, Shea told the court that there had been variations in the ICI pattern stamped on the cartridges, but he felt that Sprott's categories were basically the same. However, Shea believed the difference in the height of the C was much less than Sprott said it was. (Sprott had said the smaller C category was 1.2 millimetres, while the larger C was 1.5 millimetres).

The Crown had also managed to call as witness an ICI manager in Australia, and further evidence was admitted from the company that the categories did not exist; that any differences were due to wear and

Scientist Dr Jim Sprott was the technical brains behind the Thomas campaign. His expertise was vital in unpicking much of the evidence that had led to Thomas's conviction.

tear over time. Donald Nelson took to the stand last. He stated he had examined the Keith case and the Charles garden case and found that the height of the letter C on the cases was identical. He told the court Sprott had made a mistake.[27]

Closing arguments were heard on Saturday 14 April, an unusual weekend session of the criminal court caused by the delays the day before. Prior to the court doors being opened to the public, Sprott turned up outside, with his microscope, begging to re-examine the cartridge cases. Ryan agreed to help him, despite knowing that it would be an unpopular request, and approached David Baragwanath to see if he would ask the exhibits officer to open the safe.

But this time, the prosecution refused to let Sprott have access to the cartridges. 'We have had a gutsful of Sprott,' Baragwanath said to Ryan. 'He doesn't get to see anything.' The request never went before the judge. It was a hollow, bitter end to what had seemed a winning break for the defence team.[28]

A t 10 a.m., David Morris rose to give his closing argument. His summary of the Crown case was compelling, a legal masterclass, and as Kevin Ryan listened, his heart sank.[29] Morris opened by painting a cosy farmhouse scene — Harvey in his stockinged feet, while his wife knitted on the couch — interrupted by a single shot from the dark. As in the first trial, he described Jeannette hearing the shot and hurrying to her feet as the murderer entered the lounge through the kitchen and attacked her.

But then, Morris went further. He suggested there may have been a sexual attack before the murderer shot Jeannette. 'We fortunately do not know how long elapsed between the time Jeannette realised her husband was dying and her own death or just what happened in between,' he said.

'We do know that at some stage she received a violent blow consistent with being from the butt of a rifle to her face; and that when she was finally shot, she was lying on the floor. We also know that a long hearth mat and cushion were at some stage burned by the murderer; and also that the room was heavily bloodstained. Whether the burning of these items was, like the use of two saucepans, with a view to concealing the blood, or whether it was done to conceal other marks traceable to the killer or his treatment of Jeannette we do not know.

'The murderer was impelled by some overwhelming motive, and that motive may have been more than merely to destroy Harvey, perhaps out of jealousy, and to silence the only other witness. The evidence is equally consistent with a desire to get to Jeannette, even if this entailed first killing her husband and later Jeannette herself. Whether the murderer was impelled by a combination of these motives only he can say, but there is nothing to suggest any alternative.'[30]

Ryan — and all of Thomas's supporters — were appalled. This scenario had come out of nowhere — there was no evidence to suggest Jeannette had been raped, and Thomas hadn't been asked about it in court.

Morris next took aim at Vivien Thomas.[31] 'I wish to . . . make it quite clear that the Crown has laid no charge against Mrs Thomas, in that the question of her involvement or lack of involvement is totally irrelevant except in so far as it relates to that of her husband. The Crown does not suggest that Mrs Thomas was in any way responsible for these horrible killings. It may be that she has no more than suspicions about her husband's involvement; or it may be that she has in some way attempted to act as a loyal wife and perhaps has tried to minimise the tragedy.'

Morris closed his address with a flourish: 'This is an unprovoked, premeditated, well-executed, cold-blooded killing.'

After lunch, it was Kevin Ryan's turn to close. In later recollections, he said he was exhausted but passed up the option to make his closing address the following day. As he spoke, he could tell the jury suffered the same fatigue. He felt he had lost them.[32]

Ryan reiterated the defence position, based on Thomas's alibi that both Peter Thomas and Vivien said he was home the night of 17 June. Given the Crown had asked the jury to believe Peter Thomas about his memories of Cow No. 4 and when she had calved, they should also believe him when he said Arthur was home, Ryan told them.

He emphasised the disparity between the defence resources and those of the Crown: police experts had the wires for two months to examine while the defence had them for less than a week. 'When I referred in my opening speech to the fact that it was difficult for the individual to fight against the state I was not talking of counsel and specialist fees,' he told the jury. 'When you are in this court you can't chase around looking for witnesses. You can't have a caravan placed by the court and plugged in like the police have.'

Ryan felt unable to discuss the cartridge cases, given the Crown had seemingly discredited their evidence. Instead, he told the jury if there was any reasonable doubt, then Arthur Thomas must be given the benefit of it. 'The Crown evidence is made up like rope of many strands, but the alibi of Thomas cuts it straight through and there is no rope to link Thomas with the crimes,' he said, drawing his address to a close.[33]

The court rose for Sunday. Ryan did not enjoy his day off. He sensed he was about to lose a trial he had been confident of winning. Partly, he blamed himself, knowing he had made mistakes, particularly with the Sprott evidence. Partly, he blamed the judge, who he felt had chipped away at the defence's credibility with constant rebukes. Mostly, however, he felt as if he had been fighting a losing battle against an opponent who was more ruthless than he had anticipated, and who had worked to block his every move.

Meanwhile, after being cooped up for more than three weeks, the jury was taken fishing by police.[34]

On Monday 16 April, Justice Clifford Perry gave a lengthy summing-up. He reminded the jury of the reasons for the second trial: not that the Court of Appeal had found Arthur not guilty but rather that it had found there was new evidence that should be heard. It was now up to the jury to make a decision on the evidence put to it, he said.

In his speech, Perry did not mention the Crown allegations of sexual assault. He wrote off Bruce Roddick's sighting of a mystery woman, implying it must have been Jeannette whom he saw, on a different day. He ignored the evidence from Len Demler who said the Crewes usually ate around 7 p.m., and focused on evidence from Harvey's mother, Marie Crewe, who said they ate after 8 p.m. at least — meaning, if they were killed after dinner but before the Crewes did their dishes around 9.30 p.m., it could have been after Arthur said he went to bed at 9 p.m. Perry said the matter of whether the garden had been sieved for the

THE SECOND TRIAL   163

shell case was a case of credibility — did the jury believe the police or Graeme Hewson? On the matter of the cartridge case in the garden, Perry said on his reading of the evidence, it was in fact possible for big C cartridge cases to contain number 8 bullets.[35]

At 3.04 p.m., the jury retired to consider its verdict. By now, they were a group of 11; one had had a seizure earlier in the trial and had been excused. Rather than leaving the court, most of those in the public gallery chose to hang around, waiting. The Thomas family and the retrial committee nervously loitered in the foyer, smoking, pacing, talking. At one point, they made so much noise a judge in another courtroom sent a constable to quiet them.[36]

Kevin Ryan had a cup of tea with the Thomas family at the court cafeteria and then returned to the courtroom with Gerald Ryan to read through his papers.[37] Upstairs in the Crown prosecutors' room, David Morris took off his wig and gown and chatted to colleagues. Suddenly, court staff arrived to say the jury had reached a decision.[38]

The jury returned to the courtroom at 5.30 p.m. As the doors opened, the public surged in, so many of them that some of the Thomas supporters didn't make it inside but had to gather in the foyer and try to listen through the doors. Then Arthur Thomas was brought up from the cells and stood, waiting.

'Members of the jury, have you unanimously agreed upon a verdict?' the registrar asked the foreman.

'Yes,' Bob Rock replied.

'On the first count, do you find the accused guilty or not guilty?'

'Guilty,' Rock replied.

Arthur Thomas shook his head. He began to cry, silently. In the courtroom there was complete chaos. People were wailing, shouting. The registrar tried to get the court to quiet for the second verdict — also guilty — but it was drowned out as the noise continued. People were pushing, shoving. Someone collapsed. A group of spectators began to chant 'He's not guilty, he's not guilty'. Outside, the gathered crowd heard the chant and briefly thought the defence had won. They began celebrating, only to discover the outcome moments later.

Justice Perry asked Arthur Thomas whether he had anything to say. 'I had nothing to do with that horrible crime,' Thomas said, shaking. 'I am completely innocent.'

A distraught Ray Thomas and his wife outside the Auckland Supreme Court in 1973 after his brother Arthur Thomas was found guilty a second time.

Vivien Thomas ran to the front of the court, her friends unable to hold her back. 'What sort of people are you?' she yelled at the jury. 'He's innocent.'

Thomas joined in. 'Give me a lie detector test!'

The jury sat shocked as police flooded the courtroom, ushering the crowds out. After a brief goodbye to Vivien, Arthur was led to the police van that would take him back to Pāremoremo. People continued shouting in the foyer and the defence team was asked by court staff to try to calm the situation. Gerald Ryan spoke to the jury, reassuring them that they didn't need to be scared, that they could go. Kevin Ryan went out to the front of the court building to speak to the angry crowds. 'You're not doing any good by this,' he said. 'Please go home.'[39]

The Thomas family went back to Matakana. Vivien Thomas went to Pat Vesey's house. Kevin Ryan packed up his papers, took off his wig and gown, and went to the upstairs bar of the Station Hotel for a drink. It was a poor choice. When he walked in, the first people he saw were David Morris, David Baragwanath and Bruce Hutton. Ryan gallantly joined them for a beer, even buying a round. Hutton couldn't contain his glee.

'You didn't have a show, Kevin,' Hutton said to Ryan. 'We had the jury list weeks before the trial and we had eight A's on it.' (This means eight pro-police witnesses.)[40]

Ryan would later find out about the known connection between Detective John Hughes and jury foreman Bob Rock, as well as the judge's refusal to excuse Rock at the start of the trial — but not because court staff or the prosecution told him. A few weeks after the trial, Ryan happened to take a taxi driven by Rock.

'I suppose you know who I am,' he said to Ryan.

'How could I forget,' he answered.[41]

Ryan also learned that the jury hadn't taken two and a half hours to come to a decision. They had, in fact, reached a verdict in half an hour but had decided to loiter in the jury room to give the appearance of being cautious about making a decision to jail a man for life.[42]

CHAPTER NINE
THE GATHERING STORM

There had been a heated atmosphere around the Auckland Supreme Court that April evening when the verdict was announced; some people felt a sense of fate acting on them. One was a seasoned newspaperman named Pat Booth, deputy editor of the *Auckland Star*. He knew Kevin Ryan, and through him had signed a contract with Arthur Thomas for an exclusive in the event of the expected acquittal at the first trial. This night, at the conclusion of the second trial, he was driving past the courthouse on his way home. On a whim, he decided that if there was a vacant carpark, he would go in.

As 'destiny' would have it (so he later recounted), the very moment he drove past, a car pulled out. Booth walked into the courthouse just in time to witness the uproar following the verdict.[1] A photo of the scene captured him looking on wide-eyed as members of the public jostled around him.

It was a defining moment for him. Booth had seen court dramas before, even the dreaded moment when a judge donned the black cap to pronounce the death penalty, yet the despair of the Thomas supporters moved him unexpectedly. Deep down, he felt something was wrong. Thus began six years of hard toil.

Although sometimes a polarising figure, Booth was a formidable journalist. He had the two main traits of a successful investigative journalist: an eye for detail and perseverance. He also had a personal warmth and charm that encouraged interviewees to open up. Above all, he had a big newspaper behind him; and behind that, tens of thousands of readers and, ultimately, voters.

He obtained the transcripts of both trials from Kevin and Gerald Ryan, and doing what he called a 'straight accounting job', began comparing them and noting discrepancies. The more he read, the more disturbed he became. In particular, he noted changes in Crown witness evidence that he felt Gerald Ryan, as junior defence counsel, should have noted and raised during the second trial.[2]

First, he began checking the Crown claims of Thomas's supposedly obsessive jealousy, such that Thomas had followed Jeannette to Whanganui. He checked education department records, which showed Jeannette had applied for the Whanganui job before she left Maramarua, while a friend of hers told him Jeannette had never mentioned Thomas.

He then went to Whanganui and interviewed Clare MacGee, Jeannette's close friend and landlady there. She said she didn't believe Jeannette came to the city to get away from Thomas; she came because her best friend Beverley Ward lived there. She also told him it was not Jeannette who had asked her how to deal with unwelcome attention; rather, she had confided in Jeannette about such a situation, and Jeannette had reassured her that she should not worry, it had happened to her once and didn't last long. Realising how the Crown had twisted MacGee's evidence, Booth walked the darkened streets of Whanganui after the interview, muttering 'those bastards'.[3] *Star* 1, Crown 0.

As he read both transcripts, he noted that Detective John Hughes had given evidence in the first trial at which Thomas had said he had worked as a contractor on the Crewe farm 'and would have morning and afternoon teas in the house and had met Harvey Crewe'. In the second trial, Hughes added the word 'there' after Crewe, to imply Thomas had met the Crewes on their farm. This was a lie, and Booth proved it. He checked the records of Barr Brothers: Thomas had left the company in 1965, a full year before the Crewes moved onto the farm.

Hughes's claimed meeting, part of the web of jealousy being woven around Thomas, never happened. *Star* 2, Crown 0.

The next was the gold watch. Once the Crown realised that the family could prove Thomas had never owned a gold watch, and that William Eggleton was unreliable, it switched its story: the gold watch was Harvey's, not Arthur's, and he had ripped it off Harvey's wrist after the murder.

One morning, an unknown person called the *Star* and asked for Booth. 'If you want to know about the watch, find John Fisher,' the anonymous voice said, then hung up. Booth found him, now living in Feilding, and rang him. Yes, he did take a blood and mucus-covered watch into Eggleton's Pukekohe jewellery store in January 1971. He had been slaughtering pigs and the watch had become covered in pig blood and needed repair. Booth asked him if he still had it. Fisher put down the phone and rummaged in a child's toy box and found it.

Booth got on the next train from Auckland. The watch had Eggleton's jeweller's mark on the inside case; it was undoubtedly the watch Eggleton had wrongly attributed to Thomas. The *Star* ran a photo of Fisher holding up the watch. *Star* 3, Crown 0.

There was a chilling rider to this. Knowing the police were interested in the watch after reading the evidence from the first trial, Fisher had actually rung them and given an affidavit, but he never heard from them again, he told Booth. Once again, the police had apparently covered up.[4] Although this was a hit for the retrial committee, the actual facts may be less conspiratorial. A 1977 letter from the minister of police states that police ruled out Fisher once they had established, from the jeweller's mark on his watch, that he had taken it in for repair in January 1971. Eggleton was adamant he knew the difference between Thomas and Fisher.[5]

But the real focus was to become the cartridge case. As someone used to proofing newspaper pages, Booth had a good eye for type, and he immediately picked up on the differences in lettering on the base of the various shells. This became known as the 'Big C' theory, after the sensational intervention of Vesey.

Convinced that the claim made by DSIR, and confirmed by ICI, that there were no differences in lettering was wrong, Booth arranged to have the bases of different shells photographed and enlarged by the *Star's* photographers. Seen at this scale, the differences became even more apparent. The question was, what caused this? And was Jack Ritchie correct in his belief that Sprott's category 4 cases, with a big C on the bottom (such as the Charles case found in the Crewe garden), had never been fitted to number 8 bullets?

The photographs of the shell cases showed clearly that the C on three types of cases were markedly different from the C on the category 4 cases (such as the one found in the Crewe garden; found by Detective Mike Charles and known as the Charles case). Specifically, the gap between the horns of the C on the Charles case was, when enlarged, 1 inch (25.4 millimetres), compared to 5/8th inches (15.8 millimetres) on the small C cases. Also, on the Charles case there was a bigger gap between the C and the I: three-quarters of an inch (19.05 millimetres) compared to half an inch (12.7 millimetres) on the small C cases. These measurable differences convinced Booth that exhibit 350, the cartridge case found in the garden by Mike Charles, had to be a plant. But how to prove it?

Once again, Booth's media power was to prove crucial. His articles, accompanied by enlarged photos showing clear differences in the shell case lettering — despite Crown claims there were no differences — ran shortly after the second trial, in mid-1973.

In those days, paperboys stood on city street corners calling out the latest headlines to passers-by; Booth's scoops really gave them something to shout about. Letters started to pour in and talkback radio crackled with public concern. There were even rumours flying about the jury drinking and dancing with police.

The boost in public interest came just in time: in July, Thomas's appeal against his second conviction was rejected by the same three judges, Wild, McCarthy and Richmond, who had recommended the second trial.

But if the Crown thought it had buried the case forever, it was mistaken. This became apparent a few weeks later when members of the retrial committee argued they should go for broke and book the Auckland Town Hall for a public meeting on 28 August to raise funds to campaign for another retrial.

Auckland Star deputy editor Pat Booth was disturbed by the scenes he witnessed at the second trial. His six-year investigation with forensic scientist Jim Sprott was crucial in freeing Thomas.

Some were nervous, worrying that a small crowd would be disastrous to their cause. But the committee was encouraged by Peter Williams, an aggressive and quick-witted QC who specialised in defence work and had joined the committee. As Williams later recounted in his 1997 memoir *A Passion for Justice*, a man in a Salvation Army uniform rallied them: 'How can you not have faith in the cause? Of course people will turn out. The Auckland public is outraged by what's happened to Arthur Thomas, and as for the money, I'll guarantee it myself.'[6]

Their resolve stiffened; the committee decided the meeting should go ahead. When Williams arrived, the hall was packed with over 2000 people, and people were queuing down Queen Street waiting to get in. Roars of applause greeted Williams, Booth, Jim Sprott and Vivien Thomas as they recounted the way the trials had been stacked against Arthur Thomas.

'The meeting was a boost to the retrial committee's confidence at a low time,' says Pat Vesey. 'It was just unbelievable . . . when we got down there, to find all these people shut out. The fire brigade wouldn't allow another person in the hall. I was conducting the meeting, and once I got into the swing of things, it was okay, but initially, to suddenly be just an ordinary bloke in the street and to be addressing the Auckland Town Hall, which was the nearest we had to Buckingham Palace in Auckland? It was a tremendous responsibility.'[7]

B ruce Hutton must have been unnerved by the public backlash, but for some reason either he, or someone higher up, decided the best thing to do was remove the evidence, for good.

On 27 July 1973, police officers loaded most of the exhibits, including the highly contested Charles cartridge case and bullet fragments retrieved from the Crewes' bodies, and dumped them all in the tip at Whitford, south-east of Auckland. Strangely, although the ostensible reason for this was to save space, they did not dispose of some of the larger items, such as the axle or the Thomas rifle.

Who gave the order to dump the exhibits? According to author David Yallop, it was David Morris.[8] If so, it was a significant mistake, perhaps indicative of the growing pressure on the prosecution case. It wasn't uncommon or illegal to dispose of exhibits after a trial, but in

172 THE CREWE MURDERS

Above: More than 2000 people packed the Auckland Town Hall on 28 August 1973, four months after the second trial, as the public concern about the case became widespread. *Below:* Vivien Thomas told the town hall crowd that her husband was innocent. Behind the scenes, she knew her marriage was over.

such a controversial case, it was undoubtedly poor judgement to do so.

Kevin Ryan was first to find out the evidence had been removed. He'd run into David Morris in the street in Auckland one lunchtime and had suggested a joint approach to clear up the confusion about the cartridge cases. But Morris seemed laidback, and said an inquiry would never get off the ground.

'Why?' asked Ryan.

'You know what happens to exhibits when there is no further use for them,' Morris replied.

'I suppose they are dumped?' Ryan asked.

Ryan raced back to the office and phoned Pat Booth: 'I think they've dumped the exhibits,' he said.[9]

Booth set what he called his 'trap'. Having already sent his photos of the cartridge cases to the minister of justice, Martyn Finlay, he now asked Finlay whether he could borrow the actual cases for further study. Unaware of what had happened to the evidence, Finlay agreed.

While waiting for a response to a request that he knew would be impossible to fulfil, Booth kept busy. He had contacted forensic scientist Dr Jim Sprott and suggested they work together. At first, Sprott was wary. They were unlikely collaborators: Sprott was a meticulous scientist, conservative, and a strong Christian. Booth was a Catholic from a working-class family in Hāwera and from a radical background. His father, a painter and decorator, had planned to blow up a train carrying strike-breakers during the 1913 waterfront strike, but called it off when he realised it might kill people. But they found common cause in a determination to get to the root of the cartridge case evidence. Peter Williams joined Booth and Ryan in long evenings at Sprott's home working on the forensic detail of the case.

In late 1972, Booth and Sprott had flown to Australia to have the different shell cases photographed using a comparison microscope at the Victoria Police Centre's forensic lab. They clearly showed obvious differences in the lettering on the various shell cases. Imperial Chemical Industries (ICI) managers were astounded when Booth and Sprott then showed them what they had found.

The company realised what had happened. The lettering on the cases was produced by a machine that stamped each case using a 'hob', a metal stamp with the letters ICI engraved on it. After stamping millions of shells, the hobs wore out and were replaced. At some point, contrary to what ICI management had told the second trial in good faith, an engraver by the name of George Leighton noticed what he felt was an imbalance in the lettering, and corrected it, by altering the letter C.[10]

Why had Leighton felt there was an imbalance? Booth didn't ever explain, but Vesey has his own theory. Vesey also flew to Melbourne, and talked to Leighton. As a signwriter, he knew that the letters C and O appear differently to the naked eye and therefore have to be engraved slightly larger. Leighton confirmed to him that this was the reason he had changed the lettering of the C.[11]

Crucially, the dates when each hob was changed were recorded at the ICI factory. Thus, the period in which a shell was manufactured could be determined by the kind of lettering on its base, just as Jack Ritchie had predicted. The hob with the small C had been replaced in 1963. No small C shells had been produced after this time.

Why was this important? It became apparent when Booth and Sprott returned to Auckland and checked the company and shipping records of the Colonial Ammunition Company (CAC), which imported cartridge cases from ICI, filled them with explosive powder and fitted .22 bullets. CAC records showed that it had stopped fitting number 8 bullets to ICI cases on 10 October 1963 and that the last shipment had arrived from Melbourne on the *Kaituna* in August 1963. After October that year, when the next batch of shell cases arrived from ICI, they displayed a big C on their base and were fitted exclusively to bullets with no number 8 because CAC only used bullets with no number 8 on the base by then.

Therefore, shells with the big C (like the Charles case shown to have been fired from Arthur's rifle and found in the Crewe garden) could never have fired the fatal number 8 bullets. Number 8 bullets had never been loaded into that type of cartridge case. This was the death blow for the Crown case against Thomas. *Star* 4, Crown 0.

Incidentally, while ICI had been helpful, CAC was not, and Booth and Sprott had to rely on an unofficial contact for their information. Booth claimed that anonymous callers from the factory told them of police visiting the plant trying to get its testimony changed.[12]

Laden with sworn statements and company records from ICI, Booth and Sprott prepared to fly home. The day they were due to leave, Booth received a call from his wife, Valerie Davies, to say that Martyn Finlay had announced the original exhibits of the Thomas case had been destroyed. Saying he was 'desolate and deeply troubled', Finlay had ordered an immediate search of the tip. Booth's trap had sprung. Both he and Sprott were overjoyed, believing this time they had finally won.[13]

News that contested exhibits had been dumped so soon after a case shocked many people. Hundreds of letters poured into newspapers — most for, but some against, Arthur Thomas. Prime Minister Norman Kirk voiced concern. Members of the public offered to help search the tip. With around 3 acres of landfill at Whitford, it became apparent that the search was a lost cause. The Crown had scored a spectacular own goal. *Star* 5, Crown 0.

A week later, the *Star* published the results of Booth and Sprott's investigation: the Charles case, exhibit 350, could never have held a number 8 bullet. It was a bombshell. Many newspapers began openly calling for Thomas to be released. Public disquiet about the Thomas conviction had reached 'white heat'.[14]

L ate in 1973, the retrial committee had sent another petition to the governor-general, Sir Denis Blundell. On 1 July 1974, Finlay decided that the Court of Appeal should look at the new evidence in what would be known as the 'second referral', to determine which experts were correct about the crucial forensic evidence: the DSIR for the Crown, or Sprott and Booth for the defence.

Aware of the stakes, Bruce Hutton and Donald Nelson of DSIR worked on a rebuttal to the Booth/Sprott findings. First, Nelson came up with a new theory to explain how a number 8 bullet could have been found in a category 4 case: there must have been a mysterious master hob, since lost, which produced subtly different concave lettering, he said. Hutton and Nelson flew to Melbourne, but the theory fell apart when ICI took plaster casts of the cartridge cases and found no lettering differences.

Nelson then produced a new cartridge case, from his private collection, which had similar lettering to exhibit 350. Since he had acquired it in early 1964, it showed that those types of cases could have

Above: Allan and Ivy Thomas were unstinting in their support of their son. They were photographed in May 1974 with Pat Vesey (far left), Pat Booth, Jim Sprott and Vivien Thomas, when they met in Wellington to press yet another application for a rehearing of the case. *Below:* The Thomases at home in 1974.

been fitted to number 8 bullets, he said. His 'finding' was passed on to the assistant commissioner of police, Robert Walton, who passed it on to Martyn Finlay with the recommendation that it be kept secret and not given to the Thomas retrial committee. Fortunately for Thomas, Finlay was no fool. He did pass it on, and Sprott examined it. He quickly found that Nelson's 1964 cartridge had a different primer, known as a wet primer. These were not made in 1964. The powder, Accurex, was also from a much later production batch. Had Nelson made an honest mistake, or had he lied? Peter Williams, in his own reflections on the case, was in no doubt that Nelson lied.[15]

The appeal was heard in December 1974. Five judges sat, chaired by Chief Justice Sir Richard Wild. It was clear the case was being given the fullest possible attention. Peter Williams led the defence, backed by Kevin Ryan as second counsel.

Williams was disturbed by Wild's behaviour. He had already, Williams felt, shown bias by making public statements criticising Thomas. When the court heard of the attempt by Hutton and Nelson to get the ICI engraver George Leighton to sign a false affidavit, Wild apparently laughed.[16] But Wild could not ignore the defence evidence about the cartridge case. The court quickly dismissed Nelson's ridiculous 1964 cartridge theory. It even accepted that on balance of probabilities, exhibit 350 could not have held a fatal number 8 bullet.

Despite this, in a feat of judicial gymnastics of Olympian quality, the judges determined that it could not exclude the possibility that one might still exist.

Williams was astonished. 'It must be the first case in the history of British law where a court not only placed the onus of proof on the appellant, but made him prove his case beyond all reasonable doubt, the standard that is usually accepted by the Crown,' he told the court. 'Again evil had triumphed,' he would later write.[17]

Thomas, once more, was defeated.

I n another blow, as 1974 dragged on into 1975 and he was still in prison, Arthur's marriage disintegrated. Vivien, such a rock in public, had been finding it increasingly difficult to keep up the role of the dutiful wife. The crisis had been coming for some years. As

David Yallop explained it, Vivien had never wavered in her belief that Arthur was innocent, but she was lonely, and the strain of running the farm, the constant media attention and the visits to Arthur were taking their toll.[18] Pat Vesey saw the strain she was under. One day Vivien phoned him to see if he'd come with her to visit Arthur. She told him that whenever she saw Arthur he would be preoccupied with how she was running the farm, right down to specifics such as whether she'd got manure onto the paddocks.[19]

'I don't love Arthur anymore,' she told Vesey that day. 'It's been driven out of me. I just can't face the whole thing.'

'Well, that's going to be hard for a lot of people to swallow,' Vesey replied.

'I'm sorry,' she said. 'I've got to be honest.'

Vesey also saw how hard it was for Arthur to lose Vivien. 'When I used to go and see Arthur, he would reach out to me and say, "You will save our marriage, won't you?" And I said to him, "Arthur, I can do a lot of things, but I can't guarantee anything." It's a big responsibility when he's got tears in his eyes and he's begging you.'[20]

Vivien had stayed in the marriage long after she knew it was finished. In 1972, she was told by a doctor that she needed complete rest. In May that year, with the news that her father was unwell, she returned to England, where she was able to rest and spend time with him and friends. By then, she already knew her marriage to Thomas was over. It would have been forgivable, and entirely understandable, if she had chosen not to return to the crucible that her life in New Zealand had become. Yet she did return, to fight for him.[21]

She did not return to the farm, however, which was being run by the Thomas family; she moved to Auckland and continued her weekly visits to Arthur at Pāremoremo. She kept up the public front of being his wife, having been persuaded by Vesey and others that Arthur needed her to, but by 1975 she was well on the way to making her own life. She had a flat in the city, and a job. One night, she phoned a taxi to take her home from work. The driver was John Harrison. Something between them sparked, and they became close.[22]

Pat Vesey had to break the news to Arthur that Vivien wanted a divorce. He and Peter Williams went to the prison with the divorce papers for Arthur to sign. 'He never forgave me,' Vesey said in 2022.

'I felt that he regarded this as the last let-down. I still talk to him, but we were never close again after taking in the divorce papers.'[23]

Vivien and John Harrison were married in September 1979.

But if Vivien was drifting away, Booth, Sprott, Vesey and the retrial committee were holding the ship on a steady course. In 1975, Booth published his book *The Fate of Arthur Thomas: Trial by Ambush*, which argued for a new trial. By now, he was himself a target. One night he and his wife woke to find a masked man in a suit at the foot of their bed, rifling through his briefcase. Booth chased him out of the house. When Valerie Davies suggested he call the police, he retorted, 'That *was* the police.'[24]

The retrial committee wrote to Martyn Finlay asking the Department of Justice to review the new evidence. An opinion written by justice officials recommended no further action be taken. With that avenue closed to the committee, the only remaining legal avenue left to them was an appeal to the Privy Council in London. (Nowadays, if an appeal fails, litigants can take their case to New Zealand's Supreme Court, but in the 1970s, New Zealand used Britain's highest court, the Privy Council.)

The case was heard in 1978; and once again Thomas lost. This time, it was due to the Privy Council ruling that it had no jurisdiction to review the Court of Appeal decision, because the Court of Appeal had only been asked for a recommendation, not a judgment.[25]

With this final door slammed in his face, what was left for Arthur Thomas? There was, as it turned out, one final court, the most important of all: the court of public opinion.

Booth and Sprott had tried to keep up political pressure as well as delving into the forensic evidence. Prime Minister Robert Muldoon was familiar with the case; he had apparently spent an evening with Kevin Ryan and a bottle of whisky, inhaling the details.[26] One afternoon Booth met Muldoon to update him on the latest developments. Booth had been speaking for some minutes when he became aware that Muldoon's eyes were closed. He thought he had lost him, until he mentioned the actions and attitudes of judges. One of Muldoon's eyes snapped open, and locked on to Booth: 'What do you put their actions down to? Incompetence? Or corruption?' he asked.[27]

Above: An unlikely partnership: Jim Sprott (left), a conservative Christian, and Pat Booth, a liberal journalist, found common cause in their investigation into the mystery of the cartridge case found in the Crewe garden. *Below:* Pat Booth (left), shown here with Allan Thomas and Arthur Thomas's brother Ray, became very close to the Thomas family.

Muldoon was well aware of the political damage the Thomas case was causing. An election was due at the end of 1978 and he must have known it was a problem that needed attention. He had led National to a convincing victory over Labour only three years earlier, but an economic downturn and particularly a fuel shortage was eroding that lead. The government had had to resort to ordering 'carless days' to sustain fuel supplies.

But with the legal avenues for appeal now exhausted, and the Department of Justice firmly against reopening the case, what options were left for Thomas? The case had left the legal realm and had entered the political arena. There was, it turned out, one more hope. It came in the form of another investigative journalist, this time from London.

The writer David Yallop had come to New Zealand in 1978 for a visit. He had an interest in miscarriage of justice cases, having written a book on the notorious Timothy Evans case of 1953 in which a British man was hanged for a crime of which he was later found innocent. While staying with his friend, the novelist Maurice Shadbolt, he had become interested in the Thomas saga. He suggested to Booth they collaborate on a book, and so Booth, hoping it would help the cause, reluctantly agreed and sent him all his notes.

A few months later, Yallop told Booth he had decided to do the book on his own. He used Booth's work with little acknowledgement — a less than scrupulous approach. Carpetbagger though some may have thought him to be, Yallop's book, when it appeared in 1978 titled *Beyond Reasonable Doubt?*, was the impetus Thomas's sagging campaign needed.

It was a sensation; a strange mix of careful evaluation of the evidence, detailed reporting of the witnesses police covered up (based at least on Booth's copious notes of his own investigations), and acute and occasionally sententious summaries of the main personalities. But what clinched it was Yallop's startling claim, published at the end of the book in an 'open letter' to the prime minister, that he believed he knew the identity of the woman who had fed Rochelle Crewe.[28]

With thespian flair, Yallop did not name her, but rather announced that he had written a confidential letter to Muldoon in which he had. It was, consciously or not, a brilliant tactic; Yallop simultaneously put the case back in the headlines and gave Muldoon an excuse to act.

CHAPTER TEN

THE PARDON

I n 1979, Arthur Allan Thomas had been in prison for nine years. He had settled into his routine at Pāremoremo of working in the garden. If he still had hopes of release, they must have been starting to fade. There was a note of this in a poignant letter he wrote to Minister of Justice Jim McLay, about this time: 'I know little about justice and even less about politics but I do know that I am an innocent man and that although the pieces of evidence that convicted me have withered and fallen away over the years my convictions stands still as firm and undoubting as ever.'[1]

McLay, a 34-year-old criminal lawyer from Auckland, had been leap-frogged into one of the top positions in Cabinet after the National Party had won re-election the year before under the magnetic but divisive leadership of Robert Muldoon. 'Piggy' to his detractors, leader of 'Rob's Mob' to the party faithful, Muldoon ran his party and Cabinet like an All Blacks coach of the old school: he was disciplined, ruthless, and usually efficient.

McLay had Auckland pedigree — he was a half-brother of a previous attorney-general, Peter Wilkinson — and he had grown up around the law; his parents were friends of the recently appointed chief justice, Sir Ronald Davison.[2] He'd joined the National Party at 18 and had worked his way up, winning the traditional Labour seat of Birkenhead for National in the 1975 landslide. On the liberal wing of the party, he was thought of as something of a reformer.

When McLay arrived in his ministerial office in the Beehive after the election and sat behind the large wooden desk overlooking Wellington harbour, among the pile of congratulatory notes from friends and legal colleagues was the letter from Arthur Thomas and one from a well-known judge. After the customary recitation of praise, the latter ended with an unexpected rider: 'I hope you will take note of the Arthur Allan Thomas case and his conviction.'

McLay put the letters aside, but they stuck in his mind — he knew he would be hearing more about the Thomas case.[3]

David Yallop's open letter to the prime minister calling for an inquiry into the Thomas case had not been ignored. In late 1978, Muldoon had appointed a QC, Robert Adams-Smith, to inquire into Yallop's key claim that he knew who the woman who had fed the baby was. Some commentators believe Muldoon did this because he was 'sympathetic' to Thomas,[4] but Jim McLay believes it was just as much shrewd political management. Muldoon knew the case was continuing to attract public attention and concern. He chose the well-proven tactic of politicians and All Black first fives when under pressure: kick for touch; in this case, announce an inquiry.

Muldoon chose Adams-Smith after being cross-examined fiercely by him in a defamation case. He wanted someone tough and robust.[5] He certainly got it. Although a respected barrister, Adams-Smith soon showed he was not willing to stick to whatever brief justice officials might have had in mind for him.

In his report, he stated that he had interviewed the witness who had seen the woman on the Crewe farm, and had reviewed the evidence, and that he did not support David Yallop's view of who the mystery woman was. So far, so good for the police. But he went further and asked to conduct a second report into the wider issues of the safety of Thomas's conviction. 'Safety' is a legal term, meaning, essentially, that a jury's decision is correct — so an unsafe conviction is one where the jury has been discovered to have wrongly found someone guilty.

Asking for a second report presented a dilemma for the government. If it agreed, it could reopen issues and add fuel to the Thomas supporters' case. If it denied the request, it could look as if

Robert Muldoon, prime minister from 1975 to 1984, took a special interest in the Crewe case, but left the decision whether to pardon Arthur Thomas to his minister of justice, Jim McLay.

the government was trying to cover up for the police. However, McLay says there was never any question a second report would be authorised.[6]

Adam-Smith's report, which landed on McLay's desk in December 1979, was the beginning of the unravelling of the conviction of Arthur Thomas. It looked closely at key police evidence around the timing of the murders, interviewed witnesses, and found that the police assumption that the Crewes had been murdered late in the evening of 17 June was wrong.

The prosecution theory was that the Crewes had bought fish and chips on their way home from the stock sale in Bombay that day. This timing was important to the Crown's case against Thomas, given that the only alibi he had for that time was his wife, Vivien. But Adams-Smith interviewed the owner of the fish-and-chip shop and found the man he had served had been wearing a blue suit (Harvey was at the stock sale in a farmer's raincoat). He also argued that grease and traces of flour in the pots on the Crewe stove showed they had cooked flounder that evening.

Adams-Smith concluded that the murders could have been committed any time from around 5.30 p.m. on 17 June to the early hours of 18 June. Crucially, he concluded that he had real concerns about the safety of the Thomas conviction: 'I feel that the Crown's contention that it was late at night that Thomas came upon this couple by stealth is not warranted by the evidence as I believe it to be. This is so serious a flaw in the Crown's case, a case based mainly on circumstantial evidence, that I have real doubt whether it can properly be contended that the case against Thomas was proved beyond reasonable doubt.'[7]

What was McLay to do with this bombshell report? Much has been written about the decision to pardon Thomas, and most of that writing rehashes the view that it was Muldoon's decision. Others have alleged that he was persuaded by a friend of the Thomas family who worked in his office.[8] In fact, the truth is less conspiratorial, and much more interesting. Jim McLay has never spoken about what really happened. He does here, for the first time.

cLay asked for a meeting of an inner committee of the most senior Cabinet ministers: Muldoon, Deputy Prime Minister Duncan McIntyre, Minister of Housing Derek Quigley (the only other lawyer in Cabinet), and himself. He told them that any decision on the report had to be his, as minister of justice, and his alone. The committee accepted this.

McLay then convened a meeting of key officials from the Department of Justice. These included Deputy Secretary of Justice Jim Cameron and the powerful and long-serving solicitor-general, Richard Savage, who had written to Muldoon only days before, saying that to pardon or release Thomas 'would make a mockery of our justice system', a letter which McLay had not seen.[9] The officials advised the minister that he had three options.

First, he could simply do nothing. If he concluded the report did not provide new or cogent evidence that threw the safety of the conviction into doubt, then he did not have to take action. Second, he could refer it to the Court of Appeal, which had the option of ordering a third trial. Thirdly, there was what might be described as the 'thermonuclear' option: he could recommend to the governor-general that he exercise his prerogative of mercy and issue a free pardon. This would mean that Thomas would be deemed to have not committed the murders and could not be tried again.

It was soon obvious to McLay which option his senior officials favoured. One of them told him, 'You realise, of course, minister, that there can't be another trial?'

'Why do you say that?'

'Because much of the evidence has been destroyed. And particularly the highly controversial cartridge case,' the official replied.[10]

Exactly what was running through this official's mind when he told McLay that, we will never know, but given the tone of the department's dismissal of Thomas's previous pleas for a rehearing, it is a fair bet that at least some senior officials wanted the case buried forever. Effectively, McLay was being boxed into a corner; his officials had already looked closely at the case and had decided no action was needed, there was no real possibility of another trial, thus no point in referring it to the Court of Appeal, and the third option was obviously regarded as so far-fetched as to barely warrant mention.

McLay advised his officials and the Cabinet committee that he would return to Auckland over the weekend to write a recommendation on what action to take. He gave no indication as to which way he was leaning and officials clearly thought they had no cause for concern.

Initially, McLay recalls, 'I was still inclined to recommend that it go back to the Court of Appeal. And I started to write, but it was a bit like a compass. Each time I tried to steer it towards a reference to the Court of Appeal, the compass needle would swing back to magnetic north. I spent quite a lot of time writing, and rewriting, until I realised this wasn't making sense, so I cancelled an engagement and returned to Wellington. I felt I needed to be there, with access to officials, to get it right.'

On the afternoon of Sunday 16 December, McLay typed out his recommendation: a free pardon for Arthur Allan Thomas. The first and only free pardon of a convicted murderer ever given in New Zealand, and one of only four ever given for any offence.[11]

The next morning, McLay had a standing meeting with officials and briefed them on the options, without telling them what he was planning. 'I worked through the reasons, and I could see that some of them were coming to the same realisation, but not all of them. Remember, the solicitor-general is the person responsible for upholding convictions . . . likewise there were officials in the justice department who took the view, fairly understandably, that this man has been twice convicted by a jury, and each time the jury has reached a decision in a very short period of time, [so] we shouldn't be interfering with that. I was perturbed particularly by the fact that it wouldn't be possible to mount another trial.'[12]

Of course, one option he could have taken, and one some of his senior officials clearly favoured, was to do nothing. But McLay felt this wasn't tenable either.

'There had been a number of inquiries, two Court of Appeals, a referral to the Court of Appeal for advice, and every time the government had received these reports, no matter where they came from, they always accepted and acted on them. And if we did nothing on this one, what was different about this report? Particularly one that said

Jim McLay was just 35 when he became minister of justice in 1978. The young Auckland lawyer was given the task of deciding whether Arthur Thomas should be freed.

the case may not have been proven beyond reasonable doubt? Why accept all those previous reports and act on them when they were against Thomas, and now here was one which went the other way and we might be ignoring it? So I didn't think it was viable to leave it sitting on the desk and say there was nothing of consequence here. I had to dismiss that option. What I was doing was gradually working towards a conclusion, and my writing was taking me to that conclusion.

'But understand, I hadn't come to the Thomas case with any great feeling that injustice had been done, or for that matter that he had been rightly convicted. Other than the standard lawyer's mantra of two juries, all the evidence has been tested, who am I to interfere? The starting point probably had to be, the man's been convicted twice, don't interfere, and I had to have some reason to interfere . . . but as I started writing a memorandum justifying one course of action I found that it steered me towards another course of action.

'I suppose there was always this lingering question: Why has the government received all these reports . . . every time the government acted on the report and accepted the recommendation. Suddenly here was one that said otherwise, said something different. And to reject it didn't make a lot of sense. That could have justified sending it off to the Court of Appeal again. And Thomas's supporters — and this didn't influence me, really — could have justifiably said, why throw him back on the system that has denied him justice until now? There had to be some basis for the action that I recommended, and the basis was a report has been received, it says these things.

'One option would be to refer the matter back to the Court of Appeal, but there was no guarantee the court would recommend another trial; they might have said no further action required. So there was no certainty a new trial would be ordered. And if there was a recommendation for one, there couldn't be a new trial.'[13]

It is tempting, looking back, to attribute to McLay a sense of historical mission, or even a dramatic moment of personal revelation, such as that romanticised by great historic cases of injustice, like the Dreyfus case.[14] He was certainly aware of those cases. But he says he didn't think that at the time; he was simply trying to make the right decision on the issue before him.

Looking back, Arthur Thomas was perhaps fortunate to have

someone relatively unfamiliar with the bureaucracy in the minister's seat; a more seasoned politician might have taken a more institutional view. McLay feels vindicated by the royal commission of inquiry that would be held the following year, and the subsequent 2014 police review of the investigation. 'I took what I believed to be the appropriate course of action. Everything that happened thereafter [the various inquiries] justified it in my mind,' he says.

Is he proud of his contribution to Thomas's pardon? 'Not really. I was taking the only course of action that I could see could be justified. Pride is not the right word for it. You do what you have to do.'[15]

Back in his office in the Beehive, McLay arranged a meeting with the Cabinet committee and told them what he had in mind. He then arranged with Deputy Secretary of Justice Jim Cameron to draw up the pardon documents. Next, it was Cabinet's turn. McLay arrived part way through the Monday-morning meeting. Muldoon interrupted proceedings, saying there was an urgent and important matter to deal with.

It should have been a moment of high drama: the minister of justice reading his decision on an issue that had divided the country. No one except the three members of the Cabinet committee and McLay knew what he had decided, but just as McLay began to read, one person had a coughing fit so severe no one could hear him speak and only after it subsided could McLay tell Cabinet. There was no vote. It was not Cabinet's decision to accept it or not; all it could do was note it.

McLay then excused himself to head across town to Government House to lay his recommendation before the governor-general, as is the process under New Zealand law for a pardon. It was still possible that the governor-general might refuse to accept his minister's recommendation. When McLay was ushered in to the formal sitting room and handed his recommendation to Sir Keith Holyoake, he started to wonder if this was going to be one of those moments.

Holyoake was still a huge political presence. As New Zealand's most successful prime minister, he had won four straight elections in the 1960s for National; he was an urbane patrician and a wily politician. He was the living embodiment of the farmer-National establishment.

Holyoake took the recommendation from McLay and began to read. Minutes went by. McLay must have looked at his watch — he had hoped he would be back at the Beehive in time to brief Muldoon for the post-Cabinet press conference at 1 p.m. But still Holyoake read on. Finally, after what seemed to McLay an aeon, but which he later realised was only about 15 minutes, Holyoake looked up and started to ask questions.

McLay felt concern rising. What was Holyoake doing? Was he going to refuse to sign the pardon? After all, he had been the member for Pahīatua, Harvey Crewe's home town, and had known him personally. But it turned out Holyoake was not of a mind to turn it down. The questions were mostly about political management. Was he aware of the fallout this would cause? McLay assured him he was.

Good. The public would have forgotten all about it after Christmas, Holyoake assured him. Finally, he said, 'Good luck, Jamie, you're going to need it.'[16]

McLay dashed back to the Beehive and briefed Muldoon, who then took the unusual step of inviting him to the post-Cabinet press conference in the Beehive, where Muldoon announced the pardon. So, today, the public knows only that Muldoon announced the fateful decision, in a soundbite played repeatedly ever since: 'Cabinet has endorsed the recommendation of the minister of justice to pardon Arthur Allan Thomas for the conviction of the murder of Harvey and Jeannette Crewe.' What the public didn't know was that Muldoon had got it slightly wrong: Cabinet had not endorsed the decision, rather it had only noted it.

The press gallery reporters at the conference raced away to call their newsrooms. The presses on the afternoon papers clanged to a halt and new plates were fitted. The pardon led the news all that afternoon and the next day.

It was one of those moments that defined the end of a decade. And the backlash wasn't long in coming. Members of the Cabinet, visibly angry, told McLay he had made the wrong decision, and that it threatened to bring down the New Zealand justice system. Judges called it 'blatant political interference'.

Back in his office that afternoon, the phone on his desk rang.

'What the hell do you think you're doing?' or something to that effect, he remembers the caller asking.[17] McLay will say only that the caller was a senior judge. However, two very senior judges had already made public statements. Sir Richard Wild, whom Peter Williams described as 'a hard man who ruled with an iron rod',[18] had retired as chief justice two years earlier and had said publicly that the Thomas affair was a threat to the legal system. Earlier, in 1972, then president of the Court of Appeal, Sir Alfred North, had accused Thomas supporters of impropriety. Williams considers both judges 'breached the long-held custom that judges should keep their mouths shut on political matters and concentrate on their judgments'.[19]

In phoning to express his displeasure, it was in fact the senior judge who was out of line. New Zealand follows the Westminster model of separation of the judicial (court) and executive (Parliament) branches of government. Neither is allowed to interfere with the other's decision-making. The judge appeared to be doing just that. Perhaps he thought he could browbeat the young minister, or rely on his personal connection, seeing he'd known McLay for a long time.

McLay listened but gave no indication he would be changing his mind. He knew the law, and he knew he was on solid ground.

Meanwhile, for Arthur Thomas, the wheels of justice began their final revolution. The remorseless machinery that had whisked him from his riverside farm to a maximum-security cell in Pāremoremo prison now moved with the same efficiency to free him. First, a message was relayed to the prison superintendent, John Todd, who called Thomas to his office to give him the news of his pardon. Thomas had been weeding Todd's garden that morning. He planned to spend the afternoon watering it.

'When I walked in, Superintendent Todd says, "Look, I've got a Christmas present for you,"' he told author Ian Wishart in 2010. 'And I say, "Oh, and what's that?" "You've been pardoned". And he stood up and stuck his hand out and shook my hand. "But hang on," I said. "Do you mean my conviction has been quashed?" Because this was important; as sometimes there is a reprieve or you're released but the conviction stands, see. I wanted to know. And he said, "Yes, conviction quashed".'

Next, the superintendent was clasping his shoulder. 'It wasn't just "Thomas" anymore, it was "Mr Thomas" and "Do you want a cup of tea and bickies?", and it was just as quick as that. I would have preferred lunch.'[20]

Thomas was led back to Hut 34, his 2 x 2 metre room, to clear out his things. He put on his suit — the same suit he had bought in Dargaville in 1960 and had worn at his second trial in 1973. There was $555.87 in his wallet — his pay for six years' prison work. He recalled one awkward moment. He had a bottle of contraband whisky stashed under the bed and he wondered how to get it out in front of the warder who was accompanying him. 'But I just thought, righto, so I lifted up the covers of the mattress, right in front of his eyes, you know, lift it right up — whrrr — in the box. Quick as a flash.'[21]

After officials ascertained where Thomas wanted to be taken, there was a moment of Monty Pythonesque farce when it was realised that there was no vehicle available to drive him. The prison's car was in the workshop, and the superintendent's car was on a 'carless day'. After demurring about whether it was appropriate for the head of the country's maximum-security prison to be caught driving an inmate to freedom in an illegal vehicle, Todd eventually saw his way through the legal conundrum: 'If it's good enough for the governor-general to pardon you, Arthur, it's good enough for us to use the car, eh?' he said.

Thomas had been warned not to tell anyone, so all he could say to his cellmates as he departed was, 'Watch the news, see you chaps', and with a wave he left.[22]

On Monday 17 December 1979 he left Pāremoremo prison a free man. He was driven in the superintendent's Cortina to the home of Pat Booth and Valerie Davies, at Ararimu, south of Auckland. They were vegetarian, so Arthur's first meal as a free man was scrambled eggs.

Booth then drove Thomas on to Thomas's aunt and uncle's house in Hamilton, where he got to watch the six o'clock news of his release on the first colour television he had ever seen. When a law academic came on screen to explain that the pardon meant the offence had not been committed, there were cheers. 'Good one. I'm a new man. The conviction never happened,' Thomas said.

By 8 p.m., he was heading back to Pukekawa to stay with his youngest brother, Des; his mother, now aged 79, was not well enough to stay up

Above: Arthur Thomas's first meal as a free man, with Pat Booth (far right), Booth's partner Valerie Davies and their children, Victoria, 14, and James, 13. After the meal Thomas and Booth drove to Thomas's aunt and uncle's house in Hamilton, and then to his brother Des in Pukekawa. *Below:* Arthur Thomas eats breakfast as Pat Booth hammers out his story for that evening's *Auckland Star*, which ran under the famous headline 'My boy, my boy'.

to welcome him home that evening. Reporters had been tipped off about where he was, so Booth sneaked him out the back door of his aunt and uncle's house and into his waiting car.

Booth wrote about the drive to Pukekawa in a front-page story in the *Star* the next day: 'Arthur Thomas began to feel again what freedom meant — the green spread of Waikato pasture and the first distant sighting of Pukekawa Hill. The last time he saw the slopes was a glimpse from a prison van as he was taken to Hautu.'

'That's what I want to do, make a new life and start again,' Thomas told Booth as they drove.[23]

Freedom was still sinking in. As Thomas explained later, 'I had to unwind all that has built up in my mind over the years, and it's all getting released. The fact is, I'm a free man — I just can't believe that I can have a drink. Do my thing. I can stand on my head. No worries, you know?'[24]

The next morning, Booth drove Arthur Thomas back to his own farm, and to the waiting throng of media.

'Did you commit the murders?' one TV reporter called out.

Thomas eyeballed the camera: 'I am innocent of the Crewe murders,' he replied.

'Do you swear you are telling the truth?' someone called out.

'I am a Christian and I swear my innocence before God. There is no way I did it. My name is clear and I am innocent of the crime. I came pretty near being mental there during part of my imprisonment. I didn't know if I'd end up in Kingseat or Lake Alice.'[25]

At the end of the docu-drama *Beyond Reasonable Doubt*, made that year by director John Laing, there is actual footage of the moment Arthur Thomas returns home. Shot from the front paddock at the front of the Thomas homestead, Booth's late-model Toyota sedan is seen turning off the Mercer Ferry Road and entering the property. The car bumps over the grass and the camera pans to show a welcoming party of about 30 Thomas family members and friends shouting and waving in delight.

It is a magnificent scene, the whole Thomas tribe, with parents Allan and Ivy beaming with joy, Arthur's brothers Richard, Ray, Les,

The front page of the *Auckland Star*, 18 December 1979.

Des, his sisters Margaret and Lyrice, his cousin Peter, Pat Vesey, and of course Pat Booth. Thomas gets out of the car and is engulfed by his family. The camera zooms out, and rises to an aerial shot, showing the family, somehow now at a safe distance from history.[26]

That morning, Pat Booth continued to hammer out his report on the homecoming on his portable typewriter at the Thomas kitchen table. It ran in that evening's paper: '"My boy, my boy". Those were the only words that came from a tear-filled Ivy Thomas today when she clutched her son Arthur to her — home after nine years in jail. Only a few minutes before, Arthur Thomas and I acted on a promise we made to each other in June 1973 — that one day we would walk onto that Pukekawa farm with Arthur a free man. Pardoned yesterday of the Crewe murder convictions, Arthur Thomas came home to an emotional reunion with his mother and father Allan.

'Ivy Thomas flew to the Philippines a few months ago seeking a cure for a mysterious crippling illness. Her family felt she was better when she came home, but they knew deep down that Arthur's release would be the best possible medicine. [Arthur] was up early this morning for the last few hundred metres of his return home. Getting up was a painfully slow process for Ivy Thomas, but she was determined to be dressed and on her feet to see him. She struggled for a long time before she finally opened the door to him. She was far from the woman I had seen walking so upright and full of dignified anger at the Court of Appeal hearing in 1975. The years of sorrow and struggle had taken a terrible toll on her.

'For long minutes they just stood there clutching each other — her boy, her boy. The tears came for most in the room. Then, she sat down, with Arthur beside her and she stroked his hair, her face wide with a smile. The room emptied to leave them to these minutes they had both looked forward to for so long.'[27]

CHAPTER ELEVEN
THE ROYAL COMMISSION OF INQUIRY

As 1979 passed into 1980, it soon became obvious to the government that, despite the pardon, the Thomas affair was not over. For one thing, there was the matter of compensation. How much should be paid to Thomas? For another, there were the lurking undercurrents of allegations of police corruption. To put the public's mind at rest, and restore the reputation of the police, there needed to be a way to get to the truth of these issues.

A royal commission of inquiry is the usual vehicle. Often chaired by a judge, a commission has the power to subpoena witnesses and hear their evidence under oath. Jim McLay consulted the chief justice, who agreed that no New Zealand judge of sufficient stature was free of conflict of interest as most had already had something to do with the case. Both McLay and Muldoon also wanted someone independent.

McLay rang the Australian attorney-general, Senator Peter Durack, QC, who gave him three names. One was the Honorable Robert Taylor, a former judge of the Supreme Court of New South Wales, additional Court of Appeal judge, and was then chief judge of the Common Law Division. He was an experienced commissioner, having sat on a police corruption inquiry, and had a reputation for being robust. McLay flew to Sydney and, after meeting with Taylor, offered him the job, which he accepted.[1]

The other commissioners to accept McLay's invitation were the Right Honourable Peter Gordon, a former National Cabinet minister with a cross-party reputation for integrity, and the recently retired Anglican Archbishop of New Zealand, the Most Reverend Allen Johnston.

On 21 May 1980, the Royal Commission to Inquire into the Circumstances of the Convictions of Arthur Allan Thomas for the Murders of David Harvey Crewe and Jeannette Lenore Crewe got under way in Wellington. With the police and DSIR feeling wounded by the pardon and determined to bandage their bleeding reputations, and the Thomas supporters on a high and equally determined to show police corruption, the stage was set for a showdown. Both sides were heavily lawyered. The police had engaged John Henry QC and Robert Fisher, both of whom later became High Court judges. The DSIR had Robert Smellie QC (also later a High Court judge) and David Schnauer. The justice department was represented by John Wallace (also later to become a High Court judge).

Arthur Thomas had Peter Williams and Kevin Ryan, perhaps the country's top criminal defence lawyers at the time. They were still seething over Thomas's treatment by the police and what they saw as bias by expert witnesses, such as the scientist Donald Nelson. Williams was determined to show him no mercy. 'There was something about this man's sanctimonious, butter-wouldn't-melt-in-my-mouth attitude that really riled both Kevin and me, and we were determined to nail him to the mast for the lies he'd perpetrated over the last decade,' he later explained.[2] And nail him they did.

Perhaps the most humiliating moment for Nelson came when commission head Robert Taylor discovered that at the first and second trials, Nelson had suppressed his notes about the Thomas rifle that showed there was no match between the test-fired lead and that in the bodies. He exploded with anger, telling Nelson flatly that he did not believe him.[3]

Hutton, unhappy about being moved to the uniformed branches after the Crewe case, had retired from the police in 1976. However, as the face of the police case, he came in for aggressive questioning. Williams later summed it up: 'Again and again [Taylor] probed Hutton about why he had made a special trip to the dump and carefully hidden the Charles shell case when he knew that investigations into its authenticity were still proceeding. Hutton tried to blame Morris, but the latter refused to back him up. I believed Morris.

'Why, Taylor asked Morris, had the Thomas rifle been repossessed? Why had Hutton and Johnston gone back out to the Crewe house and fired shots there a few days before the Crewe garden was searched for the third time and the shell case found? Taylor also taxed Hutton about his interference with the court exhibits during the second trial and his going to the Station Hotel and dining with the jury.'[4]

As the clashes between Hutton and Taylor continued, the atmosphere became more and more volatile. 'The police hated him,' wrote Williams.[5] The Australian was different to any New Zealand judge the police had been used to, and he took his role as inquisitor, rather than referee, to its logical conclusion. The police were beginning to realise that, unlike the courts, they could not control this outcome, and that it was fast running away from them. They resorted to desperate methods, such as ranks of uniformed police officers filling the back of the hearing room, shouting and booing like a crowd at a football match.[6]

Methodically, piece by piece, Ryan and Williams destroyed the prosecution case against Thomas, and with it the reputations of Nelson, Hutton and Johnston. The DSIR finally conceded that Jim Sprott had been right: the Charles cartridge case could never have contained the number 8 bullet of the type that killed the Crewes. This alone decimated the Crown case. But there was more to come.

As things went from bad to worse for the police and DSIR, their counsel walked out, alleging bias — only to be persuaded by McLay to return. The commission ordered them to turn over all their documents to the defence. This, Williams said later, was 'the first occasion in

New Zealand history that the Crown, in a criminal matter, had been compelled to grant discovery to the defence'.[7]

Determined to prevent the defence finding the right documents, during the hearing the police buried them in an entire room full of other documents, making it difficult to find the significant ones. They produced deliberately unclear photostat copies, or put them out of order or upside down. Ryan and Williams also discovered that many important documents, such as the notes of their police conferences, had, like the evidence, been destroyed.[8]

Ross Meurant, one of the constables who had sieve-searched the Crewe garden, revealed years later that he was taken aside by Commissioner of Police Robert Walton before he went to give evidence to the commission, and asked what he would say. 'Of course, he already knew what I was going to say as my brief of evidence had been well prepared and repeated what I had said on oath in previous court sessions.

'In response to Walton's probing, I said that I would confirm I had been thorough and methodical, on my hands and knees at times, and that I used a sieve on occasions when searching the strips of ground that included the specific spot where Mike Charles subsequently found a cartridge case. Walton had shaken his head, and in the presence of another executive officer, who at the time was hoping to be promoted to detective chief superintendent and was dependent on the commissioner for his promotion, Walton said, "Come on! Senior detectives don't get down on their hands and knees and sift through dirt."

'Effectively, the Commissioner of Police was telling me to lie on oath to a Royal Commission. I was stunned — not least by the fact that the attempt by Walton to encourage, entice or intimidate me to change my evidence is an indictable crime punishable by 14 years' imprisonment. Needless to say, I did not alter my evidence and in fact emerged from the hearing as one of the very few police witnesses who was not castigated by the Royal Commission.'[9] (Bruce Parkes was another.)

Finally, when it was obvious they were going to lose, the police applied to the High Court to halt the hearing on the grounds of bias. Even then Peter Williams had to fight for a fair go.

One of the three High Court judges hearing the application was Justice Graham Speight, a former Crown prosecutor and legal partner of David Morris. Williams had him removed. Both the High Court and

Peter Williams joined the Thomas legal team in 1973, shortly after the second trial. Determined to reverse what he believed were outright lies by some experts, he led the team to a resounding victory over the police at the 1980 royal commission of inquiry.

eventually the Court of Appeal refused to halt the commission.[10]

What those in court did not know was that the commission was very nearly halted by Taylor. Well into the hearings, Taylor discovered that as an overseas judge, he did not have the statutory protection against defamation proceedings that New Zealand judges did. This meant anyone who felt their reputation was besmirched by the commission could sue him for damages. Alarmed, Taylor told McLay he had to change the law or he would quit. McLay, who by then had his hands full with ultimately the *more* explosive inquiry into the 1979 Erebus disaster, had to use all his political skills to persuade him to stay.

'I told him you've done what we wanted — to shake the tree and have a few rotten apples fall out. But I can't change the law, and certainly not halfway through an inquiry. I told him he could quit, but the inquiry would continue. I would simply get Peter Gordon and Allen Johnston to complete it. Of course it would have been a disaster if he had gone. Fortunately, he thought it over and decided to stay.'

In fact, a legal solution was found: the commission's report, when complete, was tabled in Parliament, and thus had the protection of parliamentary privilege; no one could sue for defamation.[11]

The hearing lasted 64 days. When the commission's 125-page report was tabled in Parliament on 28 November 1980, it was the thunderclap the Thomas family had been hoping for and that the police were no doubt dreading. In language that would not have been out of place in the King James version of the Bible, the commissioners denounced the conviction of Thomas: 'That a man is locked up for a day without cause has always been seen by our law as a most serious assault on his rights. That a man is wrongly imprisoned for nine years is a wrong that can never be put right. The fact that he is imprisoned on the basis of evidence which is false to the knowledge of police officers, whose duty it is to uphold the law, is an unspeakable outrage . . . Such action is no less than a shameful and cynical attack on the trust that all New Zealanders have and are entitled to have in their Police Force and system of administration of justice.

'Mr Thomas suffered that outrage; he was the victim of that attack. His courage and that of a very few dedicated men and women who believed in the cause of justice has exposed the wrongs which were done. They can never be put right.'[12]

But perhaps the commission's most damning finding was regarding the police actions: 'We have not been content with so much of the truth as some saw fit to put before us. With the aid of scientists we were able to demolish the cornerstone of the Crown case, exhibit 350, and demonstrate that it was not put in the Crewe garden by the hand of the murderer. It was put there by the hand of one whose duty it was to investigate fairly and honestly, but who in dereliction of that duty, in breach of his obligation to uphold the law and departing from all standards of fairness, fabricated this evidence to procure a conviction for murder. He swore falsely, and beyond a peradventure was responsible for Thomas being twice convicted, his appeals thrice dismissed, and for his spending nine years of his life in prison; to be released as a result of sustained public refusal to accept these decisions.'[13]

The commission assessed damages with the intent of putting Thomas back in the financial position he would have been in 'but for the wrongs done to him'. Based on a report from a farm valuer, it assessed the sum of compensation owing to him to be $1,087,450.35. (It noted he had been intending to gain freehold over the one-third of the farm that was leased from the Maori Affairs Department.) Of this, a total of $38,287 went to Thomas's family in recognition of their help: Ray, Lloyd and Des Thomas received just over $5000 each; his sister and brother-in-law, Margaret and Buster Stuckey, received $2100; Richard Thomas $1800; Allan Thomas $2250; and Thomas's former wife, Vivien, $10,000. A further $50,000 went to Jim Sprott, only a third of the $150,000 he claimed for the time he had put in.

One of the commissioners, Peter Gordon, objected to this payment and argued that Sprott should not have been paid given he had acknowledged it was a personal crusade. Pat Booth claimed only $1 but was commended by the commission for 'immense labour in the field of investigative journalism . . . carried out . . . at some considerable sacrifice to family life'.[14]

This left Arthur Thomas with $950,000. It also left the government with the tricky task of deciding what to do about two police officers who had been directly accused of very serious criminal offences. When the report was released, many were in no doubt there would be a prosecution. Thomas hoped there would be; it was why they had pushed for the commission, he said. Muldoon told reporters he expected the attorney-general to refer the matter to the police. Deputy leader of the opposition David Lange, himself an experienced defence lawyer, said the police had a duty to prosecute. Bruce Hutton, interviewed by journalists, was described as 'shocked and bewildered' by the commission's report, but asserted his and Johnston's innocence.[15]

And yet, despite the public expectation, nothing was done. The decision not to prosecute has been heavily criticised, so it is worth explaining in detail.

Under New Zealand law, it is up to the solicitor-general to decide whether a prosecution should be brought. The minister of justice has no say. The solicitor-general at the time was Paul Neazor QC, a former Crown counsel and devout Catholic from the well-heeled western suburbs of Wellington. He was respected in the legal profession and a trusted civil servant, as was shown by his later appointment to one of the most classified positions in the civil service, that of inspector-general of intelligence and security.

Neazor took his time to think through the issues. In a confidential opinion, dated 21 December 1981, addressed to the commissioner of police, he set out his deliberations. He considered whether Hutton (Len Johnston had died in 1978) should be prosecuted for planting the cartridge case, exhibit 350, in the Crewes' garden. Fabricating evidence is an offence, as is conspiring to prosecute for an offence, knowing the accused to be innocent, as is conspiring to obstruct, prevent, pervert or defeat the course of justice, each of which carries a penalty of up to seven years' imprisonment. For perjury that results in imprisonment for more than three years, the penalty can be up to 14 years in prison. These were clearly very serious charges facing Hutton.

Neazor concluded there was no direct evidence against Hutton; the question was whether there was sufficient evidence to establish a prima facie case that the offence was committed. He summarised the commission's findings on exhibit 350 as being that (a) this cartridge case could never have contained one of the fatal bullets; (b) it could not have reached the place in which it was found by a normal process of ejection from the rifle from the spot the prosecution claimed the fatal bullet was fired; (c) the case was not in the garden when it was first searched; (d) its physical state was too good for it to have been in the garden as long as it was claimed to have been; (e) the only explanation for it being there was that it was planted; (f) Hutton and Johnston were at the Crewe property between 30 September 1970 and 27 October 1970 (the day it was found) and planted the shell on that day; and (g) this is confirmed by Hutton arranging for another search, which found the shell after earlier searches had not.

Neazor proceeded on the basis that exhibit 350 could not have held the fatal bullets. He also said it did not matter whether Thomas had actually killed the Crewes; Hutton would be liable, regardless, if it were proved he had produced false evidence. He concluded that the cartridge likely came from a box taken from Thomas's farm on 13 October. Thomas's rifle was taken from him on 20 October; thus the first time police had both cartridge and rifle was 20 October. He said the fateful decision to plant the case must have been taken between 20 and 26 October. He decided that since any prosecution must be on a circumstantial basis, it needed to be shown that the shell could not have been in the garden before 20 October; and that Hutton and Johnston had access to the rifle and suitable cartridges at the relevant time.

He noted the commission had found that if the shell had been in the garden prior to 20 October, it would have been found by searches on 23 June or 18 August. 'The commission acknowledges that in respect of the particularly important search of 18 August this conclusion requires the rejection of the evidence of four police officers and of [Jack Handcock] then manager of the Crewe farm, and acceptance of the evidence of [Graeme Hewson] as to whether the garden was sieve searched on 18 or 19 August.'[16]

Neazor then went through the evidence of each of the above. 'The Crown would have to proceed on the basis that the garden in question was said by one witness to have been sieve-searched whereas four say specifically it was not and another expressed the view from its later state that it could not have been so searched . . . On this state of evidence I do not think the prosecution could establish the positive allegation to the required standard of proof that the shell case could not have been in the garden on 18 August 1970.'[17]

On the issue of Mike Charles changing his evidence about whether the garden had been sieve-searched to say that it had not, Neazor concluded it didn't help the prosecution. This was because while it would help the prosecution to show that Hutton would have known the garden was not sieve-searched and therefore a shell could be safely planted, it undermined the case by showing the case could have been there all along and not found because the garden hadn't been sieve-searched.

The other critical point, that the case was not sufficiently corroded, was dismissed by Neazor because the commission itself had found that 'the evidence was too inexact for heavy reliance to be placed upon it'. He noted that because the shell had been dumped in the tip, there was no way to test this.

On the issue of whether Hutton could have had access to a shell from the box taken from Thomas's farm, or the Thomas rifle, in the crucial period 20 to 27 October, Neazor concluded that due to errors and gaps in police records about where the exhibits were, Hutton could have had access to both shells and rifle.

Perhaps the most crucial evidence, Neazor said, was that of the Priests, who said they had heard shots from the Crewe farm, and shortly after had encountered Hutton and Johnston driving away. They stopped, and when they asked Hutton whether he had fired two shots at the house, Hutton had said: 'How did you know?' At the commission, Hutton had flatly denied saying this, and was interrogated by Taylor, resulting in such a shouting match that the commission transcribers had not been able to record exactly what was said.[18]

Neazor concluded that due to uncertainty from the Priests about the exact date they heard the shots, being 'sometime after 30 September', it did not reach the standard of proof. 'This material . . . is the evidence that would have to be adduced in a prosecution to prove that Mr Hutton was directly identifiable as someone who planted the cartridge case in the garden. Looked at objectively, I do not think it can be said that this evidence reaches the standard required for a prosecution to place Mr Hutton and [Mr Johnston] on the Crewe property with a rifle (let alone the Thomas rifle) between 20 October and 26 October 1970.'[19]

Finally, as to whether Hutton had committed perjury, Neazor had this to say: 'The commission clearly has not believed Mr Hutton's evidence or some part of it. That however is something that happens

After the royal commission of inquiry accused him of corruption, Bruce Hutton was described as being shocked and bewildered.

every day in Court hearings without charges of perjury being laid . . . My advice is that if the evidence does not warrant charging Mr Hutton in respect of participation in [the matters above] it equally does not warrant charging him in respect of his answers on oath denying wrongful conduct in respect of them.'

On the issue of whether Hutton deliberately withheld material evidence from the defence, Neazor concluded that even though it could be shown that Hutton knew of those matters (for example, the evidence from the Priests that three shots were fired on the night of the murders), it could not be proved that Hutton knew the evidence was material and therefore did not disclose it.[20] Neazor recommended no prosecution should be brought against Hutton on the grounds that there was not enough evidence.

He also recommended against publication of his report, firstly because it was before the Court of Appeal, and secondly because, in essence, it was not usual practice to do so. (It was, however, included in the Crewe Homicide Investigation Review of 2014.)

Neazor's opinion was, to put it mildly, a very conservative interpretation of the facts around the finding of the cartridge case. Effectively, he was saying that a jury, unlike the royal commission, would find the four police officers more credible than Graeme Hewson. He also did not think the Priests' evidence regarding the time period in which they saw Hutton was sufficiently strong. (A review of Neazor's decision in 2014 by David Jones QC reached a different conclusion. See the next chapter for a full discussion of this.)

The decision not to prosecute must have been an enormous relief to Hutton, who had been in a kind of twilight zone ever since the roasting by the royal commission. Both the decision not to prosecute and the secrecy about the reasons caused bitterness among the Thomas family and others, who wanted to see Hutton held accountable. It also encouraged speculation about yet another cover-up. Some blamed the government, but McLay points out that as minister of justice he could not direct Neazor on the matter, and it would have been improper to do so.

For Len Johnston, it was academic. There were rumours of a death-bed confession — McLay is adamant they were just that.[21]

CHAPTER TWELVE
INTEREST REKINDLED

A few weeks after Arthur Thomas was released from jail, a young, dark-haired woman stepped nervously off a bus outside the Mercer shops, just across the river from the Thomas farm at Pukekawa. Jenny Cresswell was 21. She had been following the Thomas case on television and in the papers since before she was a teenager. She had always thought Arthur and Vivien Thomas looked like a lovely couple and had found their story very sad.

Despite suffering extreme shyness, when Thomas was pardoned at the end of 1979 Cresswell had plucked up the courage to write to him from her home in Blenheim, sending not just a letter but also 112 red roses, one for each month he had been incarcerated. Among the stacks of mail sent by well-wishers from across the country, Cresswell's efforts naturally stood out. Thomas wrote back.

Soon enough he had invited Cresswell to the Mercer Ferry Road farm, where she arrived in the midst of the celebrations for Ivy Thomas's eightieth birthday. 'I pretty much met Arthur in front of all his family and friends and well wishers . . . absolutely daunting it was,' she recalled in a later interview with author Ian Wishart.[1]

To add to her anxiety, Cresswell received a disappointingly luke-warm welcome from the wider Thomas family. Many of the retrial committee members thought she might be a spy, planted in the lead-up to the royal commission hearings, and wouldn't talk to her. Others were disparaging about the age gap between the two. But 41-year-old Thomas was smitten from the start. In 1981, after the commission wrapped up, Thomas purchased a farm with his compensation money at Ōrini, 60 kilometres south-east of Pukekawa, and the couple moved in together. The land cost $750,000. Thomas employed a sharemilker to look after the cows.

A photograph taken soon after they moved shows a beaming Thomas scooping leaves out of the swimming pool. Cresswell is kneeling at the garden, bare feet, smiling over her shoulder at the camera while she holds a pair of secateurs in her hands. Behind them, a tidy brick house sits above a grassy rise. Within a year, Cresswell gave birth to a baby girl they named Bridgette. Thomas was filled with joy. 'It made me very proud, this little girl in my arms, after all the crap I'd been through.'[2]

But despite Thomas's newfound happiness with Cresswell, the first years of their life together were not entirely an easy time. After the royal commission, an exhausted, elderly Allan Thomas had suggested his son share his compensation payout with his siblings and parents, in recognition of the arduous work they had done on the campaign to free him. Thomas refused and stormed out on his father. Their relationship was never the same, causing a rift in the family. Thomas said his siblings were jealous of him. 'Money is the root of all evil,' he told the media when news of the spat reached the papers.[3]

In a flurry of newspaper articles about the feud, Arthur's brother-in-law Buster Stuckey said it was less about the money and more about Thomas's attitude after he was released from jail — 'He thought he was a king and we were to bow down to him' — while Allan Thomas, his father, was reported as saying, 'He never thought about sharing his compensation. And he never really thanked the committee.'[4]

As a result of the feud, Thomas was cut out of his father's will. Young Bridgette rarely saw her grandparents. Instead, Thomas and Cresswell mainly kept their heads down, working on the farm in Ōrini and raising

Arthur Thomas met Jenny Cresswell, 20 years his junior, after she wrote to him in prison, sending not just a letter but also 112 red roses. They were soon married, and had a baby daughter.

their daughter. Later, they spent weekends in the Coromandel, at a bach they bought in Cooks Beach. They travelled overseas, made new friends and took up hobbies, Jenny enjoying photography and Arthur flying microlight planes. When asked by a journalist why he chose that, of all pastimes, Thomas replied, 'Freedom.'[5]

B ack in Pukekawa, the focus on the murders faded. The Crewe farmhouse briefly became something of a tourist attraction, particularly after the movie adaptation of David Yallop's book was released in 1980, but largely people stopped talking about the killings. The open hostility common between neighbours during the height of the campaign became a rarity, but beneath the civility, old wounds festered.[6] Although Arthur Thomas had been formally pardoned, police weren't looking to charge anyone else with the crime. They still believed they had the right man, and some of the community continued to agree with them. For everyone else, there remained the question: If Arthur Thomas wasn't responsible for killing Harvey and Jeannette Crewe, who was?

By 1990, the case had been the subject of seven judicial hearings, six books, hundreds of newspaper articles and one feature film. The story had attracted international investigators; it was also a magnet for local amateurs — for example, in 1971, a writer named Robert W. Coombridge had attended the first trial wearing a blond wig and dark glasses and had pretended to be a police officer while making his inquiries under the alias Robert J. Williams.[7]

The case became an obsession for many who worked on it and changed the careers of others: *Auckland Star* deputy editor Terry Bell had quit his role at the paper in order to write the book *Bitter Hill* in 1972; Pat Booth shot to national fame for his detective work with scientist Jim Sprott. Ironically, Booth's work was published in the same newspaper that refused to let Bell campaign for Thomas, an editor telling him: 'It is not the role of the newspapers to attempt to try the courts.'[8]

And yet, despite all the attention, after 20 years the list of possible murder suspects remained unchanged. There was Len Demler, the focus of the initial police investigation; John Eyre, about whom Kevin

Ryan had made pointed suggestions at the second trial; and there was Jeannette Crewe, suggested last-minute by Paul Temm at the first trial in his murder–suicide theory in which she killed her husband, and then herself.

During their campaign, Pat Booth and Jim Sprott had endorsed Temm's original murder–suicide idea. Booth believed that on the eve of their wedding anniversary, Harvey and Jeannette had argued over money. Harvey struck Jeannette a heavy blow, Booth said, hard enough to cause a broken nose and jaw, causing her to lose six teeth. In Booth's theory, Jeannette then went and got a rifle and shot Harvey. Needing help to clean up, she called her father, Len Demler, who put Harvey's body in the river with the axle. They cleaned up the bloodstains in the house and burnt a bloodstained mat and cushion in the fireplace.

Over the next few days, Jeannette nursed her injury and grew desperate, realising she faced a murder charge. Some time over the weekend, she shot herself. Then, Booth said, Demler came back, got rid of his daughter's body and the gun, and faked finding the baby in the bloodstained house. In Booth's scenario, the woman seen in the front garden by Roddick was Jeannette, and she fed the baby. 'It was Jeannette who got the child out of the cot and took her into the fresh air from where she had been imprisoned in the bedroom,' Booth surmised in a television documentary in 1994.[9]

Booth's theory held some sway until 1992, when Len Demler died, leaving behind his second wife, Norma. In 1994, the 'Inside New Zealand' documentary series ran a two-part feature on the Crewe murders. The producers managed to get almost all the main players in the case to talk, including Arthur Thomas, Vivien Thomas — now Vivien Harrison — and Bruce Hutton. Thomas was interviewed on his farm, still seeming incredulous at the idea he could have ever been involved.

Hutton, meanwhile, gave the cameras a tour of Pukekawa. He was resolute. Thomas was the killer. 'I'm quite satisfied if I don't make any further progress on this homicide during my life, I'm quite sure a higher authority will make progress,' he said. 'But I don't know whether Arthur will be going to the same place as me.' He gave a little smile. He was speaking while he drove, the Pukekawa fields rushing past outside.

The documentary also asked its interviewees who they thought was responsible. Vivien said: 'I believe Len got rid of the bodies. I do.' Arthur Thomas said there must have been multiple people, given Harvey's weight. 'It's a plan, a family plan I think, two or three persons involved.' And then David Lange appeared on screen, leaning on a wall outside the Auckland High Court. 'I would not presume to know who killed the Crewes,' he said. 'If you'd asked me while he was alive I might have been man enough to say Demler. But now he's gone it would be a bit rough to put the boot in.'[10] It was a typically mischievous line from the artful Lange: if he'd given that answer while Demler was alive he would have likely faced a lawsuit. But you can't defame the dead, and Lange knew this.

In 2001, journalist Chris Birt stepped into the void left by Len Demler's death. He published *The Final Chapter*, the first book to openly argue for Demler's guilt. Birt, as a former news reporter at the *Bay of Plenty Times* in Tauranga, had followed the Crewe murders since the beginning, but became more deeply involved in the story after reporting on the retrial committee's campaign during 1976. Convinced of Thomas's innocence, he began spending his days off in Pukekawa, developing a strong respect for Allan Thomas as he struggled to free his son.

Birt's book relied on hundreds of documents obtained under the Official Information Act from the police file, such as officers' notebook entries and conference minutes, as well as 25 years of research and interviews. The case Birt laid out built on the theory that police had formed during the initial four months of the inquiry: that Len Demler had killed his daughter and son-in-law over money and property in a bid to gain back control over his late wife May Demler's estate. As evidence, Birt again highlighted the bloodstain in Demler's car, and Demler's odd behaviour after the murders, such as leaving Rochelle in her cot while he went to call the trucking company.

But Birt had new information, too. He said May's signature on her last will was forged; that Demler had access to the Chennells estate rifle, which could have fired the murder bullets; that Demler was seen, by a farm worker, on horseback at the riverbank dumping the bodies. Most dramatically, Birt said he knew the identity of the woman who fed Rochelle. He didn't name the woman in the book, for fear of a defamation suit.[11]

In early 2006, yet another television documentary aired about the Crewe case on TV One's *Sunday* programme, this one featuring Des Thomas, Arthur's younger brother. It prompted more activity, including from Pat Booth, who wrote an article defending his murder–suicide theory in the *Listener,* where he persisted with his theories: 'Jeannette garaged the family car originally seen parked alongside the house. She — and probably her father — moved stock and fed the farm dogs over those days.'[12] Around the same time, Chris Birt sent a private dossier of his evidence to police, naming the mystery woman as Norma Demler (née Thomas — but no relation to the Pukekawa Thomas family), Len Demler's second wife.

Birt provided witness statements that Norma had known Demler for longer than she had admitted publicly, and that she was around before May Demler had died. Police undertook a formal interview with Norma Demler, with detectives visiting her Auckland home to take her statement, but she denied being the mystery woman. She said she had known Len Demler for some years because her brother, Brian Thomas, had married Demler's sister, Noelene, in 1952.

She said her first visit to Pukekawa was following May Demler's death, when she had travelled to help Len Demler by cooking for the shearers. 'In attempting to isolate her first visit to a specific date, Mrs Demler stated that she remembered she'd observed signage on the Tūākau bridge, while en route to Pukekawa, which read "Arthur Allan Thomas framed".' Police wrote to Birt that this meant she could not have been there before the murders.[13]

Birt wasn't the first to suspect Norma Demler of being the killer's accomplice. Rumours had been swirling in Pukekawa since April 1972, when she and Len Demler married. (Her first marriage had ended in 1965.) In mid-May that year, Arthur Thomas's younger brother Richard decided to visit Bruce Roddick, the labourer who had made the sighting of the woman in the paddock on the Friday after the Crewes disappeared, and took him to have a look at Norma. At the time, the retrial committee was gearing up to present a second petition to the governor-general seeking a new trial. 'I was by then somewhat desperate to gather evidence that would result in the freeing of my brother and the clearing of my family name,' Richard Thomas said.[14]

He told Roddick that defence lawyer Kevin Ryan knew about the plan. The pair went in Richard's car to Sharpe Road, Pukekawa, which ran alongside Len Demler's property. Roddick said they waited for about five minutes for Demler's car to arrive at the house. Demler got out of the passenger seat and a woman got out of the driver's seat. Roddick estimated the pair were a good hundred yards away, but he said the woman he saw was of the same height and build as the first woman he'd seen at the Crewes' property after the murders, although this woman's hair was a little darker, he said.

Roddick said he told this to Richard Thomas, who said he'd tell Kevin Ryan. Richard Thomas remembered this incident differently: he said Roddick had gone further, that he'd told him that Norma Demler was the same woman he'd seen that day in the paddock. They'd had binoculars, and Roddick had looked through them for a long time, he said.

Richard's version of events was backed by retrial committee chair Malcolm McArthur, a local Pukekawa man and friend of Arthur Thomas, who'd spoken to Roddick and Richard about the sighting straight afterwards, when they turned up at his house. But, if Roddick did indeed say that to Thomas and McArthur, he changed his mind overnight, because when Roddick met Ryan to go through his statement for the court the next day, he only said it was 'possibly' the woman, not that he was sure. Kevin Ryan instructed Roddick to go back and check again.[15]

In the meantime, the police had also caught wind of this new information, most likely from the Sunday papers, which both ran stories on 28 May 1972 claiming that Roddick had identified the mystery woman. On 1 June 1972, Roddick got in a car with Detective Inspector Bruce Hutton and Detective Len Johnston and drove to the Demlers' home in the east Auckland suburb of Howick. Roddick remained in the car with Hutton as Norma Demler walked out of the house and had a short conversation with Johnston. As a result, Roddick made a further statement through his lawyer. 'She is certainly not the person I saw on 19 June 1970,' he said. Roddick wasn't asked about the sighting at the Court of Appeal or the second trial.[16]

By 1977, Bruce Roddick was fed up with dealing with the police and lawyers and the courts and moved to Australia. But he still couldn't escape the endless questions about the Crewes. In November that year, while researching his book *Beyond Reasonable Doubt?*, David Yallop sent a psychic named June Donaghie to visit Roddick at home. Donaghie presented Roddick with 16 photographs, asking him to compare them to the woman he'd seen seven years before. Donaghie reported back to Yallop that Roddick had selected two photographs. About the first one he said, 'That's her', positive it was the woman he'd seen on the Crewes' property. About the second, he said the woman was wearing the same clothes and standing in the same way as the woman he'd seen. Roddick initialled the back of these two photographs.[17]

When Yallop sent his letter to Rob Muldoon, as part of his published book, he included one of the photos Roddick had picked, but Yallop said the woman in the photo was Jeannette Crewe's sister, Heather Souter. Yallop did not mention the second photo, which was of a Scottish woman who'd allegedly never been to New Zealand.

That incident was part of what sparked Muldoon to commission the review by barrister Robert Adams-Smith into the conviction of Thomas in 1978, just ahead of the general election (Yallop also identified Norma Demler as a person of interest). However, when Adams-Smith questioned Roddick in 1978, Roddick told him that at no stage had he recognised any person in a photograph as being one and the same as the woman he had seen on Friday 19 June 1970.

Adams-Smith reported back that Roddick 'absolutely denied that he told Yallop's representative that he positively identified any woman'. Adams-Smith concluded there was no basis to suspect that Norma Demler was involved; however, due to a lack of information from overseas agencies about flights and immigration, he recommended that further enquiries be made into the whereabouts of Heather Souter at the time of the murders.

Souter was later verified as being in the United States at the time of the murders. She had flown into Auckland six days later.

Bruce Roddick died in 1990, aged 45. After his death, his family remained angry at his treatment by police, who had publicly attacked Roddick's credibility and his intelligence, even though all he'd wanted to do from the start was to help.[18]

At the same time that Chris Birt was making his case against Norma Demler, police were landed with another set of allegations against a different suspect. In December 2006, Arthur Thomas's younger brother Desmond, known as Des, sent by mail a 100-page folder of evidence he had gathered to Police Commissioner Howard Broad. Thomas's information related to the man he believed killed the Crewes: John Eyre. Eyre was known to his family as Johnny but the media and the Thomas family had always referred to him as Mickey — a macabre echo of the name of the horse allegedly ridden by the man convicted of murdering his grandfather (see Chapter 1).

Des Thomas's claims were at least the third time members of his family had made accusations about John Eyre — they had also appeared on television twice, implying that he was the murderer; once on the current affairs show *60 Minutes* in 2001 and once on *Sunday* earlier that year. Des Thomas even sent a letter to Prime Minister Helen Clark stating the police were conspiring to conceal the identity of the Crewe murder by refusing to investigate the family's concerns. Because there had been no political intervention, that conspiracy was now escalating, Des Thomas told Howard Broad.[19]

When Arthur Thomas was arrested in 1972, Des was 18 years old and still living at home. As the campaign to free his brother was waged, he'd begun undertaking investigations of his own. He had joined his older brother, Richard, and his brother-in-law, Buster Stuckey, in tracking down potential witnesses, interviewing people, and collecting evidence and affidavits. He had also paid police official fees to retrieve documents from the Crewe file. In a second letter to Broad, Thomas argued some of the same points that Kevin Ryan had raised at the second trial — that Eyre was violent, that he had been seen out late at night alone and that he had a motive. He said Eyre was owed money by the Crewes, who had refused to pay him for a job because he mowed the wrong paddock.

The Eyre gun was central to his allegations. The .22 pump-action Remington rifle was initially unable to be excluded as the murder weapon after tests in 1970 by Donald Nelson. At the royal commission, it was discovered that Nelson's tests were wrong and the gun could be excluded because it had five lands and grooves, not the six found on the murder bullets. But Des Thomas wasn't convinced by the commission's ballistics expert. He argued the gun's barrel must have been switched after the killings. He petitioned the police to examine the Remington gun again, which they did in early 2006. There was no evidence that changes had been made to the barrel of the rifle, police said.

Des Thomas, however, refused to give up. He wanted police to take John Eyre's fingerprints and compare them to the unidentified prints in the house, and to consider fresh affidavits from Pukekawa locals and the Thomas family and friends that he had collected about the axle possibly being connected to the Eyre property. 'This needs to be actioned now, in order for justice being seen to be done,' Des Thomas wrote. The police did not respond to these requests. He wrote again in June 2007, and then again three months later, submitting more evidence. Police placed his letters on the Crewe file but did not investigate the claims further.[20]

I n July 2010, on the eve of the fortieth anniversary of the Crewe murders, a ghost from the past appeared on the pages of an article in *North & South* magazine written by Chris Birt. Vivien Harrison had decided the time was right to re-enter the discussions about the case. She had been quietly watching the narrative unfold from Perth, Australia, since her departure from New Zealand in 1979. At the time of the pardon, the media had tried to find her, Harrison said, but she had a new life and a new job and didn't want to be found. For 20 years she stayed out of the limelight.

But in 2010, when journalist Chris Birt phoned to see if she wanted to return to Pukekawa for the anniversary, her instinct told her this was the time. She posed for a *North & South* photographer wearing a blue scarf and black sweatshirt, still with her trademark pixie haircut and determined tilt of the chin, outside the home where she had lived with Arthur Thomas, the scene of the worst time in her life. Harrison knew who the mystery woman was, she told Birt. The magazine didn't name her suspect, but it's clear that, like Birt, Harrison believed it was Norma Demler. The woman should come forward, Harrison said, so the murders could be solved.[21]

When asked about Detective Inspector Bruce Hutton, Harrison admitted feeling bitter towards him for a long time, particularly after the royal commission's findings about the planting of the cartridge case. 'I find it really difficult to believe that an intelligent man like him could have done what he did,' she said. But she said she knew Hutton would not change his mind. 'He has convinced himself Arthur did these terrible things and, according to the findings of the royal commission, fiddled things to prove it. Hutton will go to his grave saying Arthur did it . . . There is no way of dealing with someone like him.'

Harrison told Birt she hadn't spoken to Arthur Thomas since their divorce, but there was something she wanted the public of New Zealand to know. 'I never deserted Arthur. Had that been the case, I would not be here, saying what I'm saying now. What I did was end my marriage to Arthur. But I did not desert him. I know Arthur did not kill those people and I will declare his innocence until the day I die.'[22]

During her trip to New Zealand, Harrison wrote a letter to then Minister of Justice Simon Power asking him to appoint an independent investigator into the Crewe case. She asked him to do whatever it took to identify the woman, because it wasn't her, she said. Power declined the request.[23]

Vivien Harrison died of cancer at her home in Australia a year later. Her uncle Pat Vesey said she never got over the accusations against her or Arthur Thomas. 'It never gave her a minute's peace.'[24]

In 2010, Arthur Thomas believed the anniversary of the Crewe deaths was the right time to tell his story, too. He and Jenny had contacted former television journalist Ian Wishart, owner and editor of *Investigate* magazine, who also had a small publishing company. Wishart, a skilled investigator with an incisive mind and a conspiracy bent, decided to undertake a full review of the case at the same time as writing up his interviews with Thomas. He collated all the paperwork available, spending hours using the microfiche at the library to read old newspaper articles on the Crewe murders. He also travelled to Pukekawa and interviewed some of the key witnesses, and discovered some alleged new witnesses of his own. His book *The Inside Story*, part-investigation, part-profile, was released in September that year.

In unpicking the evidence, Wishart poured ice-cold water on the idea that Len Demler could have been responsible. Demler's strange, shambling behaviour after the murders didn't match the personality of someone who could kill two people and remove their bodies without leaving so much as a fingerprint of evidence, Wishart said.[25] Equally, May Demler's will was not the smoking gun the police had hoped it would be. Demler could keep his share of the farm until he died, unless Harvey and Jeannette bought him out, in which case he would have profited well.

Wishart therefore rejected Chris Birt's suggestion that it was Norma Demler who fed the baby (although he also didn't outright name her either, she was still a shadow at this stage). It was very unlikely she would have helped her new partner get away with murder, Wishart said, and in any case, when Bruce Roddick was presented with that set of photographs in 1977, Norma was among them. He didn't choose her.[26]

Wishart developed a theory of his own. He said Len Johnston, who came up with the louvre reconstruction, and traced the axle evidence, may have killed the Crewes. Johnston had a reputation as a 'dirty cop' who was 'physically violent and prone to making death threats', he wrote. Johnston could have planted evidence of his own to frame Arthur Thomas, including the axle and the stubs.

Wishart speculated that after Johnston had attended the burglary at the Crewes' house in 1967, he had worked out it was an insurance job and used it to blackmail the couple. According to Wishart's theory, that's what caused Jeannette to be afraid of being in the house alone. He suggested Johnston may have also been responsible for the two fires, and that he killed the Crewes when they wouldn't do what he wanted. In a final twist of the knife, Wishart said Johnston could have sexually assaulted Jeannette. However, Wishart also admitted his theory was 'entirely speculative' and that there was no evidence for his assertions.[27]

Despite this, Wishart was certain of one point: that the killing was personal, committed by someone with a deep animosity towards Harvey and Jeannette. 'It wasn't just that someone walked up to the house and killed them,' he wrote. Wishart believed that the case was capable of being solved. 'The final chapter hasn't been written,' he said in an interview in 2022.[28]

Police immediately moved to rubbish Wishart's claims. Bruce Hutton said he'd 'never heard anything like it'. Police Association

President Greg O'Connor refused to even read the book. 'I won't encourage scurrilous rubbish. You've got to ask what this guy's on,' he told the *New Zealand Herald*.[29]

But the police were about to be completely trumped. Someone intimately connected to the case, who had read Wishart's book and had also been reading commentary around it written by former police officer Ross Meurant,[30] agreed that Wishart's theory was plausible. Together with Meurant, she approached the *New Zealand Herald*, which assigned crime reporter Jared Savage to the story. On 14 October 2010, the newspaper ran a front-page story: 'Crewe murders: "Who killed Mum and Dad?" asks daughter'. The subheading ran: 'She was just a baby when her parents, Jeannette and Harvey, were murdered, only metres from her cot. For five days someone fed her. Today — for the first time in 40 years — Rochelle Crewe breaks her silence to ask police to reopen the case.'[31]

The story came as a shock to almost everyone who had been following the case. For 40 years Rochelle Crewe had maintained complete anonymity, even as an adult when reporters began to track her down and ask for interviews. The public record of her life was scant: when her grandfather Len Demler discovered the 'terrible bloody mess' in the farmhouse on 22 June 1970, he had placed her with family friend Barbara Willis. Rochelle stayed there for a time, before a Family Court case decided who would get custody. Both her grandmother Marie Crewe and her father's sister, Beverly Turner, wanted to adopt her, as did her mother's sister, Heather Souter. Rochelle initially stayed with Marie Crewe, attending St Cuthbert's College in Auckland, and then spent time in the United States with Souter before settling in the South Island and eventually raising a family of her own.

Rochelle, by then aged 41, refused to be photographed for the story or to use her new surname, but she told the *Herald* she had written to Police Commissioner Howard Broad a few weeks earlier, asking that he reopen the case and end the speculation that had been allowed to 'fester' since Arthur Thomas had been pardoned. Crewe said she had been intending to approach Broad for some time but the catalyst had been the 'pervasive corruption' exposed by Ian Wishart's book. She said she did not agree with the decision of Solicitor-General Paul Neazor not to lay charges against Bruce Hutton and Len Johnston. It concerned her, and she wanted to know more about that decision. 'Lastly, I just want to know who killed my mum and dad.'[32]

What the *Herald* didn't report was Rochelle Crewe's other motivation: clearing her family's name. For years, she felt, suspicion had unfairly fallen on her grandfather and grandmother, their names dragged through the mud.

Within a week of Rochelle Crewe coming forward, the police announced they would be reviewing the Crewe case; however, they would not be reinvestigating the crimes. Instead, police would conduct a 'thorough analysis of the file' in response to Rochelle Crewe's questions. A senior investigator, Detective Superintendent Andrew Lovelock, and a small experienced team had been appointed and a terms of reference outlined.

Rochelle again spoke to the *Herald*, saying that the refusal to open a new inquiry was no more than a 'continuation of police seeking to avoid the truth', and that she felt police were trying to protect their image. 'I feel it is not adequate enough to just review what has already been done, as this may not be a wide enough net to capture what was previously left out of the original investigation, as well as a failure to examine all evidence that was available to them at the time,' she said.[33]

If the police, and Rochelle Crewe, hoped the inquiry would dampen speculation about the murders, that hope was swiftly deflated. In June 2011, Chris Birt wrote another cover story for *North & South*, this time openly naming Norma Demler as the mystery woman. Titled 'Who Fed The Baby?' the cover carried an image of baby Rochelle in her overalls and promises of damning new revelations. The magazine had taken a paparazzi shot of Norma Demler in a grey knit blouse, sweeping the front step at her home with clearly no idea the photo was being taken.

The article also carried a quote from her after she was confronted about her alleged involvement in the murders in 2006: 'It's not true,' she told journalist Donna Chisholm. 'I had nothing whatsoever to do with it. I have a clear conscience. I can put my head on the pillow at night and go to sleep.'[34]

Birt interviewed former policeman Ross Meurant for the article. Meurant told him his superiors at the time, including Hutton, had believed Len Demler had been in the Crewe house well before the police were called, that he had attended to his granddaughter Rochelle and that he had probably been accompanied by his new female partner. 'There was considerable discussion about a woman being involved in providing care to Rochelle and deductions that Demler's woman friend was implicated,' Meurant said. His impressions, he said, were formed during the evening police conferences held during the inquiry. The conference records that are available, however, have no mention of Norma Eastman, later Demler.

As a counter to Norma Demler's assertion that she had first gone to Pukekawa after the murders, Birt wrote about two people, Len Demler's other sister, Beryl Dick, and a trustee of Harvey Crewe's estate, Colin Harvey, who both said she had been in Pukekawa some months prior to the murders. Colin Harvey told Birt that Norma was present when there were meetings regarding the Crewe estate after the killings. Beryl Dick said Norma had first gone to cook for the shearers for Len Demler when May Demler was sick in the nursing home. When asked for an interview by Birt, Norma Demler declined. Her daughter told him: 'My mother has no wish to ever discuss this matter with you.'[35]

In January 2012, the director and filmmaker Keith Hunter published his book *The Case of the Missing Bloodstain*. Its subtitle, 'Inside an incompetent and corrupt police inquiry, the truth of the Crewe murders', made Hunter's stance evident. Hunter had initially planned to work with Birt on a television documentary but it had failed to get funding, and then the pair had fallen out, Hunter citing creative differences. His book relies heavily on Birt's extraction of documents from the police file, and from Archives New Zealand, where the royal commission records are held; some, such as the commission chair's correspondence, are still restricted until 2040.

Hunter's theory was also rooted in the belief that Len Demler was the killer, but he had a few new twists. His central argument was that Bruce Hutton faked finding the axle. Rather, he planted it, along with the stub axles. Hunter contended the evidence was intended to be used against Len Demler, but was instead used against Thomas after Hutton came under pressure to make an arrest. He laid out the timeline of the investigation, and the switch in suspects from Demler to Thomas as described in the police conference reports.

He suggested that Hutton found the axle and its stubs in a shed behind Demler's property, and that on the day Harvey Crewe's body was found, he secretly concealed the axle in the bottom of the boat under some black polythene, which is pictured in the official police photographs. Before Crewe's body was removed, Hunter said Hutton had used a small pair of wire cutters to sever a piece of wire on the underside of the body's torso, allowing him to infer the wire had broken. He then dropped the axle over the side of the boat, shielding it with the polythene, where it was found by a diver.

Hunter said while the theory might seem 'unjustifiably fanciful', the marks on the axle proved it was fake. He said that careful study of the photographs showed that the wire marks did not correspond with the axle hanging vertically under the body. Therefore, he said, they must have been scratched on by someone. And therefore the axle was planted.[36]

H unter beat his former collaborator Chris Birt to the printing press. Birt's second book on the case, *All the Commissioner's Men*, was published in May 2012. Less a whodunnit — Birt still believed the killer was Len Demler — the book was more a critique of the police behaviour during the murder investigation and afterwards. Birt argued that the police were still hiding evidence. For example, he wrote, the royal commission had seen 5000 documents from the Crewe file, but in total there were 50,000. He had gained access to some of that material, and had painstakingly examined it, finding small pieces of evidence he argued were deliberately suppressed by police even during the commission inquiry: a mention on one file that the milk on the bench in the Crewes' kitchen on 22 June was fresh; that there was a second sighting of the child in the paddock the same day as the first; that there was a sighting of a woman driving the Crewe car on Thursday 18 June.[37]

Birt said he also uncovered more evidence about the so-called Chennells rifle, a gun he says belonged to May Demler's father, Newman Chennells, and then to her brother, Howard, before his death in 1950. The gun was a 'combination' rifle, part .410 shotgun, part .22, Birt wrote. Two witnesses told police they had seen the gun at the Crewe farm when it belonged to Howard Chennells. When Chennells died, Demler took the gun to his house. Birt also explained that the police had the two statements about the gun by the end of 1970 which were not raised at either trial, despite defence questioning. During the first trial, Demler said he couldn't find the gun, and that it was missing. Birt said that police tracked it down before the second trial, but again did not disclose this to the defence.

With regard to the trailer axle, Birt's theory was that the axle found with Harvey Crewe's body was not from the Thomas trailer at all. He claimed that the Thomas axle didn't have any welding when it went to engineer Roderick Rasmussen's shop and was never returned to the farm. He also contended that there was a second axle being 'hocked around' for identification purposes but that the defence was never told about that either.

Perhaps Birt's most sensational claim was about the deceased detective Len Johnston. He alleged — on the basis of a story told to him by an unnamed person — that Johnston had made a deathbed confession to an Anglican minister, the Reverend Michael Houghton, about his involvement in planting the cartridge case in the garden. Houghton had then passed that information on to Robert Muldoon. Birt did acknowledge, however, he had been unable to verify the story.[38]

Birt's book was the last substantial piece of work to come out before the police carrying out their review of the Crewe investigation completed their report. But the intervening years were not without drama. In April 2013, Bruce Hutton died in Middlemore Hospital, aged 83. At Hutton's funeral, Deputy Commissioner Mike Bush praised him and said he was known for having 'integrity beyond reproach'.[39] The outrage was swift. Bush agreed to step aside from the review process to avoid any possible perception of a conflict of interest. He later said he regretted his decision to make a speech.

Friends and family of Hutton's said it was a shame he did not live to see the review findings released, but at least, they said, he got a chance to have his say. This is because, before Hutton died, he was interviewed by Detective Inspector Andrew Lovelock, who was leading the police review. Lovelock reportedly asked Hutton if he had any regrets, or if there was anything he could have done differently. Hutton said: 'No, I've got my man.'[40]

CHAPTER THIRTEEN
SHORTFALLS

When the group of detectives began the review of the Crewe file in late 2010, they hoped it would take under a year to complete.[1] The terms of reference required the team to gather the trial transcripts, read the documents from the 1980 commission hearing, and go back through the original investigation file. The officers were then to copy the material into an electronic format, assess it, and identify whether any new avenues of inquiry could be explored by police. They were also asked to review any new information, and again decide if it required further investigation. The head of the review team, Andy Lovelock, was a very senior member of the police executive. He had also worked on the 2004 Commission of Inquiry into Police Conduct, an investigation into how police had dealt with sexual assault complaints against officers.

At the beginning the task seemed a rather dry, paper-based assignment — a lot of time sitting at a screen, reading. Rapidly, however, the team realised they were not facing a quick desk job. The documents and evidence they gathered ran to 90,000 pages even before they took into account the stack of books and newspaper articles about the case. The historic nature of the information meant even small tasks could take months.

For example, at one point, a detective tried to find any known burglars who had been operating in the Pukekawa area at the time of the murders. She spent hours in the basement of the Auckland Central police station, trawling through 'fingerprint books' that documented crimes and arrests. Some of the books were illegible, due to fire and water damage; the books for the Pukekawa area could not be located. When the police *were* able to identify offenders from the files, they sometimes spent weeks tracking them down, only to find they were dead.[2]

Where witnesses were still alive, often they were elderly or unwell. The detectives found memories had faded or had become distorted with time and their recollections were often substantially different to what they had said during the original investigation. Police put this down to the fallibility of human memory, but also to what they called the 'misinformation effect', in which the original memory becomes impaired by related or misleading information. But, equally, they noted the statements obtained by police in 1970 were not necessarily in the subject's own words in the first place, but rather in 'police narrative'. This statement style used leading questioning, with only the answers recorded, meaning there was much less accuracy and detail than in modern interviews.

Further, because in 1970 police officers did their own typing, their paperwork was usually as brief as possible. As a result, witness statements and police jobsheets lacked detail. As the review team spoke to more people, it became apparent that not all of the inquiries undertaken by the police in 1970 had been recorded, or, if they had, the records had been lost over time. Even the court transcripts were not wholly reliable — some had inaccuracies, likely the result of typing errors, and were sometimes missing responses to questions.[3]

Sometimes, police would follow 'new' information only to find it wasn't true. In one instance in 2011, two of the detectives, Gary Lendrum and Veronica McPherson, visited a husband and wife who had given information to Ian Wishart for his book. The pair had claimed that the brake lines of the Crewes' car had been cut in early 1969, soon after the house fire. Ian Wishart claimed this was evidence of a prior murder attempt. Jeannette Crewe had apparently told the wife about the brakes when the pair became friends while in the maternity ward together. The woman also claimed they had arranged to have a fish-and-chip dinner with the Crewes on the night they were killed, but on the morning of Wednesday 17 June it had been cancelled.

But when police arrived at the couple's home in 2011, the husband was not happy to see them. The wife initially hid from them at the back of the house. After investigating the woman's claims further, the officers decided it was possible that the woman was confused, but more likely that she had made the story up.[4]

By 2013, the review team was still reinterviewing key witnesses and had met several members of the Thomas family, including Arthur's brothers Des and Richard, his sister and brother-in-law Margaret and Buster Stuckey, and Arthur himself. Lendrum and Lovelock undertook these interviews. Arthur Thomas was no longer the naive young man eager to help the police he had been back in 1970. He declined to participate in a formal interview; Peter Williams QC told the team that Thomas did not believe he could add anything but he did speak to Lovelock and Lendrum informally.

Thomas later told Des that Lovelock and Lendrum asked him several questions about Buster Stuckey, including whether Stuckey went out rabbit shooting at night on his own.[5] In October 1970, Thomas had told Bruce Hutton that Buster Stuckey had the same access to items on the Thomas farm as he did. Police did not formally interview Stuckey at the time; he and his wife had demanded a lawyer be present, at the insistence of Stuckey's parents, and police had seemingly lost interest in them after that.

In 2013, a few days after their visit to Arthur Thomas, Lovelock and Lendrum arrived at the Stuckey household in Tūākau. Margaret Stuckey was surprised to see them, but let them in. She later told journalist Anna Leask of the *Herald* that, once inside, Lovelock had looked out at the view of the Waikato River from her living room and had said, 'Oh, you can see where Jeannette Crewe came out of the river from here.' Then Lendrum said, 'Did you know it's 43 years to the day that Jeannette Crewe's body was retrieved from the river?' 'It was a horrible thing to say,' Stuckey told Leask.[6]

The detectives quizzed Buster Stuckey about whether he'd worked for the Crewes, suggesting that he had argued with Harvey Crewe over a fencing job. They also asked the Stuckeys about the time they had looked after Thomas's house while Arthur and Vivien were away

SHORTFALLS   231

on holiday in April and May 1970, and about their Christian faith. Margaret Stuckey was furious. 'I know what they were thinking . . . But long before the Crewes were murdered, as a child, I was interested in Jesus. It had nothing to do with the Crewes.'

Later that week, Gary Lendrum phoned back and asked Buster Stuckey directly for an alibi. 'He asked me where I was on the night of the murder . . . He rang back the next day and asked again. I said, "You listen to me and listen real bloody good. If you carry on this way there will be a harassment charge against you." That was the finish, that was my answer,' Stuckey told Anna Leask. After that, the couple told the police they would communicate with them only if a lawyer was present. Margaret Stuckey said she didn't feel the need to justify herself to the police after what they'd done to her brother.[7]

Des and his brother Richard Thomas, however, did agree to speak with the review team. Richard, who had moved away from Pukekawa by the time of the inquiry, also provided the police with his diaries and tape recordings that described his own investigations into the murders, beginning in 1970. Back then, as well as taking Bruce Roddick to spy on Norma Demler, he had led a search along the side of Highway 22 near the Eyre property for evidence about the axle, even mowing the grass and cutting blackberry. After the interview, the police took his gun for testing. It had been collected in 1970, but it was unclear whether it had been tested at that time, police said.[8]

Des Thomas attempted to go through the evidence he and Richard and Buster Stuckey had collected over the 40 years since the murders. But the police still weren't interested in pursuing his theory that John Eyre was the killer, he told the *Herald*, or looking into the unidentified fingerprints he believed were on the file. The detectives told the Thomases that the physical evidence still pointed to Arthur Thomas's former farm.[9]

On 30 July 2014, police called a press conference at the Manukau police station to announce that the Crewe Homicide Investigation Review report had been completed. As the cameras rolled, four people walked into the room and sat at a trestle table placed in front of a huge photo of Jeannette and Harvey Crewe on their wedding day. First was Rochelle Crewe's lawyer, Natalie Walker; followed by lawyer David Jones QC, who had provided independent oversight to the review team; Deputy Commissioner Grant Nicholls, in full police uniform; and Detective Superintendent Andy Lovelock, in suit and tie. Before the waiting journalists had a chance to read copies of the report provided, Nicholls delivered the most salient news: police still did not know who had killed the Crewes.[10]

No new evidence had come to light that could implicate any specific person as being responsible for the murders, he said, nor had the review team found any information to prompt a further investigation that could realistically identify the offender.

However, Nicholls said, reading from a sheet in front of him, the report had made several other significant findings. It said the suggestion that Jeannette Crewe committed suicide after murdering Harvey had no basis. There was no credible evidence that Len Demler had been involved in the murder of his daughter and son-in-law. In fact, although back in 1970 Demler's general disposition and the fact he had left Rochelle in her cot after finding her alone in the bloodstained house had given police reason to be suspicious of him, the investigation's focus on him had 'significantly and negatively impacted the breadth of the investigation and led to a loss of objectivity on the part of the 1970 investigation team, specifically, Detective Inspector Hutton'.[11] The report acknowledged that Hutton's decision to ask Demler to identify the Crewes' bodies after they were taken from the river lacked sensitivity and was an unacceptable practice.

The report stated that the team had found no credible evidence to suggest Jeannette Crewe's sister Heather Souter or local farmer John Eyre had anything to do with the murders. It said it was unlikely anyone had fed baby Rochelle. Instead, the report said the killer was someone who had access to items from the farm, namely the wire found around Harvey Crewe's body and the axle that had been previously fitted to Allan Thomas's trailer. Police still believed Thomas's firearm was most likely to have fired the fatal bullets. 'There is significant physical evidence linking the Thomas farm with the murders. However, in the absence of new evidence, police are unable to advance this criminal investigation,' the report read.[12]

For the first time, police now conceded there was a 'distinct possibility' that exhibit 350, the cartridge case, may have been fabricated evidence, and if that were the case, then a member of police would have been responsible. Yet, despite the acknowledgement that corruption may have led to Arthur Thomas's conviction, the report repeated the opinion of Solicitor-General Paul Neazor, who had said in 1981 that there was not enough evidence to support a prosecution against any member of police.[13]

Nicholls said the public could have faith in the review because it had been supervised by David Jones QC, who provided both feedback to the review team throughout the inquiry and produced his own report on its conclusions.

Jones's assessment, a 29-page document, disagreed with the police position on the question of whether to prosecute Bruce Hutton. Jones believed there was ample evidence that exhibit 350, the empty cartridge, had been planted. Firstly, he said, it seemed unlikely that a killer who otherwise seemed prepared and forensically aware would knowingly eject a shell into the garden. Secondly, he said he couldn't imagine that no one had seen the cartridge before it was eventually found. 'It is . . . difficult to comprehend such a vital piece of evidence simply sitting in the garden unseen and unidentified for over four months,' Jones said. Further, the cartridge could not have contained the bullet that killed the Crewes. Jones said that in his opinion those three points meant there was enough evidence to prove to a 'criminal standard' that the cartridge was fabricated.[14]

Jones also gave an explanation of why he thought Hutton might have planted the case. Hutton was under intense pressure, he said. He had focused on the wrong person since the beginning of the inquiry and had tunnel vision about the case. Exhibit 350 was necessary to arrest and convict Arthur Thomas. 'Detective Inspector Hutton had the motive, means and opportunity to plant the shell casing,' Jones said, and, in his view, there was sufficient evidence for a prosecution to have been taken against him. There was not, however, sufficient evidence for a case against Detective Len Johnston.[15]

During the conference, Nicholls made no comment on Jones's findings, but he told the media that he had earlier apologised to Rochelle Crewe. He said police should have reviewed the case sooner. Some aspects of the original investigation were done well, but there were shortfalls, leaving her with 'enduring uncertainty' over the deaths of her parents. Nicholls attributed some of those shortcomings to the era, which he described as 'a time of valve radios and black-and-white televisions'.

'The past is a foreign country where they did things differently,' he said. 'But thanks to the review team's work, we now have the best understanding possible of this case. I hope the review provides Rochelle and her family with peace of mind for the future. I sincerely wish them well.'[16]

In a statement read by her lawyer, Natalie Walker, Rochelle Crewe said she was disappointed by the shortfalls in the original police investigation, and saddened that she would probably never know who killed her parents. However, she was pleased that the review stated her aunt and her grandparents Len and Norma Demler 'were not involved in any way'.[17]

Police did not apologise to Arthur Thomas.

The Crewe Homicide Investigation Review report ran to 328 pages. The technical analysis of the evidence, appendix one, was not released to the public, and was nearly twice as long again. The combined reports were methodical, detailed, fascinating. But they also had some shortcomings. There was a tendency to favour police evidence over the detective work of others, for example, which sometimes had the effect of minimising contradictory accounts. Large sections were — and remain — redacted, usually to protect the privacy of people named, or where the allegations made against them were baseless or defamatory.

But the report did not hold back in highlighting where the original investigation team had gone wrong. It was immediately obvious why police had never responded to Des Thomas's request to re-examine the unidentified fingerprints on the file, for example: the fingerprint lifts, along with the bloodstain samples, had been lost. Indeed, the report noted the lack of forensic awareness throughout the initial investigation. From the outset, the crime scene at the Crewe farmhouse was poorly managed, with numerous people trampling through, causing contamination. Police officers had eaten and discarded their rubbish outside the house, for example, and furniture and other items had been moved before photographs of the interior of the house were taken.[18]

The worst example, the report found, was the mystifying destruction of a piece of material, possibly an oilskin coat, that had been found alongside the Crewe wheelbarrow outside the back door. According to Detective Bruce Parkes' evidence to the royal commission in 1980, the material was definitely at the crime scene on 22 June, the day Len Demler raised the alarm about the bloodstained house, but during a lunch break either the next day or the day after, it apparently accidentally caught on fire when a police officer discarded a still-smouldering cigarette butt.

The royal commission chairperson, Justice Taylor, had said he believed that someone with an interest in the material, rather than the police, was responsible for burning the material. Taylor contended the coat could have been worn by the murderer. The police review said it was likely the material was used to move one or both of the Crewes' bodies, and therefore may have had some connection to the murders and should have been kept secure.

The police missteps didn't end with the lack of care taken at the farmhouse. The report noted the limited number of photographs of both the house and the evidence, the limited fingerprint records and the poor documentation of the efforts to identify the unknown fingerprints. The initial scene reconstructions by Hutton and his team did not fully explore all possible scenarios, and this had led to an 'inadequate' search of the farmhouse and surrounds. Decisions about what was relevant evidence had been left to individual detectives when they should have been sanctioned by the officer in charge of the investigation. When the area canvass was undertaken, householders had not always been required to account for their movements on the night of the murders. When new information had come to light, nothing on the file suggested that the canvassed properties had been revisited, and further questions asked.[19]

Despite the file's limitations, the review team still spent a significant amount of time trying to make sense of the more baffling elements of the crime scene, with varying degrees of success. They never got to the bottom of why the Crewes had no curtains on their living-room windows, for example, or whether the dogs had or had not been fed. They could not work out why the clothes dryer only contained one pair of men's underwear and a pair of socks. Had Harvey Crewe changed to work on the farm and got wet but hadn't wanted to put them through the wash? Possibly, but then surely his pants and shirt would also be wet, and there was no indication of soaked trousers anywhere.

Equally, they wondered, why was the outside light on? What did the offenders use to clean up the blood? What time of day did the Crewes usually collect their bread and milk? The review team was unable to find out.

There were small wins. The team reinvestigated the various witness accounts about the blinds and curtains, and decided the positions remained unchanged for the five days after the murders. A possible sighting of a fire on the Crewe property on 19 June 1970 — an incident that police said had been embellished by media over time into a report of sparks and smoke coming from the chimney — was also explained away. The report had come from an eight-year-old boy whose father told police that he was mistaken and that he believed his son had actually seen lights from a neighbouring township in the distance.

Multiple sightings of cars near the Crewe house after they had disappeared, on the other hand, were unable to be resolved. In particular, two sightings of the Crewes' green 1969 Hillman Hunter on their property after 17 June could not be made sense of, given the car was in the garage by the roadside on 22 June. Similarly, the police could not come to a firm decision about whether the three shots Julie Priest said she heard on the night of 17 June, and reported two months after the murders, were the shots that killed the Crewes. They could have been, the report said, but in that case, where was the third bullet?

Some issues were more straightforward to resolve. In clearing Len Demler, the report said there was no information to indicate that he had access to, or could have gained access to, the wire, gun or the axle. Addressing the allegations against John Eyre, the report found that although there were no records to establish whether or not Eyre's alibi that he was at home on the night of the murders had been fully investigated, equally no evidence suggested that he had access to the wire, gun and axle, despite repeated assertions by the Thomas family.

The report addressed many of the allegations raised against Eyre and various other suspects and investigated by the review team. Its introduction succinctly summarised the team's position on the detective work of amateurs: 'Since the murders, commentators have written a number of books and articles theorising who they believed murdered Harvey and Jeannette . . . None of the theories advanced are able to be substantiated by evidence.'[20]

Yet, the report also indirectly conceded a win to those same amateurs, acknowledging weaknesses in the evidence against Arthur Thomas that were first raised by either the defence team or media. For example, it said a number of people could potentially have gained access to the firearm. It said there was no evidence that Jeannette had moved to Whanganui to get away from Thomas, or that he had maintained an infatuation with her up to 1970. It also acknowledged that Detective Sergeant John Hughes had misled the court by implying that Thomas had been to the Crewe farm while Harvey and Jeannette had been living there, even when he knew that was incorrect.

But unlike Len Demler and John Eyre, the report said the evidence relating to Thomas was not strong enough to clear his name completely. Arthur Thomas was therefore left, once again, with a question mark hanging over his head.

Since the very beginning of the original inquiry, police had grappled with the baffling idea that someone may have been inside the Crewe house after the murders and fed baby Rochelle. Fuelling this theory were the two eyewitness accounts of people at the property after the murder, the dirty nappies strewn around the house, including in Rochelle's cot, and the evidence of medical professionals, some of whom thought her condition suggested she had not spent five days without food. In the review team's report, each of those pieces of evidence was summarily dismissed.

The first witness account was Bruce Roddick's. He told a detective he had seen a tall, fair-haired woman standing outside the Crewe house on the morning of Friday 19 June. The Crewe car was parked at the gate, nearby, he said. Roddick repeated this claim until his death in 1991. However, the report said no one had ever come forward to police claiming to be the woman seen that day, and there was no credible evidence which identified her. The report stated it was difficult to understand why a woman, who was likely connected to the offender, would put herself in a position where she could be seen at the property after the murders but before the crime was discovered. Perhaps Roddick did see a woman, but on a different day, the report surmised.[21]

The report was more dismissive when it came to Queenie McConachie's claim that she had seen a child in overalls in the paddock in front of the house on Friday 19 June. The review team could not reconcile why anyone would have changed Rochelle into different clothes, taken her outside, and then got her changed again. 'To have exposed Rochelle Crewe to public view would have placed the person present at serious risk of being identified as being complicit in the murders,' the report said. It concluded that if a toddler had been in the paddock then it was either not Rochelle or she had been there on a different day.

When it came to the nappies, the review team determined that perhaps Jeannette Crewe was, as the detectives of the 1970s had believed, a poor housekeeper. When Rochelle was found there was a dirty nappy in her cot, two nappies on top of the refrigerator and one on the washing machine, although there was a pre-prepared bucket of NapiSan, used to soak soiled cloth nappies, nearby. The mess could have been construed to suggest that someone other than Jeannette or Harvey may have changed Rochelle, but the team decided to go with the evidence of stock agent John Gracie, who visited the Crewes regularly, and who said that dirty nappies were commonplace in the house.[22]

During the first trial of Arthur Thomas, the police had relied heavily on medical evidence to argue that Rochelle had been fed in those five missing days in June 1970, implying that Vivien Thomas had cared for her. In the second trial, prosecutor David Morris moved to confuse the picture, introducing a second doctor who held an opposing position: Rochelle could have survived without food. The police had two other statements from doctors: again, one on each side. It was an impasse.

In September 2012, the review team engaged Professor Carole Jenny, a professor of paediatrics at the Warren Alpert Medical School of Brown University, in the United States, and a world expert on child abuse, to review all the medical evidence relating to Rochelle. Jenny said that while it was possible that Rochelle could have survived without food or drink, there were particular symptoms, including an increased breathing rate, which those looking after Rochelle would have noticed after she was found.

Among the information she reviewed, one fact stood out: investigators had described Rochelle's cot, mattress and bedding, and a nappy found in her cot, as 'very wet'. 'When children are deprived of fluid, their urine output quickly decreases to almost nothing,' Jenny said. On this basis, she told police she believed Rochelle had been fed. Her condition upon being found was 'clinically incompatible' with complete starvation and lack of fluid for five days.

The review team's analysis of Jenny's findings was that, unlike the medical experts who provided opinions in 1970, Jenny had vast experience of working with abused and neglected children and therefore her findings were more credible. Despite this, in forming their final decision, the team discounted her evidence because she had not examined Rochelle personally. The report said the lack of reported symptoms might have been because in the 1970s neither doctors nor police understood all the clinical signs of dehydration. 'The review team are of the opinion that it is improbable that Rochelle Crewe was fed or provided with fluids after being put to bed on the evening of Wednesday 17 June 1970, and prior to being found on Monday 22 June 1970 in a state of neglect,' the report concluded.[23]

What caused the review team to set aside the evidence suggesting that the killer — and perhaps an acquaintance — returned to the Crewe house? The appendices to the main report hold a clue. The review team commissioned new ballistics reports, wire analysis, fingerprint expertise and pathology advice. And in November 2012, after two years' work, and with the limitations of the historic homicide file made clear, Andy Lovelock also asked for a report from a criminal profiler.

Made famous by movies such as *Silence of the Lambs* and television shows like *Mindhunter*, profiling aims to create a psychological description of a criminal using crime-scene analysis, forensic psychology and behavioural science. Usually, a profiler strives to provide a composite of the offender, with demographic information such as their likely age, ethnic background and marital status through to more specific factors such as their criminal history, possible motive and likely area of residence.

The New Zealand Police internal criminal profiling unit assigned its psychologist Dave Scott to the Crewe file. Scott completed his report in October 2013, with a few caveats: profiling was a fallible process, he said, made more so by the limitations of the aged source information. Nonetheless, he said, the report offered another perspective on the murders. It also, clearly, provided the basis for many of the conclusions in the report about how the Crewes' killer likely thought and behaved.

Before laying out his own theory, Scott first addressed the motive advanced by the original inquiry team. The scenario of Arthur Thomas's unrequited interest in Jeannette Crewe evolving into homicidal jealousy was problematic, he said. Thomas's behaviour was consistent with how young men commonly experienced unrequited love and misinterpreted any discouraging signals. There were no signals suggesting that Thomas's feelings had turned malignant, or that he had become delusional. If he had become a 'morbidly infatuated' stalker, Scott said, there would have been some key behavioural traits, including a lack of past fixations and few relationships. Thomas, on the other hand, had many girlfriends, including sexual relationships.

If Thomas had been morbidly infatuated with Jeannette, he would have contrived opportunities to see her, and reports of people seeing him near the Crewe farm would have been likely. As the infatuation deepened, he would have become increasingly detached from his wife, Vivien, causing 'domestic discord'. Usually, stalkers also attempt to collect mementos from their victims. Scott acknowledged that if Thomas had committed the burglary, then that could be considered such behaviour. But stalkers tend to keep their treasures close, and when Thomas was interviewed by police, he readily handed over a letter to police.

Scott said that if Thomas were the killer, he would have expected him to have been more cautious in response to police inquiries about Jeannette. 'In fact the opposite appears to have occurred. Arthur was happy to talk about Jeannette and was very cooperative with the police,' he wrote.

Conceivably, Scott said, had Thomas finally realised the futility of his love he could have taken Harvey as a target. But again, the expected behaviours hadn't been reported — there was no evidence of emotional deterioration or interpersonal problems for Thomas and his wife. No one had reported any hostility towards the Crewes such as critical comments or nastiness. Nor was there anything to suggest that Thomas pathologically despised Jeannette and Harvey Crewe. 'In my opinion, harbouring such intense, long-standing, and hostile feelings would be hard to hide from others,' he said.[24]

Scott's alternative scenario was based on the assumption that the three prior events — the fires and the burglary — were linked to the Crewe murders. He said given the low prevalence of rural crime in the 1970s, four unrelated and 'significantly adverse' events happening to one farming couple completely confounded the odds. Therefore, he said, there was an escalating, persistent pattern of harm directed at the Crewes. 'In my opinion, Jeannette and Harvey Crewe's fears were well founded. Someone did not like them and their hatred was evolving over time,' Scott said.

Some aspects of the crime scene and witness evidence — Harvey Crewe's weight, and the two pots used to clean up the scene — indicated there was more than one perpetrator, but Scott believed the perpetrator had acted alone. To involve someone else before, during or after the act was too risky, he said.

Equally, he felt McConachie and Roddick must have been mistaken. 'In my opinion, it is very difficult to reconcile why the offender, or an accomplice, would allow themselves or Rochelle to be seen at the Crewe property during daylight hours so soon after the murders. Such acts would significantly increase their risk of being implicated in the crime.'

Furthermore, Scott wrote, overt sightings were inconsistent with the level of 'precautionary effort' the offender had otherwise displayed, such as leaving no bullet casings and shifting the bodies. And other factors at the crime scene argued against someone returning: the milk and bread left untouched, the clothes dryer running, the unmoved curtains, the hungry dogs. And while Professor Jenny's conclusion about whether Rochelle had been fed was sound, it was derived from what he considered 'unreliable' witness information, particularly around the wet nappy and bedding. 'Again this highlights the problems associated with eyewitness information in this case.'

Rather, the killer was likely to be a local, healthy male, possibly single, who didn't have to explain his absence to family, or who perhaps used an activity like the bowls night at Glen Murray as a cover for going out. He wasn't sexually motivated. He used his own car. He was comfortable around rural properties, and perhaps the Crewe property specifically. The direct shots to the head used to kill the Crewes suggested possibly a hunter, or a farmer, someone who was also experienced with wire and had a good knowledge of the river. However, the person probably did not arrive planning to dispose of the bodies. The use of the wheelbarrow and the bedding from the Crewe home, and the way the wires were tied without the use of a tool, suggested that was a snap decision.

Generally, however, the killer was patient and calculated, Scott said, and wary of being identified, which might suggest that he knew the Crewes well. 'Something about the perpetrator's relationship to the victims meant he spent far more than a cursory amount of time disposing of evidence. Time spent at the Crewe house significantly increased his risk of being implicated, but it was a risk he was willing to take.'

Scott hypothesised that rather than Jeannette, Harvey Crewe had been the primary target. While Harvey was a decent hard-working man who was devoted to his family, he was also described as having a dual personality: he had a quick temper, and was demanding with many people, Scott said. He was quite particular and a perfectionist. He liked to have his own way and was a domineering person. After the house fire, for example, the chief fire officer, insurance adjuster and carpenter reported finding him very difficult to deal with. In fact, one repair account was still in dispute 18 months later when Jeannette and Harvey Crewe vanished, indicating that Harvey Crewe could be extremely stubborn and drag out arguments.

Some people ended up very frustrated and upset after interactions with him. 'In my opinion, one of these people went on to commit the murders,' Scott said. 'The original issue may have been minor but this individual felt aggrieved by whatever Harvey had done. As a result he began to brood and ruminate.'

Over time, as the Crewes grew more prosperous, and with the birth of Rochelle, this person may have become further incensed and driven to punish Harvey, Scott said. But they lacked the courage to confront him. Harvey was a big man. Instead, they broke into the house, and then set the fires. When the Crewes didn't react, the perpetrator's focus shifted to murder. But they knew it wasn't safe to use their own gun. Perhaps from experience, they knew the Thomas .22 rifle was left in different places, unattended. They got the gun, and drove to the Crewe farm. Ultimately, they were still too scared to confront Harvey directly, so they approached by stealth and executed him with one shot to the head. Jeannette either saw the perpetrator or could work out who he was, therefore she had to be dispatched, Scott said. Rochelle was ignored because the perpetrator's primary grievance was with her father.

The thrill of the murder was probably short-lived. Two corpses and spreading bloodstains meant a quick return to a sense of rationality, and the killer responded by trying to clean up. But their efforts proved to be too time-consuming and were abandoned. Disposing of the bodies, however, was necessary for self-preservation. The offender thought he would be implicated quite quickly in the murders, but if the bodies disappeared, any investigation would be delayed or seriously compromised.

Afterwards, the perpetrator would have been anxious, hyper-vigilant, Scott said. In conversations about the Crewe murders this individual would have been an active listener, rather than a participant. Perhaps afterwards he left the district, to put distance between himself and the murders.

At the end of his report, Scott dedicated a couple of paragraphs to critiquing his own theory. He decided part of it had to be wrong: it was too complicated, he said, for a random perpetrator to acquire the rifle from the Thomas farm, as well as the wire and weights, without being noticed. Therefore, the most likely suspects were friends and family of either the Crewe or the Thomas families, local contractors, or neighbours. Scott ended his advice with a question: Was there someone

Arthur Thomas (left) and his younger brother Des express their disappointment at a press conference after the outcome of the police review of the case was released in 2014.

who had reason to have a grievance against Harvey who also had a link to the Thomas farm?[25]

U nlike Rochelle Crewe, the Thomas family was not invited to the police conference the day the report was released. Their lawyer was not invited to speak. Instead, *Herald* journalist David Fisher arrived in Pukekawa later that afternoon to find Des Thomas at home, leafing through the report's pages, complaining about the police.

'It's a whitewash,' Des told Fisher. 'We've been cheated, the facts haven't come out, they haven't moved on from 1970.'

His sister Margaret Stuckey, who had arrived with her husband Buster to go through the documents, said she was 'disgusted'. 'They've taken care of what Rochelle wanted — she didn't want any member of her family accused. That doesn't mean the case has been solved. Does Rochelle want to know who murdered her parents? I think she just wanted her family exonerated,' Stuckey said. 'We can say Arthur Thomas never did it and no member of the Thomas family did it.'

That afternoon, Des Thomas repeated these views to every member of the media that called. He said rather than exonerating his family, the report had unfairly cast more doubt upon them. He believed that to get the truth, there needed to be an inquiry independent from the police. 'All we want is justice, but we don't know who we're going to get it from,' he said.[26]

The Thomas family weren't the only ones left fuming over the review. In 2015, Hutton's family gave an interview to the *Herald*'s David Fisher, denying his involvement. He was an honest cop, they said, the cartridge case never would have been planted. They described how, for years, he had a picture of Rochelle Crewe on the wall; how during the investigation he'd taken home Jeannette Crewe's beloved cat, Rasty, and would talk to it when he got home after long days in Pukekawa. His daughter, Erin O'Neill, said for her father to be villainised after his death was unfair, particularly when he had been so devoted to the police. 'It's the injustice that eats at you,' she said.[27]

CHAPTER FOURTEEN
BULLETS, WIRE, AXLE

The heart of the debate over who killed the Crewes has always revolved around three pieces of evidence: the bullets, the wire and the axle. As the only physical links between the offender and the crime scene, each has undergone numerous reinterpretations to support allegations against new suspects, or to bolster new theories. In 1970, this triad of evidence formed the basis for the prosecution of Arthur Thomas (along with the now-discredited cartridge case).

In 2014, the police review team softened this view slightly, saying it believed all three items had links with the Thomas farm, rather than Arthur Thomas himself. Its findings drew from numerous expert reports about the science of ballistics and metallurgy, and a close examination of the police inquiry documents and court transcripts and from the royal commission evidence. Much of what the report said is now beyond reasonable dispute: the axle, for example, has attracted constant allegations that it was planted by Hutton. That seems highly improbable. Equally, the rifle belonging to the Eyre family simply cannot have fired the fatal bullets.

However, on a closer reading of the evidence underpinning the report, and after considering new information discovered while re-examining the evidence for this book, it appears police overstated the strength of the links to the Thomas farm. While it's almost certainly correct that the wire likely came from Arthur Thomas's property, when it comes to the bullets and the axle, the evidence is not so clear.

O f the physical evidence, the wire is one that has had least public attention, probably due to the highly technical nature of the expert opinion on it. The wire came from each of the bodies discovered in the Waikato River. The killer had wrapped Jeannette Crewe's body in a bedspread and blanket and bound them to her with copper wire. One section of wire hung out and was bent in a shape that police thought likely to have been attached to a weight. This wire was labelled exhibit 237.[1]

Harvey's body had pieces of a greenish blanket about his waist and was wrapped in two pieces of galvanised steel wire, one around his waist, and one around his chest. The wire was 16 gauge — thinner than the usual 'number 8' wire often used on sheep fences, but commonly used on farms, particularly for electric fences. There was also a piece of copper wire attached to the galvanised wire, which police believed was used to attach the axle found beneath his body. The waist wire was labelled exhibit 288(1), the chest wire exhibit 288(2), and the copper wire exhibit 288(3).

Police made considerable efforts to find the source of this wire. They collected samples from the properties of several persons of interest. On 16 August, Detective Sergeant Murray Jeffries collected copper and steel wire samples from the Crewe property. A day later, Detective Sergeant John Hughes collected copper wire from Demler's farm. On 17 September, after Harvey's body was found, Detective Sergeant Mike Charles collected more from Demler's farm, and on 22 September, Detective Bruce Parkes went round several farms and collected samples from the farms of Raymond Fox, the Chittys, the Spratts and the Priests. These wire samples were delivered to the DSIR for analysis the following day.[2]

In October, when Arthur Thomas became the focus, wire samples were collected from his farm by Detective Len Johnston on two separate occasions. On 13 October, he collected four steel and copper wire samples from the cowshed. These were labelled exhibit 328. A week later, on 20 October, he collected 11 pieces of wire from nine sites around the property. These were labelled according to the sites, exhibits 319–327. The next day, Detective Stan Keith collected two more pieces of wire, one clean and one rusty, from a wooden rail behind a garage. These were labelled exhibit 334. Two days later, Keith took them to Wellington and handed them to the DSIR.

Police say samples were also taken from nearby farms belonging to the Eyres, Tongas, Dunlops, and even the property of a former Crewe manager, James Hawker, in Cambridge, but these were not analysed.[3]

DSIR scientist Donald Nelson attempted to see whether cuts on the wire had distinctive features, but it was found they were too corroded, so analysis focused instead on the chemical composition of the wire. This analysis was done by Harry Todd, a scientist at the chemistry division of DSIR in Wellington. Todd was very experienced in one form of metallurgical analysis called Optical Emission Spectroscopy (OES) analysis. This method can measure minute or trace amounts of elements, such as carbon, silicon and chromium, present in steel wire. The amount of these elements varies in each production batch or 'heat', and so each batch has its own unique chemical signature.

Todd found only the copper wires from Harvey and Jeannette's bodies were from the same source. The two pieces of galvanised steel wire on Harvey's body had different 'signatures' and were therefore from two different production batches.

Out of all the samples collected, from all the different farms, none had the same 'signature' except some of the wires collected from Arthur Thomas's farm. The piece of wire from Harvey's waist, exhibit 288(1), was 'indistinguishable' from four separate wire samples from the farm: exhibit 320A (from the cowshed), exhibit 323 (from guttering on the implement shed), exhibit 325 (from where the so-called 'old Maori house' had stood) and exhibit 334 (from the rail behind the garage). The waist wire (288) was also in 'quite good agreement' with 328D (a piece from Thomas's implement shed). The chest wire (288/2) was in a range between 'quite good' to 'excellent' agreement with exhibit 324A — a wire from the old pig shed on Thomas's farm.[4]

Todd gave evidence at the first and second trials. Before the second trial, the defence managed to get its own expert to analyse the wire. This was Ian Devereux, a very experienced scientist who worked in Jim Sprott's private consultancy. He used a different method of analysis, called Atomic Absorption Spectroscopy (AAS). This is more precise but can only measure some elements. He used this method because he did not have OES equipment such as Todd had, but also because he had been advised by wire manufacturer NZ Steel that AAS would be more accurate.

OES can measure several elements at once and can thus compare relative amounts of each in a sample. AAS is more precise, but can only measure one at a time, and at that time could not measure carbon or silicon — two major components in steel wire. Todd argued that AAS would be good for follow-up measurements, once something was found, but would be useless for initial analysis as it could not detect some of the major elements present.[5]

Devereux's analysis appeared to blow Todd's results out of the water. He found that there was not agreement between the wire found on Harvey and the samples from the Thomas farm. He argued Todd's measurement was not precise enough and had not picked up the subtle differences in the amounts of some elements in the wire that the AAS method had picked up. The argument escalated when Sprott, Devereux's business partner, claimed Todd was unqualified to analyse the samples.

The royal commission of inquiry did not hear evidence from either, and did not try to resolve the disagreement, merely noting they disagreed. Defence counsel Peter Williams argued that it didn't matter anyway, as the killer could have been anyone who had simply taken wire from Thomas's farm. He also pointed out that the wire would have been part of a large batch, which could be on many farms in the district.[6]

The review team sought an opinion from George Ferguson, a professor of chemicals and materials engineering at the University of Auckland.[7] He pioneered the study of fracture mechanics — how cracks form in materials under stress and subsequently propagate

— and is considered a foremost expert on metallurgy in New Zealand. He was asked to review the work of both scientists to see which, if any, of their findings were correct, and to explain the apparent contradiction between their results.

His findings were conclusive, and apparently damning. Todd was right. The galvanised 16-gauge wires from Harvey Crewe's body came from two separate batches and were therefore chemically distinct from each other. Each wire was a match for specific wires from Thomas's farm. The waist wire (288/1) matched wire from the Thomas cowshed (320A), the guttering on the implement shed (323), the 'old Maori house' (325) and a piece from Thomas's implement shed (328D). All these were collected by Johnston. The waist wire also matched exhibit 334, the piece of wire collected by Stan Keith from the wooden rail behind the garage. The chest wire (288/2) found on Harvey's body was chemically distinct from the waist wire and matched 324A, the wire from the old pig shed.[8]

Ferguson was also asked to explain why Devereux's findings were different and whether this mattered. To understand his approach, you first have to understand that no two scientists measuring the composition of the same sample would ever likely get exactly the same results, due to inevitable variations in instrument calibration, operator performance and lab conditions.

The AAS method is used in very good laboratories in different countries by scientists experienced in steel and iron analysis, and thus represents international best practice. The amount of variation likely between any two competent labs has been repeatedly measured in tests by the International Organization for Standardization. As long as test results are within these accepted limits, a composition range or band in which 95 per cent of the results will fall, they are accurate. Ferguson found that Devereux's findings for AAS analysis of copper, Cu, and chromium, Cr, were within these limits. Thus Devereux's results for copper, Cu, and chromium, Cr, show there is a strong correlation between body wires and farm wires.

Ferguson also said that Todd's method was better suited because it measured more individual elements within the wire than Devereux's. He wasn't dismissing Devereux's work, rather saying that when placed in context, it actually supports the proposition that the body wires and farm wires are the same: 'Taking these findings for Devereux's analysis for chromium, Cr, and copper, Cu, together with his results for nickel, Ni, and Todd's results for C (carbon), Si (silicon), Mn (manganese), Ni (nickel), Cr (chromium), Cu, and Mo (molybdenum) and V (vanadium), one would have to conclude with a degree of confidence, that, overall the composition analysis supports the thesis that the respective body wires and farm wires have the same composition. Thus 288/2 and 320A, 323, 325, 328D and 334 have the same composition and come from the same heat and similarly 288/1 and 324A have the same composition and come from the same but a different heat,' he wrote.[9]

In 2023, to be sure that we understood his findings properly, we contacted Professor Ferguson, and asked him whether he was certain those body wires came from the same batches as the respective wires taken from the Thomas farm. 'Following my above findings I would have to conclude, yes,' he replied.[10]

A t one point, *Rolling Stone* magazine reported that Jim Sprott had tested copper wire from the Eyre property and found it to be in exact agreement with the body wires. John Martin, one of the group of Richard Thomas's friends who had been working on a vintage car on the Thomas farm around 1965, gave an affidavit saying that he had taken two pieces of copper wire from the Eyres' clothesline and given them to Richard Thomas, who had then sent them to Jim Sprott. By the time of the police review, Sprott was dead and Devereux said he didn't remember them. The police review concluded that the claims that the Eyre wire matched the body wire were 'highly improbable'.[11] Given that the defence team made nothing of it and no evidence of the findings exist, this seems a reasonable conclusion.

Essentially, therefore, the wire evidence comes down to probability. What are the chances that a piece of wire on the body would match a piece of wire on the Thomas farm? Given that wire was produced from a 'melt', or production batch, at the NZ Steel plant, and given that each melt could produce up to 2743 kilometres of wire, the chances of several farms having wire from that batch were high. On the other hand, the chances of a farm having wire from the two batches, or melts, that matched two different wires on the body were extremely low. Also, the body wires did not match wire from any of the other eight farms from which wire was sampled.

The police review considered this 'highly significant' circumstantial evidence. We would have to agree. It was an extraordinary slip by the killer to choose two pieces of wire from two chemically distinct production batches to use on Harvey Crewe's body; the fact that the wire was from two different batches that were both also found on the Thomas farm but on no nearby farm makes it almost certain the wire came from there. Whoever bound Harvey's body with that 16-gauge galvanised wire cannot have known that the two pieces they used were from different batches; if they had, they would very likely have taken care not to.

One further point is worth making about the body wire. The fact that the killer used two different wires suggests someone on the move, grabbing loose pieces lying around a farm or using bits in the back of their vehicle rather than being inside a farm workshop and cutting two lengths off a coil. One can easily imagine the killer finding the axle outside, then looking for bits of wire nearby to bind it with, also outside. It does not mean the bodies were on the Thomas farm, but simply that the wire was most likely taken from there. Given the easy access to the farm, that could have been by anyone, not necessarily a Thomas family member.

The police review, however, went further in its comments about the wire: 'When viewed in concert with other items linked to the Thomas farm, namely Arthur Thomas' Browning rifle (exhibit 317), the Nash axle (exhibit 293) and corresponding stub axles (exhibits 330 and 331), this evidence tends to significantly lessen the possibility of coincidence.'[12]

Does it? We shall see.

The finding that Arthur Thomas's rifle could have fired the fatal bullets is still considered one of the strongest pieces of evidence against him. The police have gone to considerable — and justified — lengths to determine this. There have been five ballistic reports on Thomas's and other rifles, by experts in both New Zealand and the United Kingdom.

A key strand of ballistics, the forensic science of guns and ammunition, involves studying the marks made on bullets when fired through guns, in this case, by the ridges on the inside of a rifle barrel. These ridges, called 'lands', make the bullet spin as it leaves the barrel, thus making it more accurate. Most rifles have either four, five or six lands, spiralling either clockwise or anticlockwise down the barrel, which leave distinctive marks of either four, five or six 'grooves' in fired bullets. The grooves spiral either clockwise or anticlockwise, and are measurably different in different types of rifle.

Thus, bullets have a distinctive signature showing what kind of rifling they were fired through. These are known as 'class characteristics'. In addition, individual weapons can leave distinctive 'scoring' (big grooves) or 'striae' (small marks) on bullets, due to individual barrel imperfections, such as how clean, rusty or badly manufactured they are. These individual differences are known as subclass or individual characteristics.

The first ballistic reports in the Crewe investigation were done by DSIR scientists in New Zealand. They test-fired bullets from 64 .22 rifles collected by police from within an 8-kilometre radius of the Crewe farm, plus other weapons that had come to their attention. They then compared these to bullet fragments retrieved from the victims' bodies. Unfortunately, they did not collect all the rifles within that radius, and probably should have collected more. Of these, they found that two rifles, one owned by Arthur Thomas and one owned by Jack Brewster (but being used by John Eyre), could have fired the fatal bullets.

In 1972, prior to the second trial, defence counsel Kevin Ryan arranged to have the test-fired bullets, plus Arthur Thomas's rifle, plus exhibit 350 (the 'planted' cartridge case) tested in England at the Home Office Forensic Laboratory. Scientist George Price made comparison photographs under a microscope of the fatal bullet fragments and bullets test-fired from the Thomas rifle. He reported: 'Although I have been unable to establish conclusively whether or not it was fired in the rifle exhibit 317 (Arthur Thomas's rifle), the limited individual bore characteristics it shows indicate that it could well have been fired in this rifle.'[13]

He also found that exhibit 350 was definitely fired from Thomas's rifle. He noted that of the 246 .22 rifles and pistols in the lab's collection, 15 produced similar bullet markings.

Unfortunately, Price was the last person to examine the bullets themselves as they were soon thrown in the Whitford tip. From then on, analysis had to rely on his comparison photographs.

In 1980, Price's successor at the Home Office laboratory, Peter Prescott, told the royal commission that an examination of markings on the bullet fragments retrieved from Thomas's rifle made it 'highly probable' it was the murder weapon. He said he would be very surprised if exhibit 234 (the largest portion of a .22 bullet retrieved from Jeannette's body) had been fired from any other rifle. He based this opinion on the photos taken by Price. He also found that the Eyre rifle had only five lands; thus it could never have fired the fatal bullets and should have been excluded. Extensive further analysis of the Eyre rifle has conclusively proved it was not the murder weapon.[14]

In 2014, the likelihood that Arthur Thomas's rifle was the murder weapon was again confirmed by Kevan Walsh, case manager physical evidence for New Zealand's Institute of Environmental and Scientific Research (ESR). Walsh undertook a much more sophisticated analysis, using an advanced statistical method, which first compares the likelihood of a rifle producing bullets with exactly similar markings. This is then used to calculate a 'likelihood ratio'. The fatal bullet is then assessed to see how closely the markings match, which then shows the likelihood it is fired from the suspect's rifle.

Walsh found it significant that there were a number of corresponding striae (markings) but a low number that did not correspond. 'The probability of observing the correspondence noted above for a bullet fired in another similar calibre rifle is very low. Therefore, in my opinion, the observed correspondence provides strong support for the proposition that the bullet exhibit 234 (Jeannette's) had been fired in the [Thomas] rifle,' he wrote in his report.[15]

In 2012, at the request of the review team, Sharon Fowler, senior forensic scientist at the National Ballistics Intelligence Service of the Greater Manchester Police, United Kingdom, compared photographs of exhibit 234 (the bullet that killed Jeannette Crewe) and exhibit 289 (the fragment of a bullet that killed Harvey Crewe). She also examined bullets fired from 62 of the original 64 firearms seized by police.

Based on markings she observed on the base of the fatal bullets, and comparing them to markings on all the bullets test-fired by the DSIR from the collected rifles, she found two rifles that could have fired the fatal bullets: Arthur Thomas's, and a .22 Browning pump-action rifle belonging to Arthur Eglinton, a Pahīatua farmer, which had somehow been picked up in the police sweep. Both had the same rifling, with the same size lands and grooves as those on the fatal bullets, plus the same base markings.[16]

Kevan Walsh of ESR also examined these two rifles, and Richard Thomas's rifle, also a Browning pump-action, and said that while they had the same class characteristics, they did not produce the same individual markings, or striae, on bullets. He therefore considered it unlikely that Richard Thomas's or Eglinton's rifle fired the fatal bullets. But, as stated above, he concluded there was 'strong support' for Arthur Thomas's rifle having fired the fatal bullets.

On the basis of this, the police review concluded that the weight of ballistic evidence gives strong support to the proposition that Arthur Thomas's rifle killed the Crewes. Two well-qualified experts said that; a third didn't disagree.

However, a closer look at Fowler's report throws that conclusion into question. What Fowler actually said was: 'It is not possible to determine if any of the features captured in the photographs contained in item 18 are genuine individual characteristics or subclass characteristics. Therefore, in my opinion, without a physical examination of items 234 and 289, it is not possible to reach a conclusion as to whether or not the items 234 and 289 were fired from the same barrel as items 1, 2, 3, 4, 5, 6, 7, 17 and 21, from the photographs provided, although the possibility cannot be discounted.'[17]

Effectively, Fowler was agreeing that it was that type of rifle, but she was also saying that it was not possible to say whether the markings were class characteristics, that is, from one type of rifle, or individual characteristics, from a particular rifle. In short, she disagreed with Walsh. She said it was not possible to reach an opinion as to whether Arthur Thomas's rifle had fired the fatal bullets.

Thus, the experts do *not* agree. Two say it was Arthur Thomas's rifle and one says you can't be sure. Would a jury convict on that? Unlikely. There is reasonable doubt. It could have been Thomas's rifle. Or his brother Richard's. Or Eglinton's. Or any Browning pump-action .22 or similar rifle, of which there were probably hundreds in New Zealand at that time. The ballistics are inconclusive, and don't necessarily point to the Thomas farm.

Almost all of the physical evidence from the Crewe homicide investigation now lies buried somewhere beneath the old Whitford tip in south-east Auckland. But one significant relic remains. Deep in the basement of a government building in Wellington, three floors below ground, inside a locked wire cage, sits the largest surviving piece of evidence from the Crewe murders: the axle that was apparently used to weigh down Harvey Crewe's body.

Viewing the axle requires gaining permission from Archives New Zealand, which has its headquarters near the Parliament precinct in Wellington. Inside the doors of its grey, brutalist exterior are multiple security layers. A guard checks identification. Bags must be left in a locker. No pens are allowed. A staff member escorts visitors to a lift, and down the three floors to a chilly, climate-controlled basement. A dimly lit concrete corridor leads to the cage. Inside the cage, on a wooden pallet, lies the axle. Next to it are the two wheel hubs, or stub axles.

To touch the axle, visitors must wear rubber gloves. The axle itself weighs 17 kilograms, but it's long and awkward. It's in good condition for a piece of metal almost 100 years old — and its serial number 17600 is still visible amid its coating of rust. Touching it, in the cool semi-darkness, with the knowledge it had once been tied to Harvey Crewe's body, knowing that the killer had also held this, picked it up, hefted it, judged its weight, is unnerving.

The axle was found at the same time as Harvey Crewe's body, on 16 September 1970, three months after the murders. As described earlier, the body was floating on the surface, snagged in branches of a tree, close to the shore in about 1.8 metres of water. Because the body had been in the water for three months, it was feared it might break up. Police attempted to guide a cradle beneath the body but something was obstructing it. A police diver, Constable Paul Spence, felt underneath and found a wire attached to the body. Hutton later

BULLETS, WIRE, AXLE 257

recounted many times how he reached beneath the body to try to free it from whatever was snagging it and encountered an iron object. As he did so, Spence put strain on the wire and it snapped, letting the body come free. Hutton then instructed divers to search the riverbed, and they retrieved the axle.

At no point did anyone see the axle attached to the body; it was assumed it must have been because it was found directly below the body and Hutton said there was an area on it where a wire had obviously been attached that was a light rusty colour.[18]

Analysis by James Grout, an industrial chemist, found that the level of light corrosion on the axle was consistent with it having been in the river for about three months.[19]

Others have suggested, based on the testimony of witnesses who saw it on television shortly after the finding, that the axle was later switched.[20] However, a close look at the photo showing it being held up by Hutton in the boat shows it is either the same axle, or one modified in exactly the same way; an almost impossible circumstance. Furthermore, the original negatives of the prints show there is a clear sequence from the photo of Hutton holding it up to close-ups of the axle itself.

Back in 1970, police knew they had a significant and potentially case-breaking find. That same day, 18 September, Detective Sergeant Murray Jeffries showed the axle to a TV crew, and that evening the country saw it on the TV news. The next day, the *Herald* showcased photos of it, asking anyone who could help to contact police. Detective Len Johnston joined the team two days after and was given the job of finding where it came from.

Johnston worked quickly. Within two days, he had tracked down David Keruse, who identified it as a front axle from a 1928 or 1929 Nash 420 sedan. He drove to New Plymouth to meet a Nash enthusiast, Trevor Simons, who was restoring a 420 and who also had a parts manual. This confirmed that the part number on the axle, 17600, was indeed for a 420 sedan.

The next day Charles Shirtcliffe of Te Puke approached police and told them he had built a trailer using a 1928 Nash front axle. He said he had swapped it for a fishing rod with Tony Hart, in about 1956. Johnston drove to Te Puke with Bruce Parkes, and showed Shirtcliffe exhibit 293, but Shitcliffe couldn't say whether it was the one he had used to build his trailer. He did give police a photo of his car (a Nash 420) towing the trailer and told them he had sold it to an unknown man who worked at the Meremere power station.

On 10 October 1972, the *Herald* published the photo, calling for information. A woman named Patricia Whyte, of Pukekohe, rang police to tell them she had owned a similar trailer. Her husband, Gordon Whyte, worked at Meremere. Two days later, Johnston visited Roderick Rasmussen, an engineer who moonlighted as a trailer builder. He did not recognise the axle but said the way it had been gas-cut was similar to how he would have done it.[21]

The next day, 13 October, Charles Shirtcliffe's stepdaughter, Heather Cowley, saw the photo of Shirtcliffe's trailer in the *Herald*, and rang police to tell them she remembered a 'Mr Thomas, of Mercer Ferry Road, Pukekawa' visiting to get ownership papers for the trailer. It was established that Shirtcliffe had sold the trailer to Whyte, who then sold it to Allan Thomas, Arthur Thomas's father.

When Johnston showed Arthur Thomas the axle he did not recognise it but said the trailer in the photo looked similar to his father's. Johnston then visited Allan Thomas, who didn't recognise the axle, but did recognise the picture of Shirtcliffe's trailer. As described earlier, Allan Thomas told Johnston where to search the farm tips — the first time, Johnston found nothing. Five days later, however, he arrived back at the farm with Bruce Parkes, asked for a spade, and after a short time digging in one particular tip, found two axle hubs. These were matched to the axle and became a crucial link between the killer and the Thomas farm. At trial, the axle was arguably the strongest piece of physical evidence, less complicated than the bullets and the wire.[22]

From the beginning, however, controversy surrounded the 17-kilogram axle beam. It has sparked more outlandish theories than almost any other piece of the Crewe puzzle, including that, like the cartridge case, it was planted. Defence counsel at both trials could not get to the bottom of its story; neither could the royal commission. After hearing hours of evidence from dozens of witnesses, it gave up, labelling the axle 'a morass of inconsistencies, unexplained discrepancies, and alternative possibilities'.[23]

For the axle to be linked unequivocally to the Thomas farm, two things have to be true: that it came from the Thomas trailer in the first place and that the hubs were from the farm. New evidence shows, however, that neither of those wholly adds up.

That the axle came from the Thomas trailer relies on an established chain of ownership of the axle from Hart through to Shirtcliffe, then Whyte, then Allan Thomas. There is no doubt that the Thomas trailer did have a Nash axle on it before it was removed by Roderick Rasmussen in 1965 and replaced with a tube axle. The Nash axle was then either left with Rasmussen (according to Richard Thomas) or was taken away by Richard Thomas (according to Rasmussen). However, it now seems unlikely that axle was the one found with Harvey Crewe's body.

Firstly, Shirtcliffe did not ever say it was the same axle, only that it was 'similar'. The body axle had welding in various places, to make the hubs unable to turn. He didn't ever do any welding on the axle, and nor did Whyte. Allan Thomas admitted having welding done only on one hub, not the axle itself. Thus either the welding was done after Rasmussen removed it, or it was a different axle, or someone was lying.

Secondly, Shirtcliffe was definite, in his deposition, his trial evidence and at the royal commission, that the axle came from a 1928 Nash.[24] During the trial, this was fudged by Len Johnston into a '1928 or 29' Nash.[25] No one has ever questioned why he did this, until now. It may be because he was told that the axles for a 1928 and 1929 were interchangeable.

A check of the parts manual for Nash cars, however, shows item 17600 (the front axle) was only ever fitted to a Nash 420. One of these manuals exists among the evidence boxes in Archives New Zealand; it has the same information, and next to the line listing 17600 someone has put a pencilled dot.[26] It is not clear who did this. But it seems most likely that Johnston got a parts manual — possibly the one in the archive — from Trevor Simons in New Plymouth, in which case he must have known that 17600 was only ever fitted to a Nash 420.

In July 2021, we contacted the Nash car club in the US. The club referred us to a member, Jim Dworschack, who specialises in early

Nashes. He said that the 420s were only made in late 1928 and in 1929, but were known as a 1929 car, whereas the 1928 Nash was generally considered to be a 320. The 320 had a distinctively different body to the 420.

After viewing Shirtcliffe's photograph of his car and trailer, Dworschack immediately identified the car as a 420: 'Since the person did own a '29 Nash, they would have known what a '29 looked like,' he told us. 'The '29 styling was a fairly major update of the '28, so anyone paying attention to styles and cars of the era could know a '28 from a '29 as there were so many styling updates done for the '29. Mechanically, the two cars were very similar and much is interchangeable.'[27]

On that information, Shirtcliffe was driving a 420, made in either late 1928 or 1929, towing a trailer made from a car that he always said was a 1928. As an owner of a 420, he would certainly have known the difference between the 420 and 320 models. And if Shirtcliffe is correct in his unvarying statements that his trailer axle came from a 1928 Nash, then it is more likely than not that it came from a 320, and therefore had a different parts number from the axle found with Harvey Crewe's body. Therefore, we suggest the evidence shows the axle found with the body appears unlikely to have come from the Thomas trailer.

There is another reason why the Thomas axle is unlikely to be that found with Harvey Crewe's body: the hubs. The hubs (also called stub axles) found on the Thomas farm had welding marks that matched exactly with the body axle. However, the hubs were quite different from each other. One (known as the left hub) was in good condition and roadworthy. The other (the right hub) had broken bearings and very old, congealed grease.

Reusing car axles and their hubs for trailers was commonplace in the 1950s; iron was too valuable not to be reused. But a trailer must have wheels that run straight. The axle found with Harvey's body, however, came from the front of a car, meaning it had hubs that could turn, to steer the car. On a front axle, the hubs are attached to the axle via a vertical metal rod called a kingpin, which can then rotate when the wheels are turned by the steering mechanism. When reusing a front axle on a trailer, there are two ways to lock the hubs so they can't turn; either by bolting the steering rods (which move the hubs) to the axle — usually done if the trailer builder does not have welding gear —

or by welding the hubs to the axle around the kingpin.

Shirtcliffe was adamant he used the bolting method; he never welded the hubs. So were Whyte, and Allan Thomas.[28] So why, on the axle found with Harvey's body, had the axle and matching hubs been welded together (and then later broken apart) if they came from the Thomas trailer? The Crown explanation was that someone must have welded the hubs to the axle after it was removed by Rasmussen.

During the second trial, the defence had the axle and hub assemblies examined by Allan Mowbray, a professor of engineering at the University of Auckland. Mowbray took the hubs apart and had the welding X-rayed. He made several important observations.

Firstly, he noted that the old right hub was a perfect match to the body axle. It had been welded strongly all the way around — enough to hold the weight of a trailer. When the hub had been broken off the axle, it left a jagged line in the weld, which matched the axle perfectly. He also noted that the hub was not roadworthy. The grease was old and congealed. The bearings (which bore the load of the vehicle and needed to rotate freely) were very worn, and the cage which held the bearings was broken. It would have been undriveable, and it would certainly not have got a warrant of fitness.

When we examined the hub at Archives New Zealand, the damage was obvious: the hub had half an inch of play in it. If anyone tried to drive it on the road at speed it would quickly self-destruct and the wheel would fly off. The left hub, on the other hand, was in very good condition, with newish grease and good bearings. It, too, had welding marks which matched the body axle. Thus it had been welded to the body axle.

Back in 1973, Mowbray had noticed that the left 'new' hub did not seem to align properly. It had been welded onto the axle without the kingpin in place; thus it would not have tracked straight. Also, the welding was short, and no more than what he called a 'tack weld' — it would not have held the weight of the trailer. Anyone trying to drive it on a road, especially with a load, would soon have the unpleasant experience of seeing the wheel and hub snap free from the trailer. Mowbray made some careful measurements and proved that a kingpin could not have been inserted. Mowbray also established that the welding of the tie rod end was different to that used to weld the hubs on to the axle — and thus could have been done at a different time.[29]

Mowbray concluded that the axle and hubs could not have been used together on a functioning trailer: it would not have got a warrant of fitness, let alone survive on the road. As the Thomas trailer was not only regularly warranted but also used to carry heavy loads of pigs, those hubs and axle could not have come from the Thomas trailer as they were. If they were from the Thomas trailer, they must have been welded and modified after they were removed from the trailer.

Thomas supporters argue this welding was done by Rasmussen; as proof they claim there is a cheque-book stub showing the amount he was paid for the work — they say this was a low sum as he took the hubs and axle as part payment. The stub went missing when Bruce Parkes collected the cheque-book stubs from Allan Thomas. But Roderick Rasmussen has always said the parts were useless to him and that he returned them. He said the welding was already on the axle when the trailer arrived at his workshop.

The other explanation for the welding is that the parts went back to the Thomas farm and someone then took them and tried to make a new trailer out of them. Thomas supporters have also, contradictorily, suggested a group of young men removed a similar axle from the farm in around 1965 to use on an old car and later dumped it near the Eyre farm. This was a key piece of evidence used by David Yallop to try to prove Thomas was innocent. A Thomas supporter, John Martin, claimed to have seen a similar axle in the Eyre farm workshop; Annesley Eyre, John Eyre's younger brother, had welding gear and made trailers.

The 2014 police review interviewed all the surviving men from this group and made extensive efforts to trace this lead, but there was no conclusive evidence as to whether this axle was the old Thomas trailer axle or that it had ever found its way to the Eyre farm.[30]

What does seem certain is that the hubs are not a matching pair, as has been claimed. Although they have the same part number, one is clearly old and corroded, the other uncorroded and new-looking. One is worn out through lack of maintenance; the other regularly maintained. Why, if they were used on the same axle, would one have deteriorated so badly while the other remained in good condition? Why could one have become so corroded in the five years between leaving the Thomas trailer and being found on the Thomas farm, while the other was not?

To add to this mystery, the 'new' left-hand stub was identified by Allan Thomas as coming from his trailer, while the rest of the assembly was not. He recognised it from the unusual studs (the bolts that attached the wheels to the hub), which were S.A.E. studs of 5/8ths of an inch. He remembered having these welded in place in 1963 to attach a wheel whose stud holes had become enlarged. The other right-hand hub has 9/16th-inch wheel studs. Why, then, would Allan Thomas admit that the hub, which at one point had clearly been welded to the body axle and was found on his son's farm, had come from his trailer?

The commission of inquiry considered this in 1980. 'We regard this evidence on the part of Mr Thomas as most important as far as his credibility is concerned,' the commission said. 'Had Mr Thomas not been prepared to accept the left-hand stub axle as his own, then there would have been no evidence to identify it as such. There must have been tremendous pressure on Mr Thomas to disavow any knowledge of the axle, stub axle, or anything connected with them in an effort to clear his son's name completely of any involvement in the Crewe murders. The fact that Mr Thomas was prepared to concede that the left-hand stub axle had indeed at one stage been on his trailer, in our view, does him credit and leads us to accept his evidence as that of an honest witness.'[31]

However, the police review team had a less favourable view of Allan Thomas. In a lengthy analysis of whether the axle and trailer parts were returned to the Thomas farm, including all the conflicting statements by Roderick Rasmussen and the Thomases, it noted that Allan Thomas made a statement, which he then signed, saying he 'did not know what had happened to all the trailer parts'. At the commission, he claimed he never said that.

After an extensive analysis of all the statements, the police review concluded that the trailer parts were returned by Rasmussen. It added that Richard Thomas had agreed in 1997 that he thought the parts were returned.[32]

The upshot of all this is that there is no definitive evidence as to whether the axle and hubs were returned or not. To conclude, either the axle did not come from the Thomas trailer or was heavily modified after leaving it. This raises several critical questions: Why would someone try to weld a good hub onto an axle with an unusable hub? Either they were playing, to practise their welding (which suggests an amateur), or they had another good hub they intended to weld on the other end in place of the old hub. At some point they realised it was too difficult and gave up. This suggests the welder at some point had access to another Nash 420 with a good set of useable hubs. But most importantly, if the body axle did not come from the Thomas trailer, how did the 'Thomas' hub, the good one, end up with a non-Thomas axle?

I t is certain that Len Johnston found the hubs in the Thomas farm tip on 20 October. He was in the company of Bruce Parkes, who the commission accepted was a credible police witness. Parkes has recounted for us what he remembers of finding the hubs; he told us that he believed Johnston did not plant the hubs — he appeared genuinely surprised when he found them.[33]

However, the royal commission, which also heard from Parkes (Johnston having died two years earlier), was less convinced about Johnston's incredibly good luck. It described the circumstances in which Johnston came across them as 'peculiar in the extreme'.[34]

It noted that on 15 October, at 10.45 a.m., Johnston visited Roderick Rasmussen. According to a police jobsheet, Rasmussen told him that he remembered Thomas, and that he remembered returning the parts from the trailer to Richard Thomas. At 2 p.m. that day, Johnston visited Arthur Thomas's farm, and Thomas took him down to the dump, 'where a cursory search was made without trace of the wanted trailer or parts thereof'. Five days later, on 20 October, Parkes and Johnston were back at the farm, to pick up the Thomas rifle and wire samples.

After getting the wire samples, Parkes told the commission, Johnston then borrowed a spade and began foraging around on the tip. He said that of the three tips on the farm, Johnston was interested in searching only one. After a few minutes, Parkes recalled, 'Detective Johnston located two stub axles [hubs]. One was probably partly uncovered, but the other was buried.' Parkes told the commission that Johnston knew what they were, and 'seemed quite excited by his find'. Johnston did not search the tip any further that day.

The commission was very concerned by the circumstances: 'We are very conscious that had he been here to give evidence, he may have been able to put forward a proper and innocent explanation of matters such as the finding of the stub axles from which the most serious inferences on the face of it can be drawn,' its report noted.[35] In other words, the commission was inferring, Johnston had probably planted them, or they had been planted for him to find.

The commission noted it seemed likely that the axle and stub axles were not on the farm tip in March 1970. That month, the tips had been searched closely by vintage car enthusiasts, who had found nothing but Ford Model T parts. Peter Thomas, who was living on the farm, also gave evidence that they were not there. As the commission noted, if the group of men had removed the Thomas axle in 1965, then the fact that the hubs were later found there by Johnston was irrelevant.[36]

Following this train of evidence, two scenarios are possible. In the first, the axle did not come from the Thomas trailer. Someone who had access to the Thomas trailer parts after 1965 took the Thomas 'good' hub and tried to weld it to a Nash 420 axle they had come across. At some point they gave up, probably because the other hub was useless, and discarded the hubs and axle. The axle was then used by the killer, and both hubs then found their way to the Thomas tip.

It stretches credibility to assert that Arthur Thomas, having killed the Crewes and weighted Harvey's body with the axle, would then leave the matching hubs in full view in his own tip, and encourage Len Johnston to search there. It is more likely that the killer either planted the hubs himself to incriminate Thomas, or tipped Johnston off as to where they were, and Johnston planted them. Remember, he had searched the same tip five days prior and found nothing.

It is also highly unlikely, to the point of impossibility, that they were found exactly in the spot where they were dumped after being removed from the Thomas trailer. Firstly, because the axle was welded after it was removed, and secondly, because there would have been many more trailer parts found with it.

Who had access to the 'Thomas' hub? Certainly Roderick Rasmussen and Richard Thomas. But, also, potentially any of the men who removed an axle and other parts in 1965, or anyone browsing the tip between then and 1970.

What is clear is that Johnston's actions are questionable. He appeared to ignore the repeated assertions by Charles Shirtcliffe that it was a 1928, not 1928 *or* 1929, axle; he took Roderick Rasmussen's evidence that the body axle was how he 'would have' gas cut as being that he 'had' gas cut it; but most importantly, he almost certainly either did not disclose a tip-off or, worse, actually planted the hubs himself. If the latter, then he is a strong suspect as the actual killer.

In the second scenario, the axle did come from the Thomas trailer. After being removed, and after having the fruitless attempt at welding on the hubs done on it, it was used to weight Harvey Crewe's body. The hubs were then dumped on the tip, some time after March 1970, where they were found by Johnston on his second search of the tip.

The 2014 police review essentially rejected Professor Allan Mowbray's work; it simply accepted that the hubs came from the same axle, and that it came from the Thomas trailer. It suggested that warrant of fitness standards were not always upheld; the fact that the Thomas trailer had got a warrant three months before Rasmussen worked on it did not mean both hubs were useable when he got to work. It also ignored his work on whether the trailer could have borne weight if the left-hand hub was 'tack' welded.

It discounted the idea that the Thomas tip had been combed for car parts before the murders, pointing out that the searchers were not very thorough. For example, number plates from the old Thomas trailer were later found in the tip. It put weight on Rasmussen's evidence that he remembered cutting off the hubs and giving them back, even though initially he only identified the work on the right-hand end as 'similar' to his; and gave varying answers about what he remembered at various hearings after that.

The police review did everything it could to leave open the possibility that the axle and hubs came from the Thomas trailer and went back to the Thomas farm tip and stayed there until the killer used them.[37]

The police review's conclusion turns on Rasmussen's evidence: that he could identify the trailer as the one brought to him by Allan Thomas, that the axle had been welded when he got it, and that he gave it back to the Thomases. But Rasmussen's statements have fluctuated over the years, and have put him at odds with other witnesses. In particular, on the issue of the welding, the commission noted three other people — Charles Shirtcliffe, Gordon Whyte and Allan Thomas — had said the stub axles (hubs) were not welded to the axle while these parts were in their possession. The commission accepted their evidence. Three against one is not good odds. So whom should we believe?

Roderick (or Rod as he prefers) Rasmussen lives in Pukekohe with his wife, Ann, in a single-storey brick home, up a long driveway with a remote-operated electric gate. Out front are two mobility scooters, one red, one yellow, and a giant campervan the couple use to go away fishing. When we visited in 2022, Rasmussen let us in warily, saying, 'I've had a lot of grief from some journalists. How is this going to be different?'

Rasmussen, now in his nineties, was worried we were going to report what he said back to the Thomas family. For years after Arthur Thomas was convicted, he claims, Richard Thomas pestered him to change his evidence to say he kept the hubs. He dropped notes and documents in his letterbox, and tried to set up meetings. Rasmussen told us he refused to go, saying he felt it was an ambush. At one point, he got lawyers involved, to tell Thomas to leave him alone.[38]

Ann Rasmussen, meanwhile, was worried an interview would cause her husband more stress. He was waiting for a heart operation and she didn't want him getting worked up, but the day after our first interview, Rasmussen called back. He had been thinking about what he said all night and wanted to clarify some points. We went to his home again, and later returned a third time to further check what he said.

When he refurbished the Thomas trailer in 1965, Rasmussen was living at Meremere and working at the power station. He used scrap from the station to make the trailers in a workshop under his house. In total he says he did about 100. But he remembered the Thomas trailer clearly, he said, because of the smell. 'It was a dirty, old stinking trailer, used for pigs.' The stench was so bad that his first wife had complained about it for days. Further, he said, he remembered how a week after he'd finished refurbishing the trailer, it was returned to him to be repaired. Rasmussen had made a mistake with the spacing of the springs, he said, and the new axle had bent. He fixed it for £3.

Shown a photo of the left-hand (new) hub, he said: 'I can't remember whether that weld that they had on there was cracked when I got them. I presume they must have been.' He confirmed again that on the first visit from police, Len Johnston had shown him only the axle beam. Then they turned up later with the hubs, which they told him were from the Thomas dump. When we showed him photos of exhibit 293 (the axle), he said: 'It looks to be the same axle, or very, very similar, to the one that [he worked on].

'I never worked on it. I just cut it off, and chucked it aside. I put the hubs elsewhere, hoping that they would leave them behind. They didn't.'

'Do you remember cutting the hubs off?' we asked.

'Yes. I cut them off with a gas torch. I cut the kingpins down either side so I could knock 'em out.'

We pointed to the right-hand end, with the kingpin still in place. 'But that one didn't come out.'

'No,' he said.

'Do you remember that?' we asked.

'No. It's a long time ago. Whether one of them was loose, and I was able to get it out without cutting, I can't remember. I made about a hundred trailers, all up.'

'Often with this method?'

'Yes.'

'You said this is the way you would have done it?'

'Yes,' he said.

'Any idea why they're not [both kingpins] still on the axle?' we asked.

'Unless one [kingpin] was loose, and I was able to knock 'em out. I forget. It's so long ago. Normally they have a cotter pin in one of the kingpins, to stop it dropping out. I can't ever remember not doing both ends. Both ends should have been done the same.' He was finding it difficult to remember why one popped out easily. 'It could have been just plain old wear because it was a dirty old stinking trailer.'

'So if you were to go up in court again, would your answer change?' we asked him.

'No, my answer wouldn't change. I would say to cut the stubs off, I would have cut the kingpin eyes.'

'Just like that?' We gestured to the picture of the hubs.

'Yes, and just pulled them off and knocked the hubs out. Both ends should be the same.'

'So it could easily be the axle you worked on?'

'Yes. But if the other end is not cut similar to what I'm talking about, the kingpin must have been a loose one.'

'So it could easily be the axle you worked on?'

'Yes, quite easily.'

'But you couldn't be sure?'

'No,' he said. 'I wouldn't put my hand on a Bible and say that's the axle. Because it's so long ago.'

We then went through Allan Mowbray's evidence, specifically, that if it had come into Rasmussen's workshop like that, it would not have got a warrant.

'Yeah, well it came into for me to repair because they could no longer get warrants on it. And it needed changing. And they wanted different wheels on it. They didn't want the great big [20-inch Nash] wheels on it anymore.'

'And they didn't get a warrant because?'

'I presume because one bearing was all flogged out. You wouldn't get a warrant with that.'

'Do you remember whether the axle you took off had kingpins both ends?' we asked.

'It had kingpins both ends.'

'But this one doesn't,' we pointed out.

Allan Mowbray had said that at some point someone had welded the left-hand hub back on without a kingpin.

'I would not have welded them,' Rasmussen said. 'It came in welded, for a trailer. Welded around the kingpins so the hub can't turn. It had the tie rod welded to the axle beam, also as an added thing to stop it turning.'

'You remember clearly it was all welded up when you got it?'

'Yes. It was all welded up. That was just an old-fashioned way of doing [it].'

'You're absolutely sure it was all welded up?'

'Well yeah, it had to be, otherwise the wheels would have flopped all over the place.'

'But the other way of doing it was to bolt it on,' we continued, 'but it looked like it was welded there.'

'On this one [in the photo] it was,' he said.

'But if that's not the Thomas axle?'

'Well, they say it's not the Thomas axle. Well okay, it could have been bolted. It's so long ago.' He threw his hands up in the air.

I asked him about Len Johnston.

'Nice guy. So was Parkes. They were nice people. Of course they were nice because I was helping them make the crime fit the man, or the man fit the crime.'

'When you heard about the bullet being planted, did that change your opinion of them?'

'Oh heck yeah. I thought you lying... people. After Arthur got convicted, [Thomas] started to harass us. He kept dropping literature in the box trying to get me to change my story. To say that [I] kept the hubs. But I didn't. Richard took them away. Oh no, we might be able to use them on something. But I was disappointed when they took 'em away. [I would] refurbish them. And make another trailer out of them. And restud the hubs to suit modern wheels.'

It had been a long interview, and Rasmussen was understandably getting tired. We returned one final time to the axle.

'The only bit I can really remember is they brought the beam to me, and then later they brought the hubs to me which came off the Thomas farm, so they say, [and] it all fitted together like a jigsaw.'

'Do you agree with Mowbray that the left-hand-end tack weld would not be safe?' we asked.

'The weld it showed in the photo here was not a tack weld.'

'Without a thrust bearing and kingpin, would that trailer have been safe?'

'With the size of the weld I saw, yes. Because the old saying is, an inch of weld will hold a ton. And that had a good two-inch hunk of stainless weld on that. Part way around the kingpin area.'

'Could you put a load of pigs on it?'

'It would hold, yes. Oh heck yes ... Both hubs that came back from Thomas's place were reconditionable,' he added.

'Could this welding have been done after it left your workshop, to make a trailer?'

'Why? They would have to weld up my gas cuts. Put the kingpin half-eye back on. They would have to do both sides of that. Someone would have to know what they were doing. It wouldn't be a farmer.' Rasmussen said the idea that the axle was welded after it left him is a load of hogwash. 'Why would anyone weld a heap of junk up to make it serviceable again when it was in such a horrible state?'

Thus, to sum up, Roderick Rasmussen was not sure whether the axle we saw in the vaults of Archives New Zealand and which was exhibit 293 in *Crown v Arthur Allan Thomas* is the one he worked on, but it was very similar. He cannot remember whether both ends had kingpins but he also cannot remember ever doing one that didn't. He is sure he returned the hubs to the Thomases. He is not sure the axle he was given to work on was welded. He is sure that if it had been, he would have cut them off the same way. So, what do we have that is indisputable, factual evidence?

1. The axle could have come from the Thomas trailer. But on the balance of evidence, it probably did not. One hub, however, definitely did come from the Thomas trailer.
2. The axle, wherever it came from, might have been on the Thomas farm, and been removed in 1965 or some period thereafter.
3. The hubs were both found on the Thomas farm. They might have been planted, or might not.
4. Someone, at some point, did an amateur 'farm' welding job on the axle in an attempt to attach the Thomas hub to it. There is disagreement over whether this welding would have been useable on a trailer.

So, all we can say for certain is that the axle was at some point connected to at least one of the Thomas hubs. How and why and by whom it was welded to the axle is a mystery. There is no way it can be used as evidence against Arthur Thomas, or anyone connected with the Thomas farm. It may well not have come from the Thomas trailer, and even if it did, it might have been removed from the Thomas farm well before the murders.

Considering all the above, two scenarios are possible.

Scenario one: The axle came from the Thomas trailer. Rasmussen removed it and gave it and the parts and hubs back to the Thomases. They were then dumped on the Thomas farm. The axle was taken from there by the killer. The hubs were later found by Len Johnston. All the various holes in this scenario can be explained and it was the scenario favoured by the 2014 police review.

Scenario two: The axle did not come from the Thomas trailer. Someone took the Thomas hub from the Thomas farm and had it welded onto that axle, to use as a trailer. At some point it was taken apart. The axle was used by the killer. The hubs were then dumped on the Thomas farm by persons unknown. Police then found them either by remarkable luck, through a tip-off, or they planted them.

There are more witnesses with corroborating evidence, and more convincing expert and forensic evidence for scenario two. In reality, no sensible jury would find either scenario lacking in reasonable doubt. Thus the axle is not reliable evidence.

Once again, there is a sense of frustration that something so tangible and weighty as the axle should remain opaque, but there it is. Likewise, the bullets; had they been retained, they may have been, with the benefit of modern forensics, conclusive. However, the wire sample evidence has not just stood the test of time but also been enhanced by modern expert analysis. It is reasonable to conclude that a jury would find that the killer had used wire that came from the Thomas farm.

CHAPTER FIFTEEN
A DISTRICT DIVIDED

Time in Pukekawa is measured in two halves: before the Crewe murders and after. Most of those who remember the time before have died, while the few who are left have carried its long shadow for at least half their lives.

Some have had a heavier burden than others. The Thomas family, in particular, suffered years of suspicion and abuse. They were spat on in the street, shunned by those who thought Arthur was guilty. Fighting for Arthur's freedom sucked up most of the later years of Allan and Ivy Thomas's lives. And when Arthur was pardoned, there were rows over money. The family, once tight-knit, was never as close again.[1]

When Jeannette and Harvey Crewe were killed, Peter Thomas was just 18. He had been living with Arthur and Vivien for six months before Arthur was arrested, while working for Roose Shipping at Mercer. From the beginning, he has told the same story about the day the Crewes were killed: he was at home with Arthur and Vivien that night, and he didn't hear Arthur go out. But neither his insistence that Arthur could not be the killer nor his young age stopped police from repeatedly trying to get him to change his story. At one point, late in the inquiry, Detective Inspector Bruce Hutton and Detective Len Johnston took Peter to the Tūākau police station and took turns to question him, nonstop, all day. Peter Thomas later told David Yallop that the detectives wanted him to say he'd seen the axle on the Thomas farm: 'They went on and on insisting that I had, and that I should say I had, that I must say I had. I couldn't understand why they were so desperate to get me to tell a lie, it didn't make sense,' he said.[2]

There was no jobsheet from that interview, but in their 2014 report, police acknowledged that Peter Thomas had told them about his gruelling day at the Tūākau police station. The report referred to the ordeal as 'persistent questioning', aimed at getting him to 'confirm' that he had seen the trailer on the Thomas farm. It never acknowledged that police had asked him to lie to obtain a conviction, and did not seem to consider that the extent of the corruption in the original investigation might have spread further than planting a cartridge case. The list of 80 questions at the end of the review document contains nothing about police behaviour. Instead, there is one last question about Peter Thomas: Could he have fitted the description of the woman seen on the Crewes' property on Friday 19 June 1970?[3] To anyone who has met him, as we have, it does not seem a credible question — he is shorter, and clearly has a more muscular build.

Peter Thomas lives in Tūākau now, in an immaculate brick house just up the hill from the police station where he was grilled as a teenager. He did not want to be included in this book, preferring not to dwell on the details of the case.

Peter's cousin Des Thomas, who was also 18 at the time of the murders, likewise did not want to speak with us. Des, however, is different from Peter. He maintains a strong interest in the case. He has spent many hours writing to police, reinvestigating, collecting affidavits, and working with journalists to tell his side of the story.

Most recently, Des featured in the 2018 podcast by the Stuff journalist Eugene Bingham named *The District*. The podcast was as much an exploration of the corrosive impact an unsolved murder has on a small country town as it was an investigation into lingering issues surrounding the case. At the time, the police review had only recently come out, and Des was furiously working to clear his family name. He wanted to highlight all the issues that remained after the review. He wanted an unredacted version of the review team's report — it had various names and defamatory details removed when made public — and he was still obsessed by the bullets, the wire and the axle.

'The reason I'm fighting this is because there's too many injustices in this country and this case is solvable and the police have to back down and admit they're wrong,' Thomas told Bingham. 'If somebody doesn't make a stance there's going to be more innocent people in jail.'[4]

Margaret and Buster Stuckey feature in the podcast, too. After Buster was named as a suspect in the 2014 report, they considered taking legal action, but did not proceed. The review report had said that Buster had been working on the Crewe farm just before the murders but Buster told Bingham he wasn't working there — it was another contractor called Ted Tickle who argued with Harvey Crewe about a fencing job.

Bingham interviewed Tickle, a former rodeo man, who was elderly, and dying, and yet clearly recalled being at the farm. He couldn't remember the argument so much, but said it was something to do with failing to report to the house once they finished the job. Tickle also remembered how Jeannette would follow Harvey Crewe around the farm, carrying Rochelle. 'I said she must be madly in love,' Tickle said. 'Poor girl was scared to stay at home, I think.' When Bingham took Tickle's statement to the police, they simply responded with an emailed statement pointing towards the review documents.[5]

When the podcast didn't prompt police into action, Des didn't give up. In 2018, he began a petition seeking a formal apology to Arthur Thomas from the police. In February 2019, he presented it at Parliament. Arthur Thomas himself had first raised the idea in 2017, when he was 79 years old.[6] He said he needed an apology to move on with his life. In both instances, the police said 'the door remained open' if Arthur Thomas wanted to raise any matters with police.

When Des's petition reached him, Minister of Justice Andrew Little said he had already responded to Arthur Thomas by acknowledging Thomas's pardon, the compensation, the royal commission of inquiry's report and findings, and an acceptance that he is innocent. 'I noted that

Mr Thomas accepted the then government's offer of compensation as a settlement of all his claims at the time,' Little said.

In making his plea for an apology, Des Thomas reiterated there was information in the police file that could be used to solve the murders.[7]

The story of Arthur Thomas and his family is by now well traversed. For years, they have sought justice for the hurt done to them. Many people sympathise with their crusade. Less well known is the story of another Pukekawa family whose lives were also changed by the Crewe murders.

When Jeannette and Harvey Crewe were killed, Ross Eyre was 16. Before the murders, he and his disabled brother John Eyre cut hay for Harvey Crewe. Afterwards, John was named as a possible suspect in the murders, first by defence counsel Kevin Ryan, and then by members of the Thomas family.

Ross Eyre remembers the week of the murders clearly, although he is now nearing 70. Ross and his wife Trish still live in Pukekawa, a mile or two down Highway 22 from the Eyre homestead, on the old Brewster farm. Ross is a big, burly man. He wears a Swanndri and gumboots, and has a friendly but watchful smile. He invites us into his kitchen, where two armchairs sit next to a table strewn with papers. The winter sun is bright through the window. Trish makes a cup of tea. As she sits down, a cat jumps into her lap.

Ross has never told his family's full story about the Crewe murders to a journalist before, but now he has Parkinson's disease he's decided he wants it on the record. Trish sits opposite him, chipping in as he speaks. Sometimes they finish the other's sentences.

When he was a schoolboy, he told us, he stood on Highway 22 each morning to catch a bus to school. On Thursday or Friday, the day after the Crewes were killed, but before anyone knew about it, he was waiting for his school bus at their farm gate, on the corner of Te Ahu Road. 'The Crewe car came past. And I waved out like you always do when you know everyone's cars in those days and this person glared at me, hit the pothole at the corner and nearly drove off the road and tootled off towards Tūākau. And I thought nothing much of it, I thought oh well the Crewes are snobs, she never waved to me. I remember the dog-ball eyes glaring at me. I told my mum, oh Mrs Crewe is a snob, she never waved to me as the usually do.'[8]

What Eyre means here, is that he realised that if it had been Jeannette, she would have waved to him, and would have known about the pothole. Thus, thinking it over, he realised the person in the car was not Jeannette Crewe.

Ross thought nothing of it until the news about the missing couple and the bloodstained house broke on the Monday night. His mother, Ruth, called police to report what Ross had seen. 'Next thing we know a cop comes along. That was Inspector Charles at the time in his fancy suit, smelling of perfume, etc. and all dolled up to the nines, and curly hair. He's pulled his little book out sitting there and I'm sitting here and eating scones and Christmas cake and he said, "What did you see, young fulla?" And I said, "I saw the Crewe car", and he said, "That's not possible, they've disappeared", and I said, "No, I saw the Crewe car."

'He closed his book, never even wrote anything down. "You're a little boy looking for notoriety, aren't you?"

'My mum was ropeable and . . . said, "Ross is not a liar. Ross saw the Crewe car either on the Thursday [or] Friday." I can't remember now, it was that bloody long ago but Charles didn't believe me. This is the one thing I have against the police. If they'd listened to me and the Māori boy [the witness] they would have nailed them. And the Crewes knew the pothole. Because they lived out the back and they drove there all the time.'

The Māori witness Ross Eyre is referring to is Tutu Hoeta, a local shearer. He saw a green-and-white two-toned 1964 Valiant parked in front of the Crewe house as he drove past on Saturday 20 June. He remembered the car because he had always wanted one and he remembered what day it was because he won at the TAB that day. He was able to give details of the day and time of his win, which police checked, and they were spot on. He is still alive and living in Pukekohe. We visited and asked him to confirm this evidence. However, he became agitated and asked us to leave, which we did.

Of all the vehicle sightings, this was perhaps the most significant, because there were known to be only two such cars in the district at the time. One belonged to Anthony Insoll, who lived several miles away at Glen Murray; the other to Richard Thomas. Insoll, although having been in the area on the night of the murders, was never considered a suspect.

The 2014 police review report argued that the initial investigation team was too quick to dismiss Hoeta's sighting. There is no record of Ross Eyre's statement on the file.[9]

The six Eyre children grew up near the Crewe farm. Ross is the youngest, and by the time of the Crewe murders, most of his siblings had moved out. But his older brother John was born deaf, so he always lived at home. Ross and John knew Harvey Crewe well, as they worked for him in the summer of 1969, cutting and raking hay.

Ross says Harvey was a good employer and a hard worker, tough but fair. Ross remembers driving the tractor on a steep piece of the Crewe farm, with Harvey. He remembers saying: 'This is steep, Mr Crewe, gee it's steep.' He kept saying, 'Nah, you're alright boy, you're alright.' He knew Harvey could get worked up, however: he had watched him tear strips off the hay-baler driver, telling him the bales weren't tight enough.

One day after working at the farm late, Ross went to the Crewe house and Jeannette got him a glass of orange drink. 'The little girl was there, Rochelle, clinging to her mother. Jeannette went to school with my brothers. She was a nice lady. Pleasant to talk to. She was fairly quiet from my memory of her. I never went in the house, that's the funny thing. I stood at the steps with little Rochelle there and I drunk my glass of drink at the bottom of the steps.'

In those days, he says, it was normal for children not to be invited in and he didn't see it as rude. Afterwards, Harvey Crewe took Ross home, and Ruth invited him in for a cup of tea. While Harvey was talking to his father, Annesley Eyre, known as Joff, Ross was listening in. He remembers it clearly. Harvey was wearing a new pair of boots and his father commented on them. 'Harvey said, "Yeah, things are going pretty well" and Dad said, "They must be with those boots."' He also heard Harvey say, 'Don't get Richard Thomas and Stuckey to do the fencing, they've put the fence in the wrong place.'[10]

Six months later, the Crewes were dead. For the Eyres, like many along Highway 22 who knew and liked the Crewes, the news of their likely murders was deeply shocking and upsetting. 'It was just terrible,' Ross told us. 'Absolutely terrible because we knew them and then once they found the bodies they picked all the guns up and then the forensic people made a mistake on Jack's gun.'

That mistake — incorrectly naming the Eyre rifle as one that could have fired the fatal bullets — was to spark a decades-long feud between the Eyres and Thomases that festers to this day. But that was to come later. In the days and weeks after the Crewe disappearance, most people in the district turned out to search the surrounding farmland, Trish's father included.

'My father had a boat in Glen Murray,' she said. 'He looked in all the caves and the tomo holes. Going up the river with the boat.'

Ross remembered the army parked at the top of the hill, helping with the search. 'People couldn't believe it, and God you heard all sorts of stories. It was the Americans because of Jeannette's sister. The Americans had done her in for the inheritance. Then aliens had done it. All the garbage instead of the facts.'

Later, when Arthur Thomas was arrested, the relationship between the Eyres and the Thomases turned sour. It is a moment that Ross Eyre remembers vividly. 'We couldn't believe it when they found the bodies and then they [said] that Arthur had done it. They tried Arthur and locked him up and with the second trial, Richard and his father came to see us. Old Allan Thomas turned around to Mum and said, "Ruthie, do you think Arthur did it?" and she said, "No, I don't think Arthur did it but whoever did, hanging is too good for them."'

At that, Ross claims, Richard Thomas clenched his fists. A friend of the family, Lynette Ramsey, was at one end of the table, Ross was at the other, he says, and Richard was in the middle. 'Richard pushed the chair from under him, clenched his fists and he was white and said to his father, "Dad, we've got to go", and since that day they've put the boot into us. And Mrs Ramsey turned and said to Mum, "I think they've got the wrong one." We've never believed Arthur did it.'[11]

The arrest of Arthur Thomas split the Pukekawa community into two camps, Ross says. Mostly, it was the Catholics on the Thomas side; the Protestants were neutral, but it divided a lot of families. Ross remembers incidents in town: once he was there when the jeweller William Eggleton was threatened by a local woman who was

Ross Eyre knew the Crewes, and saw the Crewe car on Highway 22 shortly after the murders. Police ignored his important evidence.

a supporter of Arthur Thomas. 'I told her three times, leave, and I had to physically remove her and she said, "You bastard Eyres, we're going to get you." She ended up going away and getting a brick and putting it through Bill's window.'

After the second trial, when Kevin Ryan had named John Eyre as a suspect, and Bruce Roddick told the court he'd seen John be cruel to animals, many of Thomas's supporters turned on the Eyres.

'I was walking down the main street and different ones I went to school with spat in my face and said, "You're just a pack of murdering bastards and you got away with it, it was nothing to do with the Thomases."' Ross says he later found out where the suggestion about his brother came from. One day, the Eyre family saw Bruce Roddick in Pukekohe and asked him why he said what he did at the trial. 'He said that Richard Thomas threatened him and said he'd better give evidence.'[12]

Things deteriorated further as some of the Thomases and their supporters became convinced John Eyre was the murderer, and that it was being covered up by his family. John Martin gave an affidavit that Richard Thomas got him to cut copper wire out of the Eyre clothesline to give to the defence to analyse to see if it matched the wire found on the bodies.[13] According to Ross Eyre, that wasn't the only intrusion onto their property in the years after the second trial. On one occasion, the family was out on a Friday night and when they got home a neighbour called to say that one of the Thomases had been going through their shed and the house. Another night, they were having dinner and looked outside to see a glow in the tree, a light going up and down, like someone puffing on a cigarette.

'So I went and got my gun, grandad's old shotgun, put two shells in my pocket and went out the back. The bugger heard me open the door, so I let rip and I ran down the driveway,' Ross told us. 'Next day the police rang up and said, "Tell the young fella to pull his head in", and Mum said, "What do you mean? He was shooting at possums."'[14]

Ross says he believes police were watching the Thomases and also watching the Eyre house. The Thomas family also claimed they'd seen an axle in the Eyre garage, or that there had been an axle in the grass verge outside their house. 'It was absolute bullshit, to put it bluntly. They were grasping at straws,' Ross says.

The Thomas theory was that John Eyre had cut the wrong paddock of hay at Harvey Crewe's farm, and they'd had a row, which is why John killed the Crewes, he says. 'Which is balderdash, because I raked the hay. And Dad did the accounts — we didn't even get paid. We did it because we were Dad's kids.' Plus, Ross says, he knows Harvey Crewe was pleased with the job because he said he would have them back the next year to do the hay again.

Ross says he believes he was targeted because he stood up for his brother, and that Richard Thomas was trying to take the heat off himself. 'I've had a shotgun put under my nose and [had somebody] say, "Admit it you bastard or we're going to blow you away" . . . that was John Martin again. I said, "What are you doing, Speedy?" and he said, "Richard wants to get the information out of you." I said, "Piss off, he did it. He's the bastard that did it, not Johnny."'

Ross claims it was Richard who had the argument with Harvey Crewe at the farm, and that it was Richard's car seen there the Saturday after the killings. Once Ross even put it to Richard that he was the one who killed the Crewes.

'He came up our drive one time and Mum said get rid of him, and I went out and he said to me, "You're the only thing stopping me getting at your mother and Mickey." And I said, "Yes, Richard, it wasn't Arthur, it was you. Now fuck off," and he just smiled.'[15]

For more than 30 years, the Eyre family did little to push back against the rumours that circulated in Pukekawa. But in 2006, when the Thomas family appeared on TV One's *Sunday* programme implying that John Eyre was the Crewe killer, it was the final straw. Ross gave a full statement to the Pukekohe police.[16] He says he did it 'just in case anything happened because I was threatened'.[17]

Des Thomas had developed a theory that John Eyre had killed the Crewes and the Eyres had the barrel of his Remington .22 rifle modified to hide the evidence. Ross took the gun with him to the police station, saying he was happy to lend it to them for any testing, but he wanted it back when they were finished.

Ross Eyre told police his whole story — about some of the Thomas family coming onto their farm, about his sighting of the woman in the car the week of the murders, about how the police never listened to him. He said since the *Sunday* programme had aired, the family had been harassed. People had been calling saying, 'How does it feel to be a murderer and get away with it?'

Police tested the Remington .22 later in 2006. They found the barrel had not been replaced at any time.[18] Ross still has the gun. Police offered to dispose of it, but Ross refused. 'I said, "Why the hell would I want to dispose of this gun when this gun is the only evidence we've got that we didn't bloody well do it?"'[19]

After the tests on the rifle came back, Des Thomas continued to insinuate that John Eyre was responsible for the murders. In 2012, Ross Eyre spoke to two of the police review team, Gary Lendrum and Detective Sergeant Veronica McPherson, who visited his house twice. They found him a credible witness, they reported.[20] He told them about overhearing the conversation about Richard and Buster and the fencing. He told them again about his sighting of the woman in the car. The sighting, of which police never found a record in the original inquiry documents, was listed as 'new information' in the report.[21] Ross Eyre says this was the first time he had felt heard by police.

The passage of time has dampened the heat of accusations about the Eyre family. The review team's findings, that John Eyre wasn't involved, has helped. Ross and Trish Eyre say it didn't ever affect their daily lives, anyway, although they sometimes worried about the impact on their two daughters, particularly while they were at school.

Ross says he knows without doubt that John did not kill the Crewes, partly because he knows his brother as a kind person, but also because of their family history. Ross and John are grandsons of Sydney Eyre, who was shot dead over 100 years ago at the Eyre homestead (see Chapter 1). Ross's father was nine years old when his own father was killed.

But the family has another story about the murder of his grandfather. Ross says when his father's older brothers, John and Phil, were young, they found a Māori gravesite on the Eyre property next to the waterfall. A little girl had been buried there. John and Phil took the skull to scare the hell out of their sister.

When he found out, their father was furious. 'Put that back where you found it,' he said. But instead of returning it, they threw it over the waterfall. Afterwards, local Māori told the family that there was a curse on the Eyres, and that's why Sydney died.

It is in part because of this history that Ross Eyre is adamant no one in his family is responsible for the Crewe murders. 'If anyone in our family had have done it, Mum would have sent them to the police because of what happened to Grandad.'[22]

John Eyre still lives in Pukekawa, too. Since Ruth Eyre died, Ross and Trish have cared for him. The police review team tried to interview him, but found it too difficult to communicate. Based on that, and what we know about his condition, we didn't think we could add anything by trying.

CHAPTER SIXTEEN
THE COURT OF LAST RESORT

n the winter of 2022, on a trip to Pukekawa, we stopped outside the former Crewe house. It was unoccupied and a 'Beware of the dog' sign hung on the fence. Trees had grown up in the front paddock; the windows were shielded from the road. It looked very different to the black-and-white photos from an earlier time.

We drove back along Highway 22 in the late afternoon, down the straight road that loops beside the rolling riverine hills. To our left was the dark mass of Pukekawa Hill. On our right, we passed a ploughed field, that rich volcanic loam, and another field with two old houses, paint long gone, windows fallen in. On the horizon, a lone nīkau stood against the darkening sky. There was, as Sarah Ballard said, a primal beauty in this land; but it seemed, that afternoon, a beauty tinged by its turbulent history.

We turned down Mercer Ferry Road, past the old Thomas farm. The little yellow house was still there. Just downstream from the Tūākau bridge, we stopped to take a photo. There was a boat ramp, just a muddy slope, and the Waikato River, in flood, beyond.

Was this where the killer put the bodies in the water? Did they take the road we just travelled, rushing to beat the chilly dawn? And the question that every book or film or story about this case has failed to answer: Who *did* kill the Crewes?

Everyone, it seems, has a theory. Over those 50 years the pieces of evidence have been sifted, jumbled, put together, taken apart and put back together in so many different ways by so many people. It is like a jigsaw puzzle of square pieces — they can be assembled almost any way you like to support almost any theory you like. To this baffling kaleidoscope we have added a few fragments.

As our discussion of the hard evidence (the ballistics, axle and wire) shows, all that can be said for certain is that the killer was someone who had access to the Thomas farm, where they got the wire to tie the bodies. It was someone who had access to a 1929 Nash 420 front axle. And someone who had access to a .22 rifle with six lands with a right-hand twist. That is all. Everything else is speculation.

What is not certain, but highly likely, is that it was a farmer, or someone who worked on a farm, someone who had a grudge against the couple and who had been watching and probably harassing them for a couple of years. Someone who had access to a hub from the Thomas trailer; someone who was strong enough to lift a 110-kilogram body into a car or van after wrapping them in bedspreads and dragging them outside. Someone who may have driven a 1964 AP6 two-toned green-and-white Valiant; someone with a female accomplice. (That accomplice, who was seen driving the Crewes' car and tending Rochelle, was someone who did not know Highway 22 well and was therefore not a close neighbour.) The killer may have been someone who lived close to the Waikato River, near where the bodies were dumped.

Above all, the killer was someone with ready-enough access to the Thomas farm to collect two different pieces of wire, most likely on their way to the river. This was not necessarily a Thomas — the farm dump was well known in the district. It would have been a convenient place to find wire for anyone who was concerned not to leave any trace of a connection to the bodies. Later, when it was known that Thomas was a suspect, it would have been a convenient place to dispose of the incriminating hubs and shift the focus to them.

Who fits this profile? Given the large number of .22 rifles in the district and the easy access to the Thomas farm, there could be many people. Len Demler has always been a suspect: he was nearby, he had no alibi, his behaviour and some comments after the murders were open to unfavourable interpretation. However, as the police review concluded, many factors make him an unlikely killer. Anyone who has read the witness reports of his apparently sincere distress when with those he trusted, as well as the lack of physical evidence, would have little regard for that.

Although, as we have shown, he had made his children rich by freeholding his brother-in-law's farm at a bargain-basement price, he personally had nothing to financially gain. On the contrary, he had consistently demonstrated exemplary stewardship of the trust assets for the benefit of others, hardly the sign of a greedy, resentful man. His supposedly guilt-ridden behaviour immediately after the Crewes' disappearance can equally be seen as the reaction of a shocked father dealing with the added horror of being treated as a suspect in the death of his own daughter.

Nor is John Eyre a credible suspect. His rifle was ruled out. He was under the close watch of his family. There is no apparent motive. There is a tenuous unproven suggestion of a link to the axle, but not to the wire.

Arthur Thomas remains a possibility for some, but he must be a remote one to any reasonable person. Although his rifle was, along with others, a possible killer weapon, and there is significant circumstantial evidence in the wire that came from his farm, that evidence alone is not anything that could not apply to persons unknown. The 2014 police review ruled him out for many reasons. He had a strong and consistent alibi from two people. Psychiatric witness evidence did not support his being the killer, nor does a criminal profile fit him. He had no credible, strong motive. Many people who knew him closely over a long time are convinced of his innocence.

His brother, Richard Thomas, has also been named as a suspect. One credible witness, Ross Eyre, has pointed to a possible motive: that he had worked for the Crewes and had a dispute over work not done correctly. He also had a reputation among some in the district for stand-over behaviour. He is one of two people who last saw the hub that fits the axle. There is a credible witness report of what may have been his car at the scene. His rifle was of the right type to have fired the fatal bullets. There is an unconfirmed witness report of him having accessed the Crewe farm and house. He was physically capable of moving the bodies.

Richard Thomas is no longer alive to speak in his own defence. If he were, he would no doubt point out his own concerted efforts to find the murderer, his consistent willingness to talk to and help police, and the lack of a demonstrated strong motive. The car at the scene may not have been his or it may have stopped there briefly for a reason unconnected with the murders and happen to have been seen at that moment. A member of the 2014 police review team told us that Richard Thomas was very open with them; he kept and readily surrendered his rifle for testing when he could easily have disposed of it.

Arthur Thomas named his brother-in-law, Buster Stuckey, as someone who could have had access to his rifle, as he was a regular visitor to the Thomas farm. The Stuckeys declined to be interviewed by the police for the 2014 review without a lawyer present. They also declined to talk to us, as is their right, and nothing should be read into that. Stuckey, like Richard Thomas, has been named by a witness as having worked on the Crewe farm; something he denies. Other than this, there is no strong evidence of their involvement. There is credible evidence of their good character; they have been married for over 50 years and are committed Christians who maintain strong relationships with their families.

Ian Wishart named Detective Len Johnston as a suspect. He knew the Crewes; he had investigated one of the earlier attacks on their home. Wishart believed Johnston formed some kind of fixation on Jeannette and that she rejected him, prompting the murders; there is zero evidence for this. Johnston is associated with some unlikely coincidences and turns of events: he joined the investigation the day after Harvey Crewe's body was found; he either fudged or carelessly misrepresented witness evidence on the origin of the axle to make it fit the Thomas trailer; within days he had found the hubs that matched the axle, in peculiar circumstances.

This was a scenario that seems so coincidental, so fortuitous, that it stretches credulity, especially when you consider that he was one of two officers named as likely to have planted the cartridge case used to incriminate Thomas. If the hubs were also planted, then either they were planted by the killer, who then tipped off Johnston, or Johnston was the killer. If the former, then Johnston did not disclose a highly significant tip-off from someone who clearly either was or knew the killer.

Against all this is the consistent evidence from a credible fellow officer, Bruce Parkes, that the hub find was genuine. There are also several witnesses as to Johnston's good character and the lack of a strong demonstrated motive — he had a happy marriage and was by all accounts a loving husband and father. Just because he may have been either careless or deliberately dishonest in his work does not make him a killer.

Apart from these, various other neighbours or relatives of the Crewes have been put forward as possible suspects, mainly on the spurious assertion that they stood to gain financially (they didn't — only Rochelle did) from the Crewes' deaths, or that they had some kind of grudge.[1] In naming these people we are not asserting they did the murders or had anything to do with it. We just want to lay out as fairly as possible the evidence for and against their involvement.

We cannot emphasise enough that while the sparse existing facts can be made to fit several of the above, it could just as easily have been someone from outside the district who had crossed or been crossed by Harvey or Jeannette years previously, and who paid periodic visits to the area to harass them before eventually killing them. That person, driving to the river, could have stopped outside the Thomas farm and snatched a couple of pieces of wire from the tip, maybe even an old axle. They may well have had an accomplice, a woman, who was seen in the Crewe car and with Rochelle. All of this fits the known facts.

Sadly, we don't have an answer to the central tragedy of this story — who it was who murdered Harvey and Jeannette Crewe. We hope, however, that we have shed light on who did *not* do it. This, more than any other case, has been one where it has been too easy to take the few broken pieces of the puzzle and put them together in a way that could point to many people. This is understandable. It remains, more than 50 years later, a horrific crime.

Most people, us included, looking at the black-and-white photos of Harvey and Jeannette, cannot help but see something of themselves in them. They became in the public mind an iconic New Zealand couple: young, optimistic, hard-working. It is a deeply human impulse to try to make sense of the few frustrating fragments of evidence. Bruce Hutton, for all his faults, is just one of many of us who evidently felt this and had a sincere desire to put things right.

But anyone wishing to draw their own conclusions should remember that unless they want to revisit the injury of unjust stigma and hurt on innocent people, they should carefully weigh the counter evidence against whomsoever they suspect. We ourselves have been down those rabbit holes — every time we have thought we were closing in on the killer, new evidence emerged to undermine those suspicions.

We conclude that unless someone comes forward with something substantial, there is simply not enough evidence to fairly and convincingly accuse anyone. What is certain is that someone, somewhere, has some knowledge that could set the mind of Rochelle Crewe at rest, and heal a rift between not just the Thomas and Eyre families, but in the district and even the country.

We could leave it there. But, as we have tried to show, this story is not just about the terribly sad events of June 1970 and beyond. Because of the way it unfolded, the unprecedented number of people involved and the way it shook society from its roots to the highest branches, it has resonance that continues to this day.

All the many accounts of this tragedy bring their own lens to it. The royal commission and 2014 review focused on police and investigation failings, as have many books. Others, such as Pat Booth, have used it to question the wider legal system. David Yallop and Booth were both journalists, and naturally highlighted the importance of journalism in freeing Thomas. The film *Beyond Reasonable Doubt* emphasised the role of family and friends.

What can we learn from this story? The first and most obvious lessons are about investigation. Much has been pointed out in the

2014 police review — the faults in the initial investigation, including inconsistent witness and suspect identification, record-keeping, scene protection. Cold-case theory also argues the importance of an evidence-based approach (evaluating all the evidence first before developing a suspect) rather than a suspect-based approach (identifying a suspect and then finding the evidence for their involvement). Clearly, the Crewe investigation is an example par excellence of the dangers of the latter.

Long-time US cold-case investigator Joe Rogan argues that successful investigations are usually the result of teamwork and of keeping an open and always doubting frame of mind. 'Doubt everything, because doubt leads to inquiry and inquiry leads to truth.'[2] Not doing so leads to tunnel vision, or confirmation bias.

Confirmation bias is one of the most studied areas in human decision-making. It has been defined as the tendency to discount information which undermines past judgements.[3] Confirmation bias usually results from overconfidence. Recent research suggests that 'existing judgments alter the neural representation of information strength, leaving the individual less likely to alter opinions in the face of disagreement'.[4] Tragically, this case and everything that has been written about it is littered with examples of people doing just that: developing a theory and seeking only the facts which support it.

Why do people do this? Confirmation bias can be adaptive; it confers social benefits if your confidence helps bend reality to your will.[5] Solving the case earns social prestige. Bruce Hutton never seemed to experience doubt and seemed not to lack confidence. This may have made him a charismatic leader, but arguably a poorer investigator. All of us, police, journalists, lawyers, judges, politicians, members of the public, like to develop a theory and win people to our view — but persuading ourselves and others does not make it true.

So many people in this case have followed a gut feeling, even been guided by fate. Some, at least in hindsight, have been vindicated: Pat Vesey, who felt something move him during the second trial; Pat Booth, for whom fate found a carpark at the courthouse; Jim McLay, whose inner compass guided him to pardon Thomas. But these are the successes. There were also many who followed their gut down a path that led nowhere: Hutton's hunches about Demler and then Thomas were by no means the only ones.

The news media was always a powerful player in this case. As David Lange said, it was an example of the power of mass media supercharging a strong cause.[6] The media was the police's eyes and ears, energising and enlisting the local community, and later the country, in the project. Key breakthroughs came through news coverage and public response. It is a partnership that, at its best, as a senior police officer once told us, is critical to many murder inquiries.

But the media is not something to take for granted, as Hutton found once Pat Booth became involved. Later, it was to prove its worth as a watchdog, investigating and bringing to light evidence and questions. Above all, it gave a voice to those who needed it; there may be no better example of the value of its role as the court of last resort. But there was a downside: the immense public interest in the case undoubtedly added to the pressure on Hutton to get a result, pressure that must have been intense.

Another lesson is how important the role of the outsider is. It is a staple of the Hollywood Western — the loner who rides in and cleans up the town. This story had at least three of them: Justice Robert Taylor from Australia, Pat Vesey from Australia, David Yallop from the United Kingdom. The power of the outsider is not just the stuff of fiction: a famous study of the Canadian police, news media and courts in the 1990s found that reporters and others could be sorted according to whether they were 'inner-circle' or 'outer-circle'. The former were trusties of the officials, dependent on them for news, and never likely to bite the hand that fed them. The latter were those few reporters who remained independent enough to criticise the court officials, police officers and even judges with whom they worked.[7]

In this story, there were several inner-circle police officers, judges, reporters, who harboured doubts yet were unable to voice them. It was arguably only the intervention of those from outside the circle — Taylor, Vesey, Yallop — who had enough social distance that the spell cast over the inner circle could be broken. And each of these outsiders built on the work of locals: Yallop on Booth, Booth on Terry Hill; Taylor was ably supported by McLay; Vesey by the Thomas family and friends. Jack Ritchie, the former policeman who took the time to record his observations accurately, pack his samples in labelled fishhook boxes and send them to Auckland, was another. It is all these people, as much as the police, judges and officials, who were so important in this case.

If we look not just at this case, but also at those murders that preceded it, it is hard not to look for resonance, an echo. That there were three similar murders in 50 years in a small area could be coincidence, but it would be wilfully blind not to look for patterns. The most obvious lesson is the cruelty of capital punishment. Due to the pitiless brevity of the court process as it was then, both Samuel Thorn and William Bayly were dead long before there was time for any retrial committees to get under way.

If the Crewe murders had come just 15 years earlier, Arthur Thomas would be dead now, too. The many extraordinary parallels between the Thomas and the Thorn and Bayly trials are partly explained by the fact that any gunshot crime will inevitably involve similar evidential processes; but they also remind us not to rush to judgment, no matter the pressures to do so.

The desire for closure is a strong and understandable one. Less understandable is the desire to avoid daylight when mistakes have been made or when the subject might attract controversy. Time and again in this story, officials were able to cloak their actions in secrecy. The first hearings were suppressed. Thomas's lawyers did not have equal access to evidence before the trials. Important witness evidence, particularly expert witness evidence crucial to the defence case? Secret. Names of jurors available to the prosecution three weeks before the trial? Secret, until three days before. The fact that the foreman of the jury who worked with and was friends with a key police witness for the prosecution wanted off the jury because he felt he was compromised? Kept secret and withheld from the defence.

Department of Justice officials and police were able to routinely keep secret their communications and opinions. The solicitor-general's reasoning for refusing to prosecute a police officer accused of corruption by no less than a royal commission of inquiry? Secret. The fact that a senior judge, no less, lobbied the minister of justice to not pardon a prisoner? Private.

In the United States, much of this would either have been available as of right to the defence or accessible under freedom of information laws. Our instinct is too often to shut down anything which might threaten the system's stability. Time and again in this story, police, justice and even scientific officials displayed a kind of confirmation bias that seemed to leave them unable to genuinely contemplate the possibility that mistakes had been made. Time and again they tried to use secrecy to shield their decisions from public scrutiny. Each person's decision may often have been over a small item, but collectively they built a wall that was near impossible to breach.

It is peculiar in the extreme, to borrow the royal commission's wording, that the Thomas pardon remains the only free pardon for homicide ever given in this country, and one of only four given at all. It took a public revolt against the police, the courts and the justice bureaucracy to free Thomas. That justice system failed Thomas, as it has arguably also failed an unknown number of wrongly convicted people, because it relied on a process for testing evidence that was demonstrably faulty, in this case at least. When the evidence was tested in a separate process, the royal commission, very different answers were found. Ultimately, Thomas was freed because he had one last appeal: to the court of last resort, public opinion.

If we take this wider view of the justice system, did it work, in this case? Yes, in a way. Because for all the concern over this case, there are some things that we as a country can be proud of. One is that despite all the heat and pain, it was conducted in a mostly civil way. Although guns were pointed and shots fired, no one appears to have been deliberately targeted, and no one killed. Secondly, it is remarkable, as Pat Vesey has pointed out, that throughout his campaign, virtually no one ever refused to see him or hear him out. In this country, even the little guy had a right to be heard, and politicians of the time took that duty seriously. It points to a level of civic trust that we should cherish.

W e began this book with one of the lingering questions that many have posed over the years: Who really freed Thomas? Muldoon has become a convenient scapegoat for the stab-in-the-back theorists who want to believe he undermined police and the judiciary due to some kind of anti-establishment whim. As we have shown, it was actually through an error of the police and the Crown prosecutor's own making that Thomas walked free, when they decided to dump the exhibits.

That decision ruled out a third trial; it also meant we will never know whether Thomas's rifle fired the fatal bullets. As we have shown, it was that decision as much as anything that propelled Jim McLay to recommend a pardon. Some may relish the irony of a plotline straight out of an episode of *Yes, Minister*. Many may simply find it sad.

That the justice system was not only unable to correct this injustice but also actively abetted it not just once, but repeatedly, is a wrong that has never been acknowledged or repaired. The police have been a con-venient scapegoat when, in fact, as we have shown, officials of the Department of Justice and leading members of the judiciary clearly took sides against what they wrongly came to believe was a threat to the judicial system. That a senior judge should think it acceptable to pick up the phone and reproach a minister of justice for granting a pardon is a constitutional wrong for which he should have resigned.

So, the final lesson of this saga is that it took politicians — accountable not to each other but to the public — to show the leadership and human instincts required to finish it. Politicians who, rather than usurping the justice system, upheld it, by listening to the people with raspy-skinned hands and grey trousers, as David Lange described them.[8] This story reminds us that justice, like democracy, cannot simply be delegated to the courts: it is ultimately the responsibility of all of us.

L et us now swing the focus back to the deepest tragedy in this story, the deaths of Jeannette and Harvey Crewe. For all that happened to Thomas and his family, to the Eyres, to all the others, it is the senseless and cruel killing of the Crewes, and the orphaning of their daughter Rochelle, that is the tragedy that cannot be undone. We hope that someone somewhere reading this, who knows anything that explains what happened, will finally come forward.

In the meantime, if we can't always find the true culprit, despite so many trying so hard and for so long, the least we can do is not find the *wrong* one.

NOTES

Introduction

1 Tim Woodhouse, *Life Sentence: The Crewe Murders*, TVNZ, 1994. www.nzonscreen.com/title/the-crewe-murders-1994

Chapter 1: Te awa, te whenua

1 www.sarahballardmusic.com/works

2 *Pukekawa Profile: A Tribute to our Pioneers 1839–1970* (Pukekohe: Alpine Printers, 1970) [no page numbers supplied in pamphlet].

3 Ibid.

4 Ibid; forms.justice.govt.nz/search/Documents/WT/wt_DOC_42317979/Wai%20898,%20A099.pdf

5 Ibid.

6 The New Zealand Constitution Act: nzhistory.govt.nz/proclamation-of-1852-constitution-act

7 Vincent O'Malley, *The Great War for New Zealand: Waikato 1800–2000* (Wellington: Bridget Williams Books, 2016), 80.

8 Ibid., 126.

9 Ibid., 150.

10 *Pukekawa Profile.*

11 Ibid.

12 O'Malley, *The Great War for New Zealand,* 370.

13 Ibid., 373.

14 *Pukekawa Profile.*

15 Six provincial councils, each with their own legislature, were established by the 1852 Constitution Act.

16 *Pukekawa Profile.*

17 Maori Roll Plan B43-ML 15226 — Boundaries of confiscated Native Land [in South Auckland Land District].

18 *Pukekawa Profile.*

19 *New Zealand Gazette* 1899, no. 88.

20 *Pukekawa Profile.*

21 'Another raid on Natives', Christchurch *Star*, 6 November 1890, 3.

22 *Pukekawa Profile.*

23 'Overland Light Four', *Franklin Times*, 1 February 1921, 1.

24 Chris Birt, *The Final Chapter: The Truth Behind New Zealand's Most Famous Murder Mystery* (London: Penguin, 2001), 24.

25 *Pukekawa Profile.*

26 Ken Brewer, *A History of the Tuakau Police 1907–2005* (Auckland: K. E. Brewer, 2005).

27 Ibid.

28 'Mrs Eyre's evidence', *Waikato Times*, 15 October 1920, 5.

29 'Evidence of deceased's son', *Waikato Times*, 16 October 1920, 7.

30 'Counsel's fighting speech', *Auckland Star*, 19 November 1920, 5.

31 Ibid.

32 'Third day of retrial', *New Zealand Herald*, 2 December 1920, 8.

33 'Thorn condemned', *Auckland Star*, 4 December 1920, 14.

34 'Thorn's employer dead', *Auckland Star*, 13 December 1920, 7; 'New trial ordered', *Auckland Star*, 11 December 1920, 6.

35 'Execution of SJ Thorn', *New Zealand Herald*, 21 December 1920, 8.

36 Mark Derby, *Rock College: An Unofficial History of Mount Eden Prison* (Auckland: Massey University Press, 2020), 189.

37 Brewer, *History of the Tuakau Police*, 11.

38 'New police theory', *Auckland Star*, 20 October 1933, 8.

39 'The Bayly trial', *Waikato Times*, 25 May 1934, 8.

40 'Records broken', *Auckland Star*, 26 June 1934, 9.

41 'Bayly convicted', *Auckland Star*, 23 June 1934, 10.

42 'Plea for Bayly', *New Zealand Herald*, 21 July 1934, 12.

43 'Both sold', *Auckland Star*, 29 June 1934, 8.

44 James Hollings (ed.), *A Moral Truth: 150 Years of Investigative Journalism in New Zealand* (Auckland: Massey University Press, 2017), 6.

45 'Bayly executed', *Waikato Times*, 20 July 1934, 5.

46 'Penalty paid', *New Zealand Herald*, 21 July 1934.

47 Ibid.

48 'Show authorities to pay', *Waikato Times*, 10 August 1934, 8.

49 'Ruawaro farmer Samuel Lakey buried 82 years after his murder', *Stuff*, 20 October 2015. www.stuff.co.nz/national/crime/73146320/ruawaro-farmer-samuel-lakey-buried-82-years-after-his-murder

50 'Bayly, William Alfred', in Dictionary of New Zealand Biography. *Te Ara — the Encyclopedia of New Zealand*. https://teara.govt.nz/en/biographies/4b15/bayly-william-alfred

51 Birt, *The Final Chapter*, 29.

52 David Yallop, *Beyond Reasonable Doubt? An Inquiry into the Thomas Case* (Auckland: Hodder & Stoughton, 1978), 24.

53 *Auckland Star*, 17 October 1936, 8.

54 'Ball at Pukekawa', *New Zealand Herald*, 9 August 1937, 3.

55 *Pukekawa School Centennial 1995*.

56 Inquest on body of Howard Geoffrey Chennells, depositions of witnesses, 2 July 1950. Cor. 1950/810.

57 Coroner's Report, 1950.

58 Certificate of Purchase of Freehold, vol. 204, folio 295, 1953, District Lands and Survey Office.

59 New Zealand median farm prices by region 2022, in statista.com.

60 Application for consent to sale or lease of land, Land Valuation Court, Auckland Registry A2/522/53 1955.

61 There are several references to 'an old Maori cemetery' in A. J. Lovelock, *Crewe Homicide Investigation Review* (Wellington: New Zealand Police, 2014).

62 Robert Bartholomew, *No Maori Allowed* (revised edition) (Auckland: Bartholomew Publishing, 2022), 146.

63 Yallop, *Beyond Reasonable Doubt?*, 25.

64 Ibid.

65 Ibid., 26.

66 Ibid.

67 Lovelock, *Crewe Homicide Investigation Review*, 2014; hereafter cited as 'Police review', 36.

68 Yallop, *Beyond Reasonable Doubt?*, 28.

Chapter 2: Return to Pukekawa

1 David Yallop, *Beyond Reasonable Doubt? An Inquiry into the Thomas Case* (Auckland: Hodder & Stoughton, 1978), 30.

2 Police review, 28.

3 Yallop, *Beyond Reasonable Doubt?*, 31.

4 Ibid., 30.

5 Pat Booth, *The Fate of Arthur Thomas: Trial by Ambush* (Auckland: South Pacific Press, 1975), 67.

6 Ibid., 67.

7 Ibid.

8 Police review, appendix 1.

9 Booth, *The Fate of Arthur Thomas*, 68.

10 Yallop, *Beyond Reasonable Doubt?*, 31.

11 Email, Veronica McPherson to Kirsty Johnston, 20 February 2023.

12 Yallop, *Beyond Reasonable Doubt?*, 31.

13 Police conference notes, 24 June 1970.

14 Ibid.

15 Police review, appendix 1, 420.

16 Ibid.

17 Ibid.

18 Booth, *The Fate of Arthur Thomas*, 68.

19 Police review, appendix 1, 420.

20 Chris Birt, *The Final Chapter: The Truth Behind New Zealand's Most Famous Murder Mystery* (London: Penguin, 2001), 35.

21 Police review, appendix 1, 422–26.

22 Ibid.

23 Ibid., 424.

24 Yallop, *Beyond Reasonable Doubt?*, 42–43.

25 Police review, appendix 1, 424.

26 Ross Eyre, interview, 2022.

27 Booth, *The Fate of Arthur Thomas*, 67.

28 Police review, appendix 1, 424.

29 Birt, *The Final Chapter*, 36.

30 Police review, appendix 1, 426.

31 Police review, 263–65.

32 Police review, appendix 1, 366.

33 Ibid., 427.

34 Police review, 118–20.

35 Police review, appendix 1, 427.

36 Yallop, *Beyond Reasonable Doubt?*, 34.

37 Police review, appendix 1, 426.

38 Booth, *The Fate of Arthur Thomas*, 20.

39 Police review, appendix 1, 20.

40 Len Demler deposition, November 1970.

41 Len Demler, police statement, 5 July 1970.

42 Ibid.

43 Police review, appendix 1, 57.

Chapter 3: A terrible bloody mess

1 Pat Booth, *The Fate of Arthur Thomas: Trial by Ambush* (Auckland: South Pacific Press, 1975), 20.

2 Police conference notes, 15 July 1970.

3 Len Demler, police statement, 5 July 1970.

4 Ibid.

5 Police review, appendix 1, 368.

6 Demler statement, 5 July 1970.

7 Bruce Hutton, Police jobsheet, 23 July 1970.

8 Ibid.

9 Len Demler deposition, November 1970.

10 David Yallop, *Beyond Reasonable Doubt? An Inquiry into the Thomas Case* (Auckland: Hodder & Stoughton, 1978), 6.

11 Ibid.

12 Craig Duncan, police jobsheet, 10 July 1970.

13 Barbara Willis deposition, 1970.

14 Ibid.

15 Police review, appendix 1, 368.

16 Demler statement, 5 July 1970.

17 Yallop, *Beyond Reasonable Doubt?*, 7.

18 Ibid.

19 First referral, Court of Appeal.

20 Police conference notes, 23 June 1970.

21 'Child alone, fears held for parents', NZPA, 22 June 1970.

22 Ibid.

Chapter 4: The investigation

1 Bruce Parkes, interview, 2022.

2 Police conference notes, 23 June 1970.

3 Parkes, interview, 2022.

4 Police review, appendix 1, 127–45.

5 Police conference notes, 23 June 1970.

6 Police review, appendix 1, 127–45.

7 Ibid.

8 Police conference notes, 23 June 1970; Police review, appendix 1, 127–45.

9 Police conference notes, 23 June 1970.

10 Ibid.

11 'Fires, jewel theft add to mystery', *New Zealand Herald*, 24 June 1970, 1.

12 Bruce Roddick statement, 23 June 1970.

13 Police conference notes, 23 June 1970.

14 Queenie McConachie deposition, 1970.

15 Police conference notes, 23 June 1970.

16 Ibid.

17 David Yallop, *Beyond Reasonable Doubt? An Inquiry into the Thomas Case* (Auckland: Hodder & Stoughton, 1978), 122.

18 Pat Booth, *The Fate of Arthur Thomas: Trial by Ambush* (Auckland: South Pacific Press, 1975), 18.

19 Terry Bell, *Bitter Hill: Arthur Thomas — the Case for a Retrial* (Auckland: Avante-Garde Publishing, 1972), 10.

20 Police conference notes, 24 June 1970.

21 Bell, *Bitter Hill*, 10.

22 Police conference notes, 23 June 1970.

23 Police conference notes, 24 June 1970.

24 Ibid.

25 Police conference notes, 25 June 1970.

26 Bruce Hutton, police jobsheet, 'An interview with Lenard Demler', 26 June 1970.

27 Parkes, interview, 2022.

28 Police conference notes, 29 June 1970.

29 Police conference notes, 1 July 1970.

30 Ibid.

31 Yallop, *Beyond Reasonable Doubt?*, 50.

32 Ibid.

33 Ibid.

34 Police conference notes, 26 June 1970.

35 Ibid.

36 Police conference notes, 27 June 1970.

37 'Theory in NI inquiry', NZPA, 29 June 1970.

38 Police conference notes, 29 June 1970.

39 Ibid.

40 Police conference notes, 2 July 1970.

41 Police conference notes, 15 July 1970, 3 July 1970.

42 Police jobsheet, 9 July 1970.

43 James Tootill, police jobsheet, 8 September 1970.

44 Hutton, police jobsheet, 9 July 1970.

45 Ibid.

46 Yallop, *Beyond Reasonable Doubt?*, 50.

47 Police conference notes, 13 July 1970.

48 Police conference notes, 15 July 1970.

49 Evan Swain, *The Crewe Murders* (Auckland: Wilson & Horton, 1971), 16.

50 John Hughes, police conference notes, 17 August 1970.

51 Ibid.

52 Francis Cairns, depositions evidence, Otahuhu Magistrates Court, December 1970.

53 Police jobsheet, 18 August 1970.

54 Police review, appendix 1, 181.

55 Police jobsheet, 18 August 1970.

56 Bell, *Bitter Hill*, 14.

57 Parkes, police jobsheet, 26 August 1970.

58 Swain, *The Crewe Murders*, 19.

59 Ian Wishart, *Arthur Allan Thomas: The Inside Story* (Auckland: Howling at the Moon Productions, 2010), 86.

60 Police conference notes, 2 July 1970.

61 First referral, Court of Appeal.

62 Wishart, *The Inside Story*, 90.

63 Police review, appendix 1, 191.

64 Parkes, interview, 2022.

65 Swain, *The Crewe Murders*, 21.

66 Yallop, *Beyond Reasonable Doubt?*, 52.

67 Swain, *The Crewe Murders*, 22.

68 Police jobsheet, 21 September 1980.

69 Swain, *The Crewe Murders*, 27.

70 Bell, *Bitter Hill*, 17.

71 Swain, *The Crewe Murders*, 29.

72 Police review, appendix 1, 243.

73 Patrick O'Donovan, evidence to Royal

Commission. In transcript, 1980.

74 Swain, *The Crewe Murders*, 28.

75 Police jobsheet, 21 September 1980.

76 Parkes, interview, 2022.

77 Police review, 31.

78 Wishart, *The Inside Story*, 88.

79 'Missing body stopped prosecution', *Rotorua Daily Post*, 21 September 2005.

80 'Cold cases: The murdered and the missing', *Rotorua Daily Post*, 28 July 2018.

81 Police conference notes, 15 July 1970.

82 O'Donovan, evidence to Royal Commission, 1980.

83 Ibid.

84 Ibid.

85 Police conference notes, 19 October 1970.

Chapter 5: The arrest

1 Pat Booth, *The Fate of Arthur Thomas: Trial by Ambush* (Auckland: South Pacific Press, 1975), 58.

2 Ian Wishart, *Arthur Allan Thomas: The Inside Story* (Auckland: Howling at the Moon Productions, 2010), 16.

3 Ibid., 20.

4 Police review, appendix 1, 456.

5 Pat Vesey, interview, 2022.

6 Booth, *The Fate of Arthur Thomas*, 52.

7 David Yallop, *Beyond Reasonable Doubt? An Inquiry into the Thomas Case* (Auckland: Hodder & Stoughton, 1978), 88.

8 Booth, *The Fate of Arthur Thomas*, 52.

9 Police review, appendix 1, 461.

10 Yallop, *Beyond Reasonable Doubt?*, 90.

11 Wishart, *The Inside Story*, 84.

12 Yallop, *Beyond Reasonable Doubt?*, 72.

13 Terry Bell, *Bitter Hill: Arthur Thomas — the Case for a Retrial* (Auckland: Avante-Garde Publishing, 1972), 17.

14 Johnston deposition, 1970.

15 Wishart, *The Inside Story*, 95.

16 Police review, appendix 1, 244–45.

17 Patrick O'Donovan, evidence to Royal Commission, 1980.

18 Ibid.

19 Ibid.

20 Police conference notes, 19 October 1970.

21 Ibid.

22 Police review, appendix 1, 189–91.

23 Police conference notes, 19 October 1970.

24 Ibid.

25 Wishart, *The Inside Story*, 95.

26 Johnston deposition, 1970.

27 Police conference notes, 244–45.

28 Yallop, *Beyond Reasonable Doubt?*, 59.

29 Johnston, police jobsheet, 27 October 1970.

30 Evan Swain, *The Crewe Murders* (Auckland: Wilson & Horton, 1971), 32.

31 Hutton evidence, first trial, in transcript.

32 Wishart, *The Inside Story*, 101.

33 Booth, *The Fate of Arthur Thomas*, 58.

34 Yallop, *Beyond Reasonable Doubt?*, 72.

35 Ibid., 70.

36 Booth, *The Fate of Arthur Thomas*, 38.

37 Swain, *The Crewe Murders*, 35.

38 Bruce Parkes, interview, 2022.

39 Yallop, *Beyond Reasonable Doubt?*, 75.

40 Ibid., 76.

41 Booth, *The Fate of Arthur Thomas*, 49.

42 Hutton first trial evidence, in transcript.

43 Wishart, *The Inside Story*, 111.

44 Ibid., 113.

45 Parkes, interview, 2022.

46 Ibid.

Chapter 6: The first trial

1 Pat Booth, *The Fate of Arthur Thomas: Trial by Ambush* (Auckland: South Pacific Press, 1975), 52.

2 Ian Wishart, *Arthur Allan Thomas: The Inside Story* (Auckland: Howling at the Moon Productions, 2010), 115.

3 David Yallop, *Beyond Reasonable Doubt? An Inquiry into the Thomas Case* (Auckland: Hodder & Stoughton, 1978), 6.

4 Jim Tully, interview, 2023.

5 *Auckland Star*, 14 December 1970.

6 Bruce Roddick, Depositions, Otahuhu Magistrates Court, December 1970, retrieved from Archives New Zealand.

7 Ibid.

8 Ibid.

9 Yallop, *Beyond Reasonable Doubt?*, 94.

10 Ibid., 95.

11 Ibid., 94.

12 Wishart, *The Inside Story*, 115.

13 Yallop, *Beyond Reasonable Doubt?*, 94.

14 'Isolating jury not common', *Truth*, 17 February 1971.

15 Yallop, *Beyond Reasonable Doubt?*, 113.

16 Transcript, first trial.

17 Ibid.

18 Ibid.

19 Ibid.

20 Ibid.

21 Ibid. For a full explanation of the wire evidence, see Chapter 14.

22 Ibid.

23 Ibid.

24 Ibid.

25 Yallop, *Beyond Reasonable Doubt?*, 158.

26 Transcript, first trial.

27 Yallop, *Beyond Reasonable Doubt?*, 160.

28 Transcript, first trial.

29 Tully, interview, 2023.

30 Transcript, first trial.

31 Ibid.

32 Court of Appeal Judgment of North P and Haslam J, delivered 18 June 1971.

33 Transcript, first trial.

34 Tully, interview, 2023.

35 Transcript, first trial.

36 Tully, interview, 2023.

37 Wishart, *The Inside Story*, 147.

Chapter 7: The backlash

1 David Yallop, *Beyond Reasonable Doubt? An Inquiry into the Thomas Case* (Auckland: Hodder & Stoughton, 1978), 193.

2 Ibid.

3 Pat Vesey, interview, 2022.

4 Yallop, *Beyond Reasonable Doubt?*, 193–94.

5 Ibid.

6 *New Zealand Weekly News*, 23 August 1971.

7 Yallop, *Beyond Reasonable Doubt?*, 195.

8 Ibid., 199.

9 Ibid., 202.

10 Ibid.

11 Ibid.

12 Vesey, interview, 2022.

13 Ibid.

14 Ibid.

15 Ballistics report, G. Price, Crewe Homicide Review, appendix 8, 3.

16 Yallop, *Beyond Reasonable Doubt?*, 216.

17 Ibid., 217.

Chapter 8: The second trial

1 David Yallop, *Beyond Reasonable Doubt? An Inquiry into the Thomas Case* (Auckland: Hodder & Stoughton, 1978), 222.

2 Kevin Ryan, *Justice Without Fear or Favour* (Auckland: Hodder Moa Beckett, 1997), 136.

3 Ibid., 136–37.

4 Pat Booth, *The Fate of Arthur Thomas: Trial by Ambush* (Auckland: South Pacific Press, 1975), 25.

5 'Crown Prosecutor: horrible killings', *Auckland Star*, 27 March 1973.

6 Ryan, *Justice Without Fear or Favour*, 137.

7 Ibid., 133–35.

8 Yallop, *Beyond Reasonable Doubt?*, 223.

9 Transcript, second trial.

10 Ibid.

11 Ibid.

12 Jack Handcock, witness evidence, second trial, retrieved from Archives New Zealand.

13 Ryan, *Justice Without Fear or Favour*, 133.

14 Transcript, second trial.

15 Ibid.

16 Ryan, *Justice Without Fear or Favour*, 141.

17 Yallop, *Beyond Reasonable Doubt?*, 246.

18 See Chapter 4 for details of these cases.

19 Transcript, second trial.

20 Ibid.

21 Yallop, *Beyond Reasonable Doubt?*, 209.

22 Transcript, second trial.

23 Yallop, *Beyond Reasonable Doubt?*, 234.

24 Pat Vesey, interview, 2022.

25 Ibid.

26 Yallop, *Beyond Reasonable Doubt?*, 263–64.

27 Transcript, second trial.

28 Yallop, *Beyond Reasonable Doubt?*, 266.

29 Ryan, *Justice Without Fear or Favour*, 147.

30 Transcript, second trial.

31 Yallop, *Beyond Reasonable Doubt?*, 268.

32 Ryan, *Justice Without Fear or Favour*, 147.

33 Yallop, *Beyond Reasonable Doubt?*, 271.

34 Ryan, *Justice Without Fear or Favour*, 147.

35 Transcript, second trial.

36 Yallop, *Beyond Reasonable Doubt?*, 273.

37 Ryan, *Justice Without Fear or Favour*, 147–48.

38 Booth, *The Fate of Arthur Thomas*, 24.

39 Ibid., 24–29.

40 Ryan, *Justice Without Fear or Favour*, 150–51.

41 Ibid., 152.

42 Yallop, *Beyond Reasonable Doubt?*, 273.

Chapter 9: The gathering storm

1 Pat Booth, in *Deadline: My Story* (UK: Penguin, 1997) cited in James Hollings, *A Moral Truth: 150 Years of Investigative Journalism in New Zealand* (Auckland: Massey University Press, 2017), 118–19.

2 Pat Booth, interview, 2009.

3 Hollings, *A Moral Truth*, 120–25.

4 Ibid., 123.

5 David Yallop, *Beyond Reasonable Doubt? An Inquiry into the Thomas Case* (Auckland: Hodder & Stoughton, 1978), 360.

6 Peter Williams QC, *A Passion for Justice* (Christchurch: Shoal Bay Press, 1997), 157.

7 Pat Vesey, interview, 2022. See also Williams, *A Passion for Justice*, 157.

8 Yallop, *Beyond Reasonable Doubt?*, 120.

9 Hollings, *A Moral Truth*, 120–23.

10 Ibid.

11 Vesey, interview, 2022.

12 Hollings, *A Moral Truth*, 129.

13 Ibid.

14 Yallop, *Beyond Reasonable Doubt?*, 281.

15 Williams, *A Passion for Justice*, 160.

16 Ibid., 161.

17 Ibid.

18 Yallop, *Beyond Reasonable Doubt?*, 206.

19 Vesey, interview, 2022.

20 Ibid.

21 Yallop, *Beyond Reasonable Doubt?*, 209.

22 Ibid.

23 Vesey, interview, 2022.

24 Hollings, *A Moral Truth*, 130.

25 Kevin Ryan, *Justice Without Fear or Favour* (Auckland: Hodder Moa Beckett, 1997), 154.

26 Williams, *A Passion for Justice*, 163.

27 Hollings, *A Moral Truth*, 131.

28 Yallop, *Beyond Reasonable Doubt?*, 294–307.

Chapter 10: The pardon

1 Arthur Thomas, letter to the Minister of Justice, quoted in unpublished manuscript of Jim McLay.

2 Jim McLay, interview, 2022.

3 Ibid.

4 Police review, appendix 1, 471.

5 McLay, interview, 2022.

6 Police review, appendix 1, 464–70.

7 Ibid.

8 Ross Eyre, interview, 2022.

9 David Fisher, 'Robert Muldoon ignored pardon advice', *New Zealand Herald*, 11 October 2014. www.nzherald.co.nz/nz/crewe-murders-robert-muldoon-ignored-pardon-advice/B4NK5E7KKD2XZ3MZCXQQE3CNGE/

10 McLay, interview, 2022.

11 The governor-general has the power to exercise the royal prerogative of mercy, and either give a free unconditional pardon (as in the case of Arthur Thomas), reduce the sentence, or refer the case back to the Court of Appeal. Apart from Thomas, the Ministry of Justice says it is aware of only three previous cases when the royal prerogative of mercy appears to have been exercised to grant a free pardon to a living person. One was for a Mr Spiller, the secretary of a 1941 Patriotic Committee, who took the blame for the sale of beer with sandwiches at a meeting; and one for Mr Brown, the salaried chairman of a county council who voted unlawfully in an election. Atenai Saifiti, who was convicted for assaulting a prison officer, was pardoned in 1972 after an investigation by the chief ombudsman concluded there were substantial grounds for believing he was innocent of the offence. There was one earlier case where Parliament granted a statutory pardon, contained in the Meikle Acquittal Act 1908, to James Meikle, who had been convicted of sheep stealing (see Neville Trendle, *The Royal Prerogative of Mercy: A Review of New Zealand Practice* [Wellington: Ministry of Justice, 2003]). Since 1995 there have been 19 successful applications where the minister of justice has recommended the governor-general exercise the royal prerogative of mercy and have the case referred to the Court of Appeal (email, Ministry of Justice). To date, 15 of those have been quashed, but many more have been declined. For example, Neville Trendle found that of 63 applications between 1996 and 2002, only seven were referred. Many simply do not apply because the test for getting a referral, that of showing fresh evidence, is too high. One study found that 'if Māori and Pacific Islanders applied for the prerogative at the same rate as Pākehā, during the period from January 1995 to December 2018 there should have been approximately 114 applications for the prerogative from these groups compared to the 12 that actually occurred' (see Gianna Menzies, 'Walking in Circles: Why the Criminal Cases Review Commission Proposal Does Not Break the Circularity in Addressing Miscarriages of Justice', Bachelor of Laws dissertation, University of Otago, 2019, 18. www.otago.ac.nz/law/research/journals/otago734251.pdf). Recently, following the example of the United Kingdom and other jurisdictions concerned over mounting evidence of wrongful convictions, a Criminal Cases Review Commission has been established. Starting from 2020, by 2023 it had received 368 applications (59 relating to murder or manslaughter) and referred only one case, an assault case, to the Court of Appeal. There has been criticism of this process, that it reinforces a circular process, as the Court of Appeal remains too focused on whether procedure was

followed, rather than testing evidence, and that the bar of providing fresh evidence is still too high (see Menzies, above). There has also been criticism of the free pardon — that it is subject to political whim and that ministers may be pressured or lobbied. See, for example, Minister of Justice Phil Goff's argument for setting up the Criminal Cases Review Commission: Audrey Young, 'Goff plans tougher pardon rules', *New Zealand Herald*, 3 January 2004, www.nzherald.co.nz/nz/goff-plans-tougher-pardon-rules/4KXZ432MJTS3YA4J7ESCJR6IQM

12 McLay, interview, 2022.

13 Ibid.

14 Alfred Dreyfus was a French officer convicted of treason and later exonerated in what became France's most infamous case of wrongful conviction.

15 McLay, interview, 2022.

16 Ibid.

17 Ibid.

18 Peter Williams QC, *A Passion for Justice* (Christchurch: Shoal Bay Press, 1997), 151.

19 Ibid., 152.

20 Ian Wishart, *Arthur Allan Thomas: The Inside Story* (Auckland: Howling at the Moon Productions, 2010), 206.

21 Ibid., 207.

22 Ibid.

23 'My boy', *Auckland Star*, 17 December 1979, 1.

24 Wishart, *The Inside Story*, 208.

25 Ibid.

26 *Beyond Reasonable Doubt*, 1979, directed by John Laing.

27 'My boy'.

Chapter 11: The royal commission of inquiry

1 Jim McLay, interview, 2022.

2 Peter Williams QC, *A Passion for Justice* (Christchurch: Shoal Bay Press, 1997), 165.

3 Ibid., 167.

4 Ibid.

5 Ibid.

6 Ibid., 169.

7 Ibid., 168.

8 Ibid., 169.

9 Ross Meurant, retrieved from www.thedailyblog.co.nz/2018/12/19/guest-blog-ross-meurant-the-real-story-behind-the-crewe-murders

10 Judicial Review: High Court Judgment; Judicial Review: Court of Appeal Judgment, 1982.

11 McLay, interview, 2022.

12 Robert Taylor, Report of the Royal Commission to Inquire into the Circumstances of the Convictions of Arthur Allan Thomas for the Murders of David Harvey Crewe and Jeanette Lenore Crewe, 1980, 116.

13 Ibid., 115.

14 Ibid.

15 'Walton rejects criminal interrogation of Hutton', *Dominion*, 29 November 1980, 1.

16 Paul Neazor, Opinion of the Solicitor-General Paul Neazor as to the Prosecution of Bruce Hutton. Cited in appendix 16, Crewe Homicide Investigation Review, 2014.

17 Ibid., 7.

18 Ibid., 11.

19 Ibid.

20 Ibid., 14–16.

21 McLay, interview, 2022.

Chapter 12: Interest rekindled

1 Ian Wishart, *Arthur Allan Thomas: The Inside Story* (Auckland: Howling at the Moon Productions, 2010), 210–11.

2 Ibid., 210–12.

3 'Public feud escalates in Thomas case', *New Zealand Herald*, 30 June 2000.

4 'Jealousy blamed for split', *New Zealand Herald*, 30 June 2000.

5 Wishart, *The Inside Story*, 210–22.

6 Ross Eyre, interview, 2022.

7 Police review, appendix 1, 349, 436.

8 Russell Brown, 'The war over a mystery', *Public Address*, 16 April 2012, https://publicaddress.net/hardnews/the-war-over-a-mystery

9 Cited in *Life Sentence: The Crewe Murders*, TVNZ, 1994, www.nzonscreen.com/title/the-crewe-murders-1994

10 *Life Sentence: The Crewe Murders.*

11 Chris Birt, *The Final Chapter: The Truth Behind New Zealand's Most Famous Murder Mystery* (London: Penguin, 2001).

12 Pat Booth, 'Dead ends', *New Zealand Listener*, vol. 203 (April 2006): 30–31.

13 Chris Birt, 'Who fed the baby?', *North & South* (June 2011): 37–49.

14 Ibid.

15 Ibid.

16 Police review, appendix 1, 78–80.

17 Ibid., 85.

18 Ibid., 86.

19 G. Wycherly, 'Brothers say Crewe killer is still living in Pukekawa', *New Zealand Herald*, 27 November 2000.

20 Police review, 160–61.

21 Chris Birt, 'A life sentence', *North & South* (July 2010): 38.

22 Ibid.

23 J. Ihaka, 'Crewe case killed my marriage and my ex-wife', *New Zealand Herald*, 11 April 2011.

24 Pat Vesey, interview, 2022.

25 Wishart, *The Inside Story*, 42–43.

26 Ibid., 81–83.

27 Ibid., 252–54.

28 Ian Wishart, interview, 2022.

29 David Fisher, 'Book claims dead cop killed Crewes', *New Zealand Herald*, 26 September 2010.

30 Ross Meurant, 'Too many loose ends to ignore Crewe Case', *New Zealand Herald*, 9 October 2010.

31 Jared Savage, 'Crewe murders: "Who killed Mum and Dad?" asks daughter', *New Zealand Herald*, 14 October 2010.

32 Ibid.

33 'Police avoiding truth: Crewe', *New Zealand Herald*, 22 October 2010.

34 Birt, 'Who fed the baby?, 37–49.

35 Ibid., 47.

36 Keith Hunter, *The Case of the Missing Bloodstain* (Auckland: Hunter Productions, 2012).

37 Chris Birt, *All the Commissioner's Men* (Taupō: Stentorian, 2012).

38 Ibid.

39 'Eulogy shows police still have a long way to go', *New Zealand Herald*, 12 April 2013, web.archive.org/web/20130412054111/http://www.nzherald.co.nz/opinion/news/article.cfm?c_id=466&objectid=10877023

40 David Fisher, 'Our dad was an honest cop', *New Zealand Herald*, 20 May 2015, www.nzherald.co.nz/nz/crewe-murders-our-dad-was-an-honest-cop/UKGTY3IMDJ4737LYNPGUNUNNBE

Chapter 13: Shortfalls

1 Veronica McPherson, interview, 2022.

2 Police review, appendix 1, 437.

3 Ibid., 25–26.

4 Ibid., 435.

5 Anna Leask, 'Crewe killings: Cold-case review officers question Thomas', *New Zealand Herald*, 31 August 2013, www.nzherald.co.nz/nz/crewe-killings-cold-case-review-officers-question-thomas/YJ3RKJUTJZMVVEM4JYL3Z57TMI

6 Ibid.

7 Ibid.

8 Police review, appendix 1, 218.

9 Leask, 'Crewe killings'.

10 'Crewe murders: Police admit cartridge case planted', *Stuff*, 30 July 2014, www.stuff.co.nz/waikato-times/10327013/Crewe-murders-Police-admit-cartridge-planted

11 Police review, 26.

12 Ibid., 29.

13 Ibid., 27.

14 Police review: Independent report by David Jones, QC, 16–19, www.police.govt.nz/about-us/publication/crewe-review-report-independent-counsel-mr-david-jones-qc

15 Ibid., 24.

16 'Crewe murders: Police admit cartridge case planted'.

17 Ibid.

18 Police review, 109.

19 Ibid., 17.

20 Ibid., 26.

21 Ibid., 16.

22 Ibid., 97.

23 Ibid., 16.

24 Ibid., appendix 13, (2013) Criminal

Profiling Unit Report on the CREWE Murders.

25 Ibid., 30.

26 'Crewe murders: Thomases "feel cheated"', *Otago Daily Times*, 31 July 2014, www.odt.co.nz/news/national/crewe-murders-thomases-feel-cheated

27 Fisher, 'Our Dad was an honest cop', *New Zealand Herald*, 20 May 2015, www.nzherald.co.nz/nz/crewemurders-our-dad-was-an-honest-cop/UKGTY3IMDJ4737LYNPGUNUNNBE

Chapter 14: Bullets, wire, axle

1 Police review, appendix 1.

2 Ibid.

3 Ibid.

4 Ibid., 227.

5 Ibid., 230.

6 Police review, 180.

7 William George Ferguson: PhD UoA, Post Doc. Berkeley 1964, Research Fellow Oxford 1966, C&M Engineering staff 1968, Cambridge 1975 and again Sheffield University & British Steel Research Laboratory 1983.

8 Police review, 170.

9 Police review, appendix 12. A keen reader may have noticed that Ferguson appears to invert Todd's findings — switching the label for the waist and chest wires. According to the 2014 police review, this is because he is following Todd's table of results in the court transcript, in which Todd inadvertently switched the labels for the body wires; calling the chest wire '288/1' and the waist wire '288/2'. Detective Matthew Cook, who was in charge of the body and received the exhibits from the pathologist who removed them from the body, told the court the correct labelling was 288/1 for the waist and 288/2 for the chest. In practice, as the 2014 review pointed out, this does not materially affect the implication of the results.

10 George Ferguson, interview, 2023.

11 Police review, appendix 1, 236.

12 Police review, 182.

13 Police review, appendix 8, 2.

14 Ibid.

15 Ibid., 20.

16 Police review, appendix 8.

17 Ibid., 14.

18 Police review, appendix 1, 241.

19 Ibid.

20 See Keith Hunter, *The Case of the Missing Bloodstain* (Auckland: Hunter Productions, 2012).

21 Police review, appendix 1, 244.

22 Ibid.

23 Royal Commission, 71.

24 See depositions, trial transcripts, Royal Commission.

25 Trial transcripts.

26 Nash parts manual, held in Archives New Zealand as part of the Royal Commission papers.

27 Email to authors from Jim Dworschack, 28 July 2021.

28 Royal Commission.

29 Police review, appendix 1, 273.

30 Ibid.

31 Royal Commission, 67.

32 Police review, appendix 1, 260–62.

33 Bruce Parkes, interview, 2022.

34 Royal Commission, 66.

35 Ibid., 66.

36 Ibid., 70.

37 Police review, appendix 1.

38 Roderick Rasmussen, interview, 2022.

Chapter 15: A district divided

1 'Jealousy blamed for split', *New Zealand Herald*, 30 June 2000, www.nzherald.co.nz/nz/jealousy-blamed-for-split/LZCTG3NY5XATSPG24ZIXSWNIAU

2 David Yallop, *Beyond Reasonable Doubt? An Inquiry into the Thomas Case* (Auckland: Hodder & Stoughton, 1978), 70.

3 Police review, 246.

4 Eugene Bingham, *The District*, Episode 2, 'The Brother', *Stuff*, www.interactives.stuff.co.nz/2018/12/the-district

5 Ibid., Episode 4, 'The Tale of Ted Tickle'.

6 'Still no closure for Thomas family', *Stuff*, www.stuff.co.nz/waikato-times/

news/110834905/apologise-still-no-closure-for-thomas-family

7 Ibid.

8 Ross Eyre, interview, 2022.

9 Police review, appendix 1, 126.

10 Eyre, interview, 2022.

11 Ibid.

12 Ibid.

13 Police review, appendix 1.

14 Eyre, interview, 2022.

15 Ibid.

16 Police review, appendix 1.

17 Eyre, interview, 2022.

18 Police review, appendix 1, 9.

19 Eyre, interview, 2022.

20 Police review, appendix 1.

21 Police review, appendix 1, 125–26.

22 Eyre, interview, 2022.

Chapter 16: The court of last resort

1 Police review, appendix 1.

2 Joe D. Rogan and Hogan Hilling, *Solving Cold Cases: Investigation Techniques and Protocol* (North Carolina: Exposit, 2023), 18.

3 A. Kappes, A. H. Harvey, T. Lohrenz et al., 'Confirmation Bias in the Utilization of Others' Opinion Strength', *Nature Neuroscience* 23, no. 1 (2020): 130–37.

4 Ibid.

5 Uwe Peters, 'What Is the Function of Confirmation Bias?', *Erkenntnis* (2020): 1351–76.

6 Cited in *Life Sentence: The Crewe Murders*, 1994, TVNZ, www.nzonscreen.com/title/the-crewe-murders-1994

7 Richard Ericson, Patricia Baranek and Janet Chan, *Negotiating Control: A Study of News Sources* (Toronto: University of Toronto Press, 1993).

8 Cited in *Life Sentence: The Crewe Murders*.

BIBLIOGRAPHY

Books and journal articles

Bartholomew, Robert. *No Maori Allowed* (revised edition). Auckland: Bartholomew Publishing, 2022.

Bell, Terry. *Bitter Hill: Arthur Thomas — the Case for a Retrial.* Auckland: Avante-Garde Publishing, 1972.

Birt, Chris. *The Final Chapter.* Auckland: Penguin, 2007.

—— *All the Commissioner's Men.* Taupō: Stentorian Publishing, 2012.

Booth, Pat. *The Fate of Arthur Thomas: Trial by Ambush.* Auckland: South Pacific Press, 1975.

—— *Deadline.* Auckland: Hodder Moa Beckett, 1997.

Brewer, Ken. *A History of the Tuakau Police 1907–2005.* Auckland: K. E. Brewer, 2005.

Derby, Mark. *Rock College: An Unofficial History of Mount Eden Prison.* Auckland: Massey University Press, 2020.

Ericson, Richard, Patricia Baranek and Janet Chan. *Negotiating Control: A Study of News Sources.* Toronto: University of Toronto Press, 1993.

Hilling, Joe D., and Hogan Hilling. *Solving Cold Cases: Investigation Techniques and Protocol.* North Carolina: Exposit, 2023.

Hollings, James. *A Moral Truth: 150 Years of Investigative Journalism in New Zealand.* Auckland: Massey University Press, 2017.

Hunter, Keith. *The Case of the Missing Bloodstain.* Auckland: Hunter Productions, 2012.

Kappes, Andreas, Ann H. Harvey, Terry Lohrenz, P. Read Montague and Tali Sharot. 'Confirmation Bias in the Utilization of Others' Opinion Strength'. *Nature Neuroscience* 23, no. 1 (2020): 130–37.

Nash Motors Company. *Nash Car Parts Manual.* USA, 1920.

O'Malley, Vincent. *The Great War for New Zealand: Waikato 1800–2000.* Wellington: Bridget Williams Books, 2016.

Peters, Uwe. 'What Is the Function of Confirmation Bias?'. *Erkenntnis* 87 (2020): 1–26. https://doi.org/10.1007/s10670-020-00252-1

Pukekawa Profile: A Tribute to Our Pioneers 1839–1970. Pukekohe: Alpine Printers, 1970.

Pukekawa School Centennial. Pukekawa: Pukekawa School, 1995.

Ryan, Kevin. *Justice Without Fear or Favour.* Auckland: Hodder Moa Beckett, 1997.

Williams, Peter. *A Passion for Justice.* Christchurch: Shoal Bay Press, 1997.

Wishart, Ian. *Arthur Allan Thomas: The Inside Story.* Auckland: Howling at the Moon Productions, 2010.

Yallop, David A. *Beyond Reasonable Doubt? An Inquiry into the Thomas Case.* Auckland: Hodder & Stoughton, 1978.

Official reports

Application for consent to sale or lease of land. Land Valuation Court, Auckland Registry A2/522/53, 1955.

Certificate of Purchase of Freehold volume 204 folio 295. District Lands and Survey Office, 1953.

Transcript of hearing of the Royal Commission to Inquire into the Circumstances of the Convictions of Arthur Allan Thomas for the Murders of David Harvey Crewe and Jeanette Lenore Crewe. Ministry of Justice, 1980.

Coroner's Report, 1950.

Davison, C. J., Richardson, Cooke, Casey and Somers, J. J. Judicial Review: Court of Appeal Judgment. Wellington: Court of Appeal, 1982.

Depositions before First Trial of Queen v Arthur Allan Thomas. Magistrates' Court. Held at Archives New Zealand, 1971.

Lovelock, A. J. *Crewe Homicide Investigation Review.* Wellington: New Zealand Police, 2014.

Maori Roll Plan B43 — ML 15226 —

Boundaries of confiscated Native Land [in South Auckland Land District]. Archives New Zealand.

McCarthy, J. First Referral. Wellington: Court of Appeal, 1973.

Moller, Holland, and J. J. Thorp. Judicial Review: High Court Judgment. Auckland: High Court, 1982.

Neazor, P. Opinion of the Solicitor-General Paul Neazor as to the Prosecution of Bruce Hutton. Ministry of Justice: In appendix 16, Crewe Homicide Investigation Review, 1981.

New Zealand Constitution Act 1852.

New Zealand Gazette. New Zealand Government, 1899.

New Zealand Police. Police Jobsheets. 1970.

New Zealand Police. Statements to Police. 1970.

New Zealand Police. Police Conference Notes. 1970.

North, P. The Queen v Arthur Allan Thomas. Wellington: Court of Appeal, 1971.

Queen v Arthur Allan Thomas: Transcript of first trial. 1971. Held at Archives New Zealand.

Queen v Arthur Allan Thomas: Transcript of Second Trial. 1973. Held at Archives New Zealand.

Taylor, R., P. Gordon and A. Johnston. Report of the Royal Commission to Inquire into the Circumstances of the Convictions of Arthur Allan Thomas for the Murders of David Harvey Crewe and Jeanette Lenore Crewe. 1980.

Wild, C. J. Second Petition: Court of Appeal Judgment. Wellington: Court of Appeal, 1973.

Wild, C. J. The Queen v Arthur Allan Thomas. Wellington: Court of Appeal, 1973.

Wild, C. J., P. McCarthy, J. Richmond, J. Macarthur and J. McMullin. Second Referral: Court of Appeal. Wellington: Court of Appeal, 1975.

Online sources

Bayly, William Alfred. Dictionary of New Zealand Biography. *Te Ara — the Encyclopedia of New Zealand*. https://teara. govt.nz/en/biographies/4b15/bayly-william-alfred

'The Bayly Case, 1934'. *Te Ara — the Encyclopedia of New Zealand*. https://teara. govt.nz/en/1966/trials-notable/page-15

Edwards, Brian. *Life Sentence: The Crewe Murders*. TVNZ, 1994. www.nzonscreen. com/title/the-crewe-murders-1994

Interviews and personal correspondence

Booth, Pat. Interview with James Hollings, 2009.

Dworschack, Jim. Email correspondence with James Hollings, 2021.

Eyre, Ross. Interview with Kirsty Johnston and James Hollings, 2022.

Ferguson, George. Interview with Kirsty Johnston and James Hollings, 2023.

McLay, Sir James. Interview with Kirsty Johnston and James Hollings, 2022.

McPherson, Veronica. Interview with Kirsty Johnston and James Hollings, 2022.

Parkes, Bruce. Interview with Kirsty Johnson and James Hollings, 2022.

Rasmussen, Roderick. Interview with Kirsty Johnston and James Hollings, 2022.

Tully, Jim. Interview with James Hollings, 2023.

Vesey, Pat. Interview with Kirsty Johnston and James Hollings, 2022.

Wishart, Ian. Interview with Kirsty Johnston and James Hollings, 2022.

ACKNOWLEDGEMENTS

There are so many people who make a book happen. We might have had the privilege of drawing it all together, but all these people have given time and thought and practical help; this book is as much theirs as it is ours. Firstly, we acknowledge the journalists and writers before us: Terry Bell, Pat Booth, David Yallop, Chris Birt, Keith Hunter, Ian Wishart, Jared Savage, David Fisher and Eugene Bingham; and the lawyers Kevin Ryan and Peter Williams for their records. Our book builds on their work. Keith Hunter and Chris Birt generously gave us access to their records without restriction.

We are grateful to Dave Lynch and Veronica McPherson of the New Zealand Police for giving us access to the file and helping where they were able to and for being professional and courteous. The staff at Archives New Zealand were always helpful, dragging the boxes out time and time again. Vincent O'Malley was hugely helpful and generous in showing us how to search the early history of the land.

Professor Stephen Croucher and Associate Professor Sean Phelan of Massey University provided encouragement and practical support in giving James time to finish the book. Bernadette Courtney and Keith Lynch at Stuff gave Kirsty time to undertake field research, for which we are grateful.

We are especially grateful to Nicola Legat, an outstanding publisher, for taking on the idea, for guiding, encouraging, for helping in so many ways. In many ways this is her book, too. Her team at Massey University Press, particularly Anna Bowbyes, managed the production process superbly; we feel very lucky to be publishing with them. Thanks also to Jude Watson for her tenacious and careful editing, and Robert Stewart for his wise legal counsel.

Kirsty would like to thank Janet Tatham for lending us her beautiful home; her friends Anke, Kate, Naomi, Michelle and Noelle for their constant advice and validation; and especially her very patient husband, Stephen, for the endless cups of tea and unwavering faith that, eventually, it would be done.

James would like to thank above all his partner Kate for all the practical and emotional support, for always listening and not least for looking after the children while he went away on research trips to Pukekawa and Auckland.

Thanks also to his brothers Charles and Tom and sister-in-law Siobhan Donnellan for being such generous hosts on our periodic research trips; we greatly valued your warmth and valuable contributions and hospitality.

Lastly, we would like to thank all those who trusted us with their stories. They are named in this book. It was a privilege to tell them.

ABOUT THE AUTHORS

Kirsty Johnston is an award-winning investigative journalist with an interest in inequality, gender and social justice. Her work has helped to change lives, through the banning of seclusion rooms in primary schools, and the repeal of a law that discriminated against family carers for the disabled. She began her career at the *Taranaki Daily News*, and has worked at Stuff, the *Sunday Star-Times* and the *New Zealand Herald*. She has made two documentaries. She was named Reporter of the Year at the 2022 Voyager Media Awards. She now works at RNZ.

James Hollings is Associate Professor of Journalism at Massey University, Wellington. He is the author of *A Moral Truth: 150 Years of Investigative Journalism in New Zealand* (Massey University Press, 2017) as well as numerous academic articles on journalism. At Massey he teaches investigative journalism, among other things. Before joining Massey he was a journalist for newspapers and radio both in New Zealand and overseas. He has also made two documentaries.

INDEX

Page numbers in **bold** refer to images

60 Minutes, television programme 220

Abbott, Graham 64
Adams, Joseph 82
Adams-Smith, Robert 184
  report into safety of Thomas's conviction 184, 186–88, 190–91, 219
  report into woman who fed Rochelle Crewe 184
Archives New Zealand 226, 257, 260, 262
Atomic Absorption Spectroscopy (AAS) 250, 251
Auckland Star 167, 168, 169, 170, 175, 176, **197**, 198
Auckland Supreme Court (now High Court) 116, **145**, 146–47, 149, **165**, 167
Auckland Town Hall 170, 172, **173**
Austing, George 79
axle found with Harvey Crewe's body 10, 86–87, **88**, 89, 101, 110, 117, 124, 132, 172, 215, 253, 257–73, 287
  allegations that Hutton planted the axle 226–27, 246, 247, 259
  allegations that Johnston planted the hubs 223, 265–66, 267, 272, 289
  hubs 106, 120, 124, 257, 259, 260, 261–65, 266–68, 269, 271, 272, 287
  possible connection to Eyre property 221, 282
  question of whether from Thomas trailer 97–99, 104, 105, 106, 107–09, 114, 120, 130, 155–56, 228, 233, 259, 260–61, 262–63, 264–65, 266–73, 275, 288, 289

Baker, Wally 91–92, 101, 104
Ballard, Sarah, *Bitter Hill* (symphony) 15, 286
Baragwanath, David 120–21, 127, 141, **148**, 149, 161, 166

Baron, Eric 48
Barr Brothers 49, 94, 113, 152, 168
Bartholomew, Robert 37
Batkin, Beverley 113, 125, 126, 149–50
Bayly, Frank 30
Bayly, Phyllis 30
Bayly, William Alfred 28–32, 294
Beard, Jennifer Mary 90, 154
Bell, Terry, *Bitter Hill* (1972) 14, 141, 214
Beyond Reasonable Doubt
  book by David Yallop 14, 182, 214, 219
  docu-drama, directed by John Laing 196, 214, 291
Bingham, Eugene, *The District* (podcast, 2018) 275–76
Birt, Chris 14, 226
  All the Commissioner's Men (2012) 227
  The Final Chapter (2001) 33, 216–17
  North & South magazine articles 221–22, 225–26
Blundell, Sir Denis 176
books about the Crewe murders 14, 214, 238, 291; *see also* under names of authors
Booth, Pat 10, 42, 167–70, **171**, 172, 174, 175–76, **177**, 180, **181**, 182, 194, 196, 198, 205, 214, 215, 216, 291, 292, 293
  The Fate of Arthur Thomas: Trial by Ambush (1975) 14, 180
Brant, Percy 129
Brewster, Jack 254
Broad, Howard 220, 224
Brown, Lloyd 78
Brown, Ronald Geoffrey 49
Browne, Thomas Gore 17, 18
bullet testing 102, 103, 104, 110–11, 114, 116, 120, 121–22, 153, 158–59, 161, 200–01, 207, 253–57, 273; *see also* cartridge case found in Crewe garden; rifles; Thomas, Arthur Allan: rifle
Bush, Mike 228
Byrne, Paddy 81

Cairns, Francis 61, 79, 82, 82, 87, 119–20, 123
Cameron, Jim 187, 191
capital punishment 30
Carter, Nick and Edna 94
cartridge case found in Crewe garden 116, 181
  Booth's investigation 169–70
  claim to have been fired from Thomas's rifle 110, 121, 130, 141
  decision not to prosecute police accused of offences 205–08, 210, 234
  planted by police 132, 141, 151, 156, 205, 206, 207, 208, 222, 228, 233–34, 246, 290
  police dumping of exhibits 172, 174, 187, 201, 208
  prediction of cartridge case carrying a no. 8 bullet 158–59, 161, 162, 164, 169–70, 174–76, 178, 201, 206
  searches of garden 107, **109**, 135, 201, 202, 207
  sieving of garden and finding of cartridge 108, 110, 120, 121, 122–23, 131, 135, 138, 141, 142, 151, 153, 156, 163–64, 202, 207–08
  Victoria Police Centre comparison microscope photographs 174
  see also bullet testing; Thomas, Arthur Allan: rifle
Cathcart, Mervyn 94, 128–29
Caughey, Ronald 73, 153
Charles, Mike 74, 86, 87, 89, 108–10, 112, 120, 170, 248, 278
Chennells, Howard 33, 34, 35–36, 38, 41, 47, 77, 84
Chennells, Nellie 33
Chennells, Newman 33, 34, 227
Chennells estate rifle 118–19, 216, 227–28
Chennells family 24
Chisholm, Donna 225
Chitty, Carolyn 46, 248
Chitty, Ron 46, 65, 151, 248
Christie, Keith 49
Churton, A. K. 19, 23

313

Clark, Helen 220
Colonial Ammunition Company (CAC) 159, 175
Commission of Inquiry into Police Conduct, 2004 229
compensation to Arthur Thomas, family and Jim Sprott 199, 205, 212, 277
confirmation bias 292, 295
Coombridge, Robert W. 214
Court of Appeal 204, 210
hearing, 1973 141–42, 144, 146, 152, 163, 188
option for a third trial 187, 188, 190
second referral, 1974 176, 178, 180, 188
Cowan, John 25
Cowley, Heather 259
Crawford, Nancy 60
Cresswell, Jenny 211–12, **213**, 214
Crewe, David Harvey 9, 41–42, 50
apparent bad temper and brusqueness 49, 65–66
farming life 41, 42, 43–44, 46, 47, 48, 49, 51, 52–53, 56, 279, 283
fatherhood 10, **11**, 47, 48, 50
financial position, compared to Jeannette 123, 130
meeting and marriage with Jeannette 40, 41, 42–43, **45**, 130
Crewe, Jeannette Lenore (née Demler)
birth and childhood 34–35, 93, 279
descriptions given to police 66
farm bequeathed by Howard Chennells 36, 41
fearfulness after burglary and fires 47, 48, 50, 51, 223, 276
financial position compared to Harvey 123, 130
inheritance from May Demler 50, 52, 74, 76
life as a farmer's wife in Pukekawa 43–44, 46, 47, 51–53
meeting and marriage with Harvey 40, 41, 42–43, **45**
move from Maramarua to Whanganui 40, 150, 168
overseas trip 39, 44, 94
poor housekeeper 66, 239
teaching career 38, 39, 40, 168
Crewe, Marie Lal 42, 51, 142, 156, 163, 224

Crewe, Rochelle Janeane 10, **11**, 14, 47, 50, 51, 52, 53, 131, 244, 246, 276, 279, 290
care by Barbara Willis 59–60, 64, 68, 78
discovery after parents' murders 9, 56, 59, 62, 65, 114, 216, 233
medical assessment 68–69, 73
Nicholls' apology for shortfalls of investigation 234–35
police conversation with Demler 73–74
request to police to reopen the case 224–25
Crewe, Rochelle Janeane: feeding after parents' murders 68–69, 117, 141, 147, 182, 184, 215, 224, 233, 287, 290
likelihood of survival without feeding 73, 147, 153, 239
Norma Demler as the woman who fed Rochelle 216–18, 223, 225–26
review team findings 238–40, 243, 246
Vivien Thomas as the woman who fed Rochelle 114, 119, 128, 130
Crewe, William David Candy 41–42
Crewe farm and house, Pukekawa
burglary of farmhouse 46–47, 72, 89, 91, 92, 101, 103, 113, 223, 241, 242
clean up of house after murders 65, 77, 79, 92, 130, 215, 237, 242, 243, 244
contamination of crime scene 61, 235–36
Crewes' car moved and driven after their disappearance 66, 82, 114, 217, 227, 237, 277–79, 283, 284, 287, 290
fire at farmhouse 47–49, 51, 72, 91, 92, 101, 103, 113, 223, 230, 242, 243, 244
fire in hay barn 50, 72, 91, 92, 101, 103, 113, 223, 242, 244
house 43–44, **96**, **109**
land leased from Maori Affairs Department 205
no curtains on living-room windows 51, 130–31, 236–37
police searches 63–64, 84, 85, 98–99, 104, **109**, 108, 122, 125, 135, 151, 156, 201, 202, 207, 259, 265–66, 267, 272, 273

sighting of a child outside house 68, 82, 114, 227, 239, 242, 290
sighting of a mystery woman outside house 66, 68, 81, 110, 114, 119, 128, 156, 217–18, 238–39, 242, 275 290
Stuckeys looked after house while Thomases on holiday 231–32
tourist attraction 214
Crewe Homicide Investigation Review, 2014 191, 210, 225, 228, 229–32, 250–53, 263, 267–68, 273, 285, 288, 289, 291
report 232–46, 247–48, 276, 279, 284
Crewe homicides
alleged earlier murder attempt 230–31
alleged sexual assault of Jeannette 162, 163, 223
evidence linking Thomas farm 97–99, 114, 232, 233, 246, 247, 248–51, 259, 260, 287
finding of empty house and blood stains 56, 59–60, 61–62, 77, 114, 147, 161–62, 215, 216, 224, 226, 233, 236
funerals 84
hypothesis that Harvey was primary target 243–44
identity of the killer 72, 214–15, 287–91 (*see also* Demler, Lenard [Len]; Thomas, Arthur Allan)
initial assumption of domestic cause 66
knocking down and shooting of Jeannette 83, 84, 117, 120, 159, 161–62, 215
map showing neighbouring farms and location of bodies **58**
profiler's description of killer 240–44, 246, 288
recovery of Harvey's body 9, 86–87, **88**, 154, 227, 233, 257–58
recovery of Jeannette's body 9, 82–84, 135, 231, 233
search for bodies 59, 62, 63, 70, **71**, 72, 79–81, 82, 86, 89, 103, 105, 135, 280
shooting of Harvey through kitchen louvre windows 99, 101, 108, **109**, 117, 119–20, 123, 129, 130, 138, 161, 201, 223

314   THE CREWE MURDERS

time of murder 84, 163, 186

see also murder–suicide theory; police investigation

Cummings, James 25, 27

Dagg, John 55

Davies, Valerie 176, 180, 194, **195**

Davison, Sir Ronald 183

Demler, Heather see Souter, Heather (née Demler)

Demler, Jeannette Lenore see Crewe, Jeannette Lenore (née Demler)

Demler, Lenard (Len) 24, 33, 34, 35–36, 38, 39–40, 44, 46, 47–48, 52, 54, 55, 62, 64, **75**, 78, 135, 142, 215, 216

Birt's case for guilt 216–17, 225, 227–28

blood stain in car 77, 78, 91, 118, 150, 216, 235

Crewe Homicide Investigation Review finding 233, 235, 237

cross-examination, first trial 118–19

cross-examination, second trial 150–51, 163

finding of empty Crewe house and blood stains 56, 59–60, 61, 62, 77, 114, 216, 224, 226, 233, 236

identification of Jeannette's and Harvey's bodies 83, 87, 233

inheritance from May Demler 50–51, 74, 76, 77, 216

lawyers 78, 82

police suspicions of guilt 69–70, 73–74, 76–82, 83–84, 89, 90–91, 92, 101, 105, 116, 118–19, 123, 214, 225, 226–27, 288, 292

rifle ownership 119, 216, 227–38

Wishart's rejection of guilt 222–23

Demler, May (Maisie, née Chennells) 33, 34, 35–36, 38, 39, 44, 46, 47, 48, 70, 225, 226

will 50–51, 74, 76, 92, 216, 223

Demler, Norma (née Thomas) 215, 217–18, 219, 221, 225–26, 232, 235

Demler, William 24, 33

Demler family 24

Department of Justice 180, 182, 187, 294, 296

Department of Scientific and Industrial Research (DSIR) 79,

82, 85, 91, 101, 102–03, 110, 121, 153, 169–70, 176, 200–01, 249–50, 251, 254, 256

depositions hearing, 14 December 1970 112–15, 116, 135

Devereux, Ian 250, 251–52

Dick, Beryl (née Demler) 226

dogs on Crewe farm 42, 59, 62, 142, 154, 156, 217, 237, 243

Donaghie, June 219

Duncan, Craig 73–74

Dunlop family 249

Durack, Peter 200

Dworschack, Jim 260–61

Eaton, Anthony 49

Eggleton, William 124, 126, 130, 136, 141, 142, 154, 169, 280, 282

Eglington, Arthur 256

Evans, Timothy 182

evidence 91

circumstantial evidence 114–15, 118, 130, 134, 186, 207, 253

covering up and suppression of evidence 169, 200–01, 210, 227, 228, 294

Crown compelled to grant discovery to defence 201–02

destruction of material found outside Crewe house 236

disclosure of police evidence withheld from defence at trials 115–16, 117, 154, 228, 294

fake evidence 10, 168–69, 206, 207, 226–27

faulty process of testing 295

lies and twisting of evidence 168, 178, 202, 204, 206, 208, 210

planted evidence 170, 205, 206, 207, 208, 222, 223, 226–27, 233–34, 246, 247, 259, 265–66, 267, 272, 289

police dumping of exhibits after second trial 172, 174, 176, 187, 201, 255, 257, 296

Eyre, Annesley (Joff) 25, 263, 279

Eyre, Bruce 156

Eyre, John (Mickey) 25, 26, 156–57, 214–15, 220, 232, 233, 237–38, 277, 279, 282, 283–85, 288

rifle 102–03, 220–21, 247, 254, 255, 280, 283, 284

Eyre, Millicent 25, 26

Eyre, Philip 25, 26, 284–85

Eyre, Ross 49, 277–80, **281**, 282–85, 288

Eyre, Ruth 157, 278, 279, 280, 283, 285

Eyre, Sydney 24–25

murder 25–27, 284, 285

Eyre, Trish 277, 280, 284, 285

Eyre family 24, 38, 85, 86, 102, 121, 249, 252, 263, 282, 283–84

Ferguson, George 250–51, 252

fingerprints 62, 69, 72, 114–15, 221, 232, 235, 236, 240

Finlay, Martyn 138, 174, 176, 178, 180

Fisher, David 246

Fisher, John 169

Fisher, Robert 200

Fleming, David 50

Forbes, George 31

Fowler, Sharon 255–56

Fox, Charles 68–69, 73

Fox, Raymond 248

Fox, Thomas 114, 153

Gaines, Pat 62, 70, 72, 79–81

Gee, Kevin 151

Gerbowitz, John 82

Glen Murray 23, 33, 53, 54, 103, 156, 278, 280

Gordon, Peter 200, 204, 205

Gracie, John 52–53, 239

Graham, Peter 48

Granville, James 25, 26–27

Grout, James 258

Handcock, Jack 77, 151, 207

Harrison, John 179–80

Harrison, Vivien see Thomas, Vivien (née Carter, later Harrison)

Hart, Tony 259, 260

Harvey, Colin 226

Hawker, James 249

Henry, John 200

Henry, Trevor 116–17, 124, 129, 132, 134

Hessell, Grace 39

Hewlett, C. J. 31

Hewson, Graeme 42, 43, 46, 47, 50, 73, 135, 141, 142, 151, 154, 156, 164, 207, 210

Hewson, Mary 42, 46, 47

Higgins, Leslie 151

Hill, Terry 293

Hodgson, Alfred 36

Hoeta, Tutu 278–79

Holyoake, Sir Keith 191–92

Houghton, Michael 228

Hughes, John 64, 69, 72, 73, 78, 83–84, 85, 87, 117, 125, 126, 146, 166, 168–69, 238, 248

INDEX 315

Hunt, Din 25
Hunter, Keith, *The Case of the Missing Bloodstain* (2012) 226
Hutchesson, Thomas 76
Hutton, Bruce 61–62, 66, **67, 80**, 84, 90–91, **96, 209**, 218, 223, 246, 291, 292, 293
  allegations that Hutton planted axle 226–27, 247, 259
  attempt to get Peter Thomas to change evidence 274–75
  case against Arthur Allan Thomas 10, 101, 104–11, 122–23, 127, 215, 226–27, 234, 293
  case against Len Demler 69, 70, 73, 74, 76, 77–78, 79, 81, 82, 83, 92, 225–26, 233, 234, 293
  Court of Appeal second referral, 1974 176, 178
  death and funeral 228
  decision not to prosecute over planted cartridge 205–08, 210, 225, 234, 294
  first trial 117, 122–24
  freeing Harvey Crewe's body from axle 86–87, **88**, 257–58
  royal commission of inquiry 201, 205–06, 208, 210
  second trial 147, 149, 153–54, 158–59, 166
  Vivien Harrison's bitterness 221–22

ICI Australia 159–60, 169–70, 174–75, 176
'Inside New Zealand' feature on Crewe murders 215–16
Insoll, Anthony 278–79
Institute of Environmental and Scientific Research (ESR) 255
Irvine, Alexander 53

Jack, Sir Roy 138, 139
Jeffries, Murray 62, 64, 84, 89, 151, 248, 258
Jenny, Carole 239–40, 243
Johnson, Henry Ernest 32
Johnston, Allen 200, 204
Johnston, Len 46–47, 92, **96**, 106, 107–09, 110, 127, 132, 152, 218, 225, 271
  attempt to get Peter Thomas to change evidence 274–75
  Birt's allegation of planting cartridge 228
  investigation of the axle 89, 97, 98–99, 104, 108, 120, 173, 258–59, 265–66, 267, 269

royal commission of inquiry, 1980 201, 205–06, 207, 208, 210
suspected of Crewe murders 223–24, 289–90
theory about shot through louvre windows 99, 101, 108
wire sample collecting 103, 249
Jones, David 210, 233, 234
Judge, Edith 38
justice system 192–93, 294, 295–96

Kaihau, Henare 22
Kaka, Tahi 30
Kauahi 16
Keith, Stan 65, 92, 104, 111, 120, 121, 126, 249, 251
Kelly, Gregory 29
Keruse, David 97, 258
Kīngitanga 16, 17–19, 20, 22
Kirk, Norman 141, 176
Kukutai, Waata 20

L. M. Bernard & Son 50
Laing, John 196
Lakey, Samuel and Christobel 28–32
Lange, David 13–14, 206, 216, 293, 296
Leask, Anna 231, 232
Leather, Odette 138
Leighton, George 175, 178
Lendrum, Gary 230, 231, 232, 284
Liddell, Charles 152–53
Lightbody, John 60
Little, Andrew 276
Lovelock, Andrew 225, 228, 231, 233, 240
Lumsden, Evelyn and Robert 194
Lundbrook, Samuel 73

MacGee, Clare 40, 44, 46, 51, 150, 168
Magon, Thomas 35
Māori
  land and trade, Pukekawa district 16–17
  land loss by purchase and confiscation 16, 17, 19–20, 22, 36–37
  segregation and racist discrimination 37–38
  see also Kīngitanga; Waikato War
Maramarua 34, 39, 40, 94, 113, 125, 150, 168
Marshall, Charles 16, 18, 20

Marshall, Jack 139
Martin, John 156, 252, 263, 282, 283
McArthur, Malcolm 38, 218
McCarthy, Thaddeus 141, 170
McConachie, Queenie 68, 81–82, 114, 128, 239, 242
McGregor, George 138–39, 141
McGuire, George and Ella 142, 154
McIntyre, Duncan 187
McKay, Betty 90, 154
McLay, Jim 183–84, 186, 187–88, **189**, 190–93, 199–200, 201, 204, 210, 292, 293, 296
McPherson, Veronica 230, 284
media coverage and representation 9, 10, 89, 113, 134, 136, 146, 214, 216, 218, 224, 293
  Thomas's pardon and homecoming 192, 194, **195**, 196, **197**, 198
Meurant, Ross 84, 151, 202, 224, 225–26
Mickey (horse allegedly ridden by Samuel Thorn) 25–27, 220
Miller, Ian 158
'misinformation effect' 230
Monteith, Douglas 52
Moore, Joseph 55
Moreton, G. E. 31
Morris, David **80**, 90, 113, 141, 142, 202
  dumping of exhibits after second trial 172, 174, 201
  first trial 117, 118, 119, 120, 121, 124, 126, 129–30
  Hutton's update on police case, July 1970 79, 81, 82
  second trial 147, **148**, 149, 155, 159, 161, 164, 166, 239
Mount Eden Prison 26, 27, 28, 30, 31–32, 111, 116, 142
Mowbray, Allan 262–63, 267, 270, 271
Muldoon, Robert 139, 141, 180, 182, 183, 184, **185**, 186, 187, 191, 192, 200, 206, 219, 228, 295–96
Mullins, Mrs 23
murders
  Pukekawa district 16, 25–27, 28–32, 294
  unsolved murders 90–91, 154
  see also Crewe homicides
murder–suicide theory 10, 82, 130–31, 132, 215, 217, 233
Murray, Brian 106–08, 115, 128
Murray, Tom 25

National Ballistics Intelligence Service, Greater Manchester Police 255–56
Neazor, Paul 206–08, 210, 225, 234
Nelson, Donald 82, 101, 102, 103, 121–22, 161, 220–21, 249
Court of Appeal second referral, 1974 176, 178
royal commission of inquiry, 1980 200–01
New Zealand Constitution Act 1852 17
New Zealand Herald 31, 34, 55, 62, 98, 138, 224, 225, 231, 232, 246, 258, 259
Newman, Joseph 19–20
Newton, Kenneth 129, 134
Ngā Iwi o Tainui 16, 36–37
Nicholls, Grant 233, 234–35
North, Sir Alfred 193
North & South 221, 225
Northcroft, E. 31

Oakley Hospital, Auckland 111
O'Connor, Greg 224
O'Donovan, Patrick 91–92, 101, 104
Official Information Act 14
O'Malley, Vincent, *The Great War for New Zealand* 17, 19, 20
O'Neill, Erin 246
Onewhero Block 19, 20, 37
Chennells and Demler farm, block XVI, section 7 20, **21**, 36
Crown ownership of block XVI, section 7 36–37
Onewhero Rugby Club 23, 24, 55, 78
Optical Emission Spectroscopy (OES) 249, 250
Ōpuatia 24, 33, 34, 54
Ōrākau 18–19
Ōrini 212, **213**, 214
outsiders' roles 293–94

pardon for Arthur Allan Thomas 13, 187, 188, 191–94, 196–98, **197**, 200, 214, 292, 294, 295–96
Pāremoremo prison 133, 142, 166, 179, 193–94
Parkes, Bruce 63–64, 85, 89, 92, 97, 98, 101–02, 103, 104, 108–10, 111, 120, 152, 202, 236, 248, 259, 263, 265–66, 271, 290
Payne, David 106
Perry, Clifford 144, 146, 150, 163–64, 166

petitions 138, 176, 276–77
Pirrett, Thyrle 53
police investigation 10, 291, 292
corruption 13–14, 199, 200, 202, 204, 205, 234, 275, 294
disappearance of Jeannette and Harvey 61–66, 68–70, **71**, 82
documents and records 14, 72, 73, 201–02, 216, 227, 292
forensic methods 63–64, **71**, 235–36
suspect-based approach 292
unresolved issues and shortfalls 14, 234–35
weapons searches 62, 63, 84, 108
see also axle found with Harvey Crewe's body; bullet testing; cartridge case found in Crewe garden; evidence; rifle; wire found with the bodies
police review of investigation, 2014 *see* Crewe Homicide Investigation Review, 2014
political aspects of the case 13, 296
Porritt, Sir Arthur 138
Pōtatau 17
Power, Simon 222
Prescott, Peter 255
Price, George 254–55
Priest, Julie 84, 108, 136, 208, 210, 237, 248
Priest, Owen 50, 56, 59, 61, 84, 108–10, 136, 208, 210, 248
Privy Council appeal, 1978 180
profiler engaged by review team 240–44, 246
public opinion 13, 134, 138, 172, 176, 180, 205, 295
Pukekawa and district 13, 14, 15–16, 43, 54, 135, 149, 194, 196, 286
burglaries 229–30
divisions and feelings after Crewe murders 136–37, 274, 280, 282, 291
early Pākehā settlement and social life 16, 19–20, 23–24
Home Guard unit 34
Māori land and trade 16–17, 19–20, 22, 23
map showing Crewes' neighbours and location of bodies **58**
Tāwhiao's settlements 20, 22, 37
Pukekawa Hill 20, 25, 196, 286

Pukekawa Profile 22
Pukekawa Ratepayers' Association 24, 54, 85, 103, 106
Pukekawa School 23, 24, 33, 35, 38, 43, 93
Pukekohe 24, 26, 33, 37–38, 52, 72, 278

Quigley, Derek 187

Raglan and Waikato Native Company 16
Ramsey, Lynette 280
Rangiaowhia 19
Rangiriri 18
Rasmussen, Ann 268
Rasmussen, Roderick (Rod) 99, 107, 156, 228, 259, 260, 262, 263, 264, 265, 267–72
ratepayers' meeting, Glen Murray *see* Pukekawa Ratepayers' Association
Reeve, Harold 49
retrial committee 135, 136, 138, 141, 158, 164, 169, 170, 178, 180, 212, 216, 217, 218
public meeting 1973 170, 172, **173**
Richmond, Clifford 141, 170
rifles 256, 257, 287, 288, 289
collection and testing 83–86, 102–03, 104, 105, 106, 200–01, 207, 220–21, 232, 254–57
see also bullet testing; cartridge case found in Crewe garden; Chennells estate rifle; Thomas, Arthur Allan: rifle
Ritchie, Jack 158, 170, 175, 294
Roberts, John 65–66, 68, 70, 73
Rock, Bob 146, 164, 166
Roddick, Bruce 66, 68, 81, 96, 110, 114, 119, 128, 141, 142, 147, 152, 154, 156–57, 163, 217–18, 219, 222, 232, 238–39, 242, 282
Rogan, Joe 292
Roose Shipping Company, Mercer 93–94, 107, 274
royal commission of inquiry, 1980 9, 191, 199–201, 212, 220–21. 226, 227, 229, 236, 250, 255, 260, 264, 265–66, 291
Crown compelled to grant disclosure to defence 201–02
findings about cartridge case 205–06, 210, 222, 294
police application to halt hearing on grounds of

INDEX 317

bias 201, 202, 204
protection of parliamentary
privilege 204
report 204–06, 276
Ruawaro 28
Rumble, Eric 35
Ryan, Gerald **145**, 147, 149, 157,
164, 166, 168
Ryan, Kevin 135, 141, 142, 167,
174, 178, 180, 218, 277
Justice Without Fear or Favour
(1997) 151
royal commission of
inquiry 200, 201, 202
second trial 144, **145**, 146,
147, 149–52, 154, 158–59, 161,
162–63, 164, 166, 168, 214–15,
220, 282

Savage, Jared 224
Savage, Pat 111
Savage, Richard 136, 187
Schnauer, David 200
Schultz, Leslie 77, 92, 102
Scott, Dave 240–44, 246
Seaman, Phil 70, 85–86, 97
Shadbolt, Maurice 182
Shanahan, Rory 101, 110, 122,
153
Sharpe, Herman 34, 35
Shea, John 159
Shenkin, Brian 78
Shirley, Emmett 54–56, 114
Shirtcliffe, Charles 97–98,
258–59, 260, 261, 262, 267, 268
Simons, Trevor 258, 260
Slater, John 28
Smellie, Robert 200
Smith, Ted 138
Souter, Heather (née
Demler) 34–35, 38, 39, 50–51,
74, 76, 78, 83, 85, 219, 224, 233
farm bequeathed by Howard
Chennells 36, 41, 43
Souter, Robert (Bob) 50, 74
Speight, Graham 202
Spence, Paul 86–87, 257–58
Spratt, Ian 138, 248
Sprott, Jim 157, 158–59, **160**, 161,
163, 170, 171, 172, 174, 175–76,
177, 178, 180, **181**, 201, 214, 215,
250, 253
compensation 205
St Cuthbert's College,
Auckland 23, 38, 39, 89–90,
224
Stuckey, Buster 205, 212, 220,
231–32, 246, 276, 279, 284, 289
Stuckey, Margaret (née

Thomas) 198, 205, 231–32,
246, 276, 289
Stuckey family 38
Sturrock, Colin 36, 76
Sturrock & Monteith Solicitors,
Tūākau 52, 76
Sunday, TV One programme 217,
220, 283–84

Tāwhiao 17, 20, 22, 37
Taylor, Robert 200–01, 204, 208,
236, 293–94
Temm, Paul 107, 110, 113, 135
appeal against first trial
verdict 134
first trial 115–16, 118–20, 121–22,
123–24, 125–26, 128–29,
130–31, 132, 134, 135, 155, 215
lack of access to police
evidence 115–16, 119
Thomas, Allan 24, 33–34, 38, 93,
95, 98, 99, 115, **177**, **181**, 196,
198, 205, 212, 214, 216, 259,
260, 261, 264, 274
Thomas, Arthur Allan 9, 54,
93–95, 97, **245**
admirer of Jeannette
Demler 38–40, 85, 92, 94,
97, 101, 105–07, 110, 113, 114,
117, 128, 130, 134, 150, 152–53,
155, 168–69, 238, 241–42
alibi 85, 101, 106–08, 108, 110,
117–18, 125, 127–28, 155, 162,
163, 186, 274–75
brush and comb set given to
Jeannette 39–40, 85, 94, 98,
105, 113, 117, 120, 132, 150, 152
compensation 199, 205, 212,
277
divorce from Vivien 178–80
finances 103, 113
framing 10, 106, 107, 110,
155, 217
gold watch accusations 124,
126, 130, 136, 141, 142, 154,
169
illegitimate child 115, 116
'Inside New Zealand' feature
on Crewe murders 215
interviews and
questioning 85–86, 97, 102,
105–07, 110–11, 123, 125,
241–42
knowledge of the Crewe
farm 101, 168–69, 238
letter to Minister of Justice, Jim
McLay 183, 184
no apology from police 235,
276–77

profiler assessment 241–42,
288
psychiatric assessment 111,
134, 288
purchase of bach at Cooks
Beach 214
purchase of farm at Ōrini 212,
213, 214
return to Pukekawa after
pardon 194, **195**, 196, **197**,
198
statements about Harvey
Crewe 117, 132, 168–69
Thomas, Arthur Allan: legal
matters
charged with murder 111, 112
committed to trial 115
first trial evidence 125–26
imprisonment 9, 111, 116, 133,
142, 166, 179, 183
name not cleared
completely 238
pardon 13, 187, 188, 191–94,
196–98, **197**, 200, 214, 292,
294, 295–96
petitions for a retrial **12**
second trial evidence and
reaction to verdict 153,
155–56, 164, 166
weaknesses in evidence against
Thomas noted by defence
team or media 238
Thomas, Arthur Allan: rifle 85–
86, 97, 101, 104, 105, 110–11, 117,
118, 130, 159, 172, 207, 233, 244,
253, 289, 296
ballistic reports 253–54
DSIR reports 102–03, 121,
200–01, 254, 256
Home Office Forensic
Laboratory testing 141,
254–55
Kevin Walsh's analysis
(ESR) 255, 256
review team's expert analysis
and conclusion 255–57
see also bullet testing; cartridge
case found in Crewe garden;
rifles
Thomas, Brian 217
Thomas, Bridgette 212, 214
Thomas, Desmond (Des) 107,
194, 198, 205, 217, 220–21, 231,
232, 235, **245**, 246, 275–76, 284
Thomas, Edward 24, 33
Thomas, Ivy (née Wilkins) 34,
38, 93, 115, 146–47, **177**, 194,
196, **197**, 198, 211, 274
Thomas, Les 196

318   **THE CREWE MURDERS**

Thomas, Lloyd 107, 115, 205
Thomas, Lyrice 115, 198
Thomas, Margaret, *see* Stuckey, Margaret
Thomas, Peter 85, 107–09, 118, 127, 152, 162, 198, 266, 274–75
Thomas, Ray 93, **165**, **181**, 196, 205
Thomas, Richard 156, 196, 205, 252, 278, 279, 280, 282, 283, 284, 288–89
  part in campaign to free Arthur 217–18, 220
  review team questioning 231, 232, 289
  rifle 256, 257, 289
  suspected guilt 283, 288–89
  trailer, axle and hubs 99, 107, 260, 264, 265, 267, 268, 271, 288
Thomas, Vivien (née Carter, later Harrison) 54, 85, 94–95, 97, 99, 101, 102, 104, 112, 115, 120, 126, 135, 142, 205, 211, 215, 216, 241, 242
  Arthur's alibi 117–18, 125, 127–28, 131, 162, 222
  disintegration of marriage to Arthur 178–80, 222
  face of the Thomas campaign 136, **137**, 172, **173**, 177, 179
  first trial 127–28, 130, 131, 132, 134
  identification parade 110, 127
  marriage to John Harrison 179–80
  North & South article by Chris Birt 221–22
  police questioning 105, 107, 127
  second trial 155, 162, 166
  suspected feeding of Rochelle 114, 119, 128, 130, 141, 147, 156, 239
Thomas family 24, 33, 38, 99, 115, 132, 134, 135, 136, 164, 166, 181, 210, 211–12, 231, 246, 274, 277, 282, 283, 294
Thompson, Bruce 25
Thorn, Samuel 25–27, 294
Tickle, Ted 276
Todd, Harry 91, 120–21, 249–50, 251
Todd, John 193–94
Tonga family 38, 249
Tootill, James 68, **80**, 84, 92
trial (first), 15 February 2 March 1971

appeal, May 1971 134
closing arguments 129–31
Court of Appeal hearing, February 1973 141–42, 144, 152, 163
Crown case 117, 118–24, 132, 136, 138, 141
defence case 117–18, 125–29, 132, 134, 135
jury 116–17, 294
Martyn Finlay's concerns 138
summing up 132
verdict 132–33, 134, 280
trial (second), 27 March 16 April 1973
appeal 170
closing arguments 161–63
Court of Appeal second referral, 1974 176, 178, 180
Crown case 147–54, 168
defence case 144, 155–61, 262
disparity in resources between defence and Crown 149, 162–63
jury 144, 145, 146, 163, 166, 170, 201, 294
summing-up 163–64
verdict 164–66
Tūākau 18, 23, 24, 26, 33, 34, 38, 43, 48, 51–52, 136, 275
Tūākau police 61–62, 85–86, 275
Tuakau Transport Limited 56
Tully, Jim 113, 127, 132–33
Turner, Beverly Elizabeth (née Crewe) 42, 224

Underwood, Richard 23

Vesey, Joyce 94, 115
Vesey, Pat 94, **140**, 166, 172, **177**, 179–80, 198, 222, 293, 294
  cartridge cases 157–58, 169, 175
  second trial 149, 156, 157–58, 292
  support for Arthur Thomas 115, 135, 138–39

Waikato River 9, 10, 15, 17, 18, 20, 23, 43, 70, 82–83, 86–87, **88**, 89, 117, 124, 128, 130, 151, 231, 286–87
Waikato War 18–19
Waikato–Tainui Raupatu Claims Settlement (1995) 22, 36–37
Walker, Natalie 233, 235
Walker, Olive 90, 154
Wallace, John 200
Walsh, Kevin 256

Walton, Robert 79, 82, 90–91, **96**, 178, 202
Webb, Brian 113, 125, 127
Westminster model 193
Whanganui 40, 42, 43, 51, 150, 155, 168, 238
Whyte, Gordon 98, 259, 260, 261, 268
Whyte, Patricia 259
Wild, Edward 48
Wild, Sir Richard 141, 142, 170, 178, 193
Wilkinson, Peter 183
Williams, Peter 172, 174, 178, 179, 193, 200, 201–02, **203**, 231, 250
  A Passion for Justice (1997) 172
Willis, Barbara 59, 60, 68, 224
Willis, Beverley (née Ward) 40, 42, 47, 150, 168
Willis, Tony 40
Willis family 46
wire found with the bodies 124, 248
  defence expert analysis 250, 251–52, 282
  DSIR testing 249–50, 251
  evidence for Thomas farm as the source 248–49, 250–53, 273, 287, 288
  police sample collection 87–88, 89, 91, 98, 103, 105, 114, 117, 120–21, 153, 162–63, 233, 265
  review team expert opinion and conclusion 250–53
Wishart, Ian 193
  The Inside Story (2010) 222–24, 230, 289–90
Wright, Ronald 56
Wyllie, Gerald 61, 86

Yallop, David 38, 46, 61, 138, 172, 178–79, 182, 263, 275, 291, 293
  Beyond Reasonable Doubt? 14, 182, 214, 219
  'open letter' to Muldoon 182, 184

INDEX 319

First published in 2023 by Massey University Press
Private Bag 102904, North Shore Mail Centre
Auckland 0745, New Zealand
www.masseypress.ac.nz

Text copyright © Kirsty Johnston and James Hollings, 2023
Images copyright © Stuff Media Ltd, except for page 21: Archives New Zealand Te Rua Mahara o te Kāwanatanga; page 57: New Zealand Police; page 195: Courtesy Victoria Carter; page 281: Kirsty Johnston and James Hollings
Map page 58 by Janet Hunt

Cover design by Gideon Keith
Internal design by Kate Barraclough
Cover images copyright © Stuff Media Ltd (front) and New Zealand Police (back)

The moral rights of the authors have been asserted

All rights reserved. Except as provided by the Copyright Act 1994, no part of this book may be reproduced, stored in or introduced into a retrieval system or transmitted in any form or by any means (electronic, mechanical, photocopying, recording or otherwise) without the prior written permission of both the copyright owner(s) and the publisher.

A catalogue record for this book is available from the National Library of New Zealand

Printed and bound in China by Everbest Investment Ltd

ISBN: 978-1-99-101647-8
eISBN: 978-1-99-101661-4